DO YOU KNOW

*WHAT AN "X" ENGRAVED ON THE BACK OF YOUR NEW TV MEANS . . . AND HOW THAT CAN MEAN YOU'VE BEEN SCAMMED?

*HOW A GUM WRAPPER CAN SHORT CIRCUIT YOUR AIR CONDITIONER AND COST YOU HUNDREDS?

*WHY YOU COULD GET "SPANKED" BY YOUR MOVER IF YOU GO FOR THE LOWBALL RATE?

*WHAT "THE GRIND" IS AND HOW CAR DEALERS GET YOU TO LOSE ON A LEASE?

*WHAT A "SPIFF" IS AND HOW IT CAN SEND YOUR SALESPERSON TO THE CARIBBEAN AND YOU TO THE POORHOUSE?

*HOW YOUR FREE GETAWAY DREAM VACATION CAN END UP A COSTLY NIGHTMARE?

*WHY "GRAY-MARKET GOODS" WILL ALWAYS LEAVE YOU IN THE RED . . . AND PROBABLY RIPPED OFF?

SHOP SMART WITH . . .

TRICKS OF THE TRADE

TRICKS of THE TRADE

A Consumer Survival Guide

JANICE LIEBERMAN

WITH JASON RAFF

A DELL TRADE PAPERBACK

A DELL TRADE PAPERBACK

Published by
Dell Publishing
a division of
Bantam Doubleday Dell Publishing Group, Inc.
1540 Broadway
New York, New York 10036

The trademark Dell® is registered in the U.S. Patent and Trademark Office.
Library of Congress Cataloging-in-Publication Data
Lieberman, Janice.
    Tricks of the trade; a consumer survival guide / by Janice Lieberman
  with Jason Raff.
        p.   cm.
    Includes index.
    ISBN 0-440-50825-8
    1. Consumer education—United States.   I. Raff, Jason.   II. Title.
  TX336.L53   1998
  640'.73'0973—dc21   98-19624
                                                                        CIP

Printed in the United States of America

Published simultaneously in Canada

September 1998

10   9   8   7   6   5   4   3   2   1

BVG

To all those who, despite their trust,
good faith, and intelligence,
have been ripped off, deceived,
and scammed . . . Take charge!
—JANICE LIEBERMAN

To my wife, Sue, for her love and support.
—JASON RAFF

ACKNOWLEDGMENTS

We want to express our appreciation to our editor, Amanda Kimmel, who presented us with the opportunity to do this book, and who had the patience and perseverance to deal with and believe in two first-time authors.

I would like to thank my mother, who has been my role model in every way, and my father, who has taught me the fine art of bargain hunting. My gratitude also extends to my sister, my most honest critic, who shares with me . . . everything (like it or not!).

This book could not have been completed without Coleen Murphy, whose enormous talent and sense of humor helped to bring these pages to life.

My appreciation to the management at both ABC and NBC for believing in the importance of consumer reporting and for affording me the opportunity to do this book.

To Michael Glantz, my friend first, and agent second, and to Dean Tassy, for always being there, many thanks.

My sincere appreciation to all those who helped me with the research and editing of this book, including, Lamar Goering, Mary Murray, Bonnie Teller, and Patrice Schneider.

—JANICE LIEBERMAN

I owe an enormous debt of gratitude to my wife, Sue. As a freelance writer, she helped convert my writing style from television journalist to author. In addition, she spent countless hours helping to research, edit, write, and fact check parts of this book.

Special thanks goes to my colleagues at NBC News, particularly *Today* show executive producer, Jeff Zucker, who gives me the freedom to pursue stories I feel strongly about. I'm also grateful to NBC attorney Roberta Brackman and the executive producer of broadcast standards, David McCormick, who ensure that my investigative stories are aggressive but fair.

I'd also like to thank my family for their support, especially my father, who taught me the value of a buck, but also that the stingy man pays the most.

Finally, we both would like to recognize our fellow consumer reporters, investigative journalists, and consumer advocates. Their drive to expose fraud and fight for consumer rights has contributed to this book both directly and indirectly.

—JASON RAFF

Table of Contents

Introduction

It's tough to be a consumer. Let's face it, the retail marketplace isn't exactly a level playing field. With misleading ads, high-pressure sales tactics, and industry dirty tricks, how is the average consumer supposed to get a fair deal? Don't get us wrong, there are plenty of honest salespeople and reputable businesses out there, but in our work as investigative reporters, we've learned that the most important thing consumers can do to avoid being taken for a retail ride is to look out for themselves. The more you know, the less chance you have of being ripped off.

According to Webster's Dictionary, the word "scam" was coined in 1965, but we all know that scams were operating long before that. In our investigative TV reports, we've turned the tables on many dishonest retailers and revealed the particular tricks of their trades. We've interviewed hundreds of experts, salespeople, and consumers, and taped hours of hidden camera footage to bring their scams and rip-offs to public attention. Unfortunately, the reports we do for television are fairly short, so we often have to edit out a great deal of valuable information. That's why it's been such a pleasure for us to write *Tricks of the Trade*. In it we've been able to share all the information gained from our various investigations as well as let you in on some of the behind-the-camera activities that go on when we produce our stories.

Our book will save you money by showing you how to shop smart. In each chapter we reveal how a different industry works, then we offer you a shopping strategy—tips to help you make informed purchases. In our TV work, we've received hundreds of calls from consumers who were scammed and want to know where to turn for help. Here we've included all the resources you'll need to do your own investigating before you buy as well as places to lodge a complaint that will get results if you're dissatisfied with a company or service. They say knowledge is power. *Tricks of the Trade* will give you the power to level out the playing field and get the best value for your dollar.

CHAPTER 1

AUTOMOBILES

BUYING/LEASING

Walking is slow. And since the invention of the wheel some several thousand years ago, we've decided that the automobile is a necessity. Food, water, shelter, car. Driving is the only way to go! The vibrancy of our love affair is evidenced by the more than 50 million automobiles manufactured annually. You are well aware of the magnitude of such a purchase. If you weren't you wouldn't be reading this book.

But recognizing the importance of getting a good deal is as far as many of us get. Why? Because it's *confusing!* So many decisions. So much emotion. Your options are staggering. Buy? Lease? New? Used? . . . Corvette? Jeep? Gremlin? And each and every option represents an opportunity to save money, *or* spend more of it. Your money!

Everyone in the automobile business, from the manufacturer to the guy who changes your oil, makes a buck off of you, the motorist. It's quite a setup. Did you ever notice that you need (or want) a new car as soon as your payments (and warranty) end?

WHERE TO START
The first thing to do is sort through the most rudimentary of those staggering options. You need a car. And you have these basic options: buying a new or used vehicle or leasing a new vehicle. Used car leases are rarely available. You must decide in advance which is the smartest choice for you. Are you a leaser or a buyer? Do not walk into a dealership looking for direction; believe us, the salespeople will be happy to direct you to the best and most financially sound choice—*for them!*

Buying New

The appeal of owning a new car is obvious. New cars have that fabulous olfactory option: smell! And if money were no object, we'd all have a shiny new ride. But high initial cost and rapid depreciation are a major concern for those who don't want to hold on to a car forever. So, should you go for it?

Buying a new car may be for you if . . .

- You intend to keep the car for more than five years.
- You're willing to spend more for the latest safety features and a factory warranty.
- You've decided on a make and model that depreciates slowly.* (Pickup trucks and sport utility vehicles generally hold their value well.)
- Prestige is more important than resale value. (Large luxury sedans depreciate quickly.)
- You expect your mileage to significantly exceed that allowed by a new car lease (a miserly 10,000 to 12,000 miles per year on many leases).

---

*Depreciation rates are available in the car pricing sources listed later in the chapter.

Buying Used

Industry estimates report that two out of every three cars sold this year will be preowned. One sales manager told us, "Used cars are like liquor. They sell well when the economy is good and when the economy is bad, they sell well!" Since new cars can depreciate as much as 40 percent in the first year, it is understandable that bargain-hungry consumers choose to bypass the new car prestige *and* the biggest hit on depreciation.

Buying a used car may be for you if . . .

- Your budget is limited.
- You are mechanically savvy *or* are willing to spend the time and money to have the car mechanically evaluated.

- You want to use the lower price tag to pay cash and avoid finance costs and monthly payments.
- You would exceed the allowable mileage on a lease.
- The thought of making payments on a car that is not yours or that is depreciating rapidly makes your wallet hurt.

Leasing

Look at the automotive advertising section of any newspaper. Leasing appears to be a quick and inexpensive way to get behind the wheel of a new car. Of course, the down side to leasing is that you own nothing. Your monthly payment covers only the depreciation in the car and an interest charge, and if you are a lifelong leaser, your payments never end.

Leasing can be tricky, and consumers have complained about hidden charges and misleading contracts. Some even have been led to believe they were buying when they actually were leasing! (More on leasing problems later.)

This is not the option for someone who has been conditioned to think of a car as an investment. But even Remar Sutton, a major critic of leasing, states in his book, *Don't Get Taken Every Time*, "If leasing is done *right*, it is an excellent way to drive a new vehicle and save your hard-earned money."

Leasing may be for you if . . .

- You want to drive more of a car than you can afford.
- You want to drive more of a car than you can afford *and* you use the car for business. (You'll be able to deduct more of the costs than if you bought the car.)*
- You need a car *today* and don't have the money for a down payment.
- You have down payment money but prefer to invest those funds and earn interest.
- You want to avoid the headache of selling the car down the road.
- You can deal with the Scrooge-like mileage allowance.

---

*Check with a tax accountant for specific regulations.

Never Say Lease!

Inside industry sources recommend that you never enter a dealership and disclose your desire to lease. They advise that you first negotiate a sale price for your car and *then* bring up leasing. This will give you a fair price from which to begin leasing negotiations. If you are responding to an advertised leasing special at a particular dealership, however, this tactic probably won't be of help.

DIRTY DEALS

Once you have made your new/used/leasing/buying decision, it is not yet time to whip out your checkbook. But it is time to start getting nervous!

Tarnished by Trickery

Let's take a quick look at how the auto industry's reputation became so tarnished in the first place. Here are a few favorite frauds on record.

Keys Please?

In the 1950s and 1960s, a slick trick was to hide a customer's car keys (which the salesman had taken to evaluate the trade-in) when negotiations had broken down and the customer wanted to take his or her business elsewhere. This stranded the buyer and gave the sales force (emphasis on *force*) more time to harrangue and harass the customer into signing a deal.

Pure as the Undriven Snow?

Another favorite ploy was rolling back odometers. It was common to see used car lots filled to the brim with vehicles of miraculously low mileage. Half the fun of selling used cars was inventing scenarios in which the former owner was kinder and gentler than Gandhi and drove the car so rarely that it still had its original tank of gas.

No Sticker Shock

Federal law requires that all cars sold in the United States have a window sticker that displays the MSRP (manufacturer's suggested retail price). This was not always the case. Once upon a time, "asking price" was created by the salesman (usually much higher for female customers), after he had sized up the customer's wallet size and gullibility.

Small May Not Mean Safe

It is unlikely (but not impossible) that a major dealership would attempt such false imprisonment, odometer tampering, or other shenanigans in this day and age, but do beware of independent used car lots, especially small ones, where renegade tactics may still be alive and well.

THE TUNEUP OF THE AUTO INDUSTRY

Indeed, the automobile industry is thought of as notorious. Notorious for lots of things: false advertising, repair scams, collusion, Teamster tensions . . .

It is a law of nature (practically) that bad news gets more air time than good news. News of the Garkfinkle family's safe vacation trip in their new station wagon, which was sold to them by a pleasant and knowledgeable salesperson, does not interest the producers at *Hard Copy*. But rumors of a potential automaker recall of air-bag–containing vehicles that are putting children at risk gets us knocking on the door of Detroit mansions, cameras rolling, to confront fat-cat executives.

So is there any good news that will affect your pocketbook? Yes. And while those of us in the investigative media can take some credit for the improved state of affairs, there is one single invention that has single-handedly saved motorists millions and millions of dollars. This little miracle worker is called the consumer survey.

Did Consumer Surveys Save the World?

In 1968 J. D. Power III founded a marketing information company. By the 1980s the J.D. Power "Customer Satisfaction Index," or "CSI," had saved the world. Well, sort of. All new car owners are surveyed one year after purchase, and the myriad of questions they answer result in the CSI. The industry takes this rating very seriously because it impacts sales immensely. You'll see it prominently referred to in automobile advertising. The ratings take into account service, reliability, safety, and hundreds of other factors. Many dealers and manufacturers do their own surveys, as do other research firms, but the J.D. Power name carries clout. The surveys are independently financed and results are extremely reliable. What this means to consumers is that the makers and sellers of cars are now *accountable*.

According to one Toyota sales manager, "We live and die by our CSI number. It means everything to us. In my opinion it protects buyers from getting ripped off or gouged. Women are treated better. A good rating means we'll have the best allotments [cars in stock]. It keeps dishonest dealers out of the business."

But before you let your guard down too much, remember, the goal remains the same. The car business wants to get as deeply into your wallet as it can. And while the old tricks now seem blatant, the new tricks are sophisticated, slick, and high tech. And the thing to remember about old tricks is that they always can resurface.

Leasing

Consider this story, which was reported by those of us at CNBC's *Steals & Deals* in 1996. A CNBC employee, Alison Pederson, came across a deal she just could not resist: a thirty-eight-month lease on a Nissan Pathfinder with low monthly payments. Alison's truck would come with all the latest equipment.

The only extra item she requested was GAP insurance. GAP insurance covers the difference between what your insurance company will pay and what you still owe on your lease in the event of an accident or theft. Alison signed an order form with Ramsey Nissan of New Jersey. The form stated that her payment would be $157 a month plus tax. Two days later, when she arrived to pick up her truck, she was presented with a lease that totaled her payment at $184 a month. Her payment had jumped $27 a month, which would come to a grand total of $1,026 over the life of the loan!

Needless to say, Alison was upset. Ramsey's explanation was that the extra money covered the GAP insurance, taxes, and a window etching antitheft system that it claimed Alison had agreed to buy, although Alison said she was told on her first visit that the GAP had already been figured in and that she had been offered the antitheft system for free. At her wits' end, she signed the lease and left with her truck. But the questions persisted when she reread the lease. Nowhere in her contract did it say how much she was being charged for GAP.

So she did some checking. To her surprise, she found that GAP insurance was included as part of her financing! Who knew? So she was being double-charged for something she already had. Alison headed back to the dealership, this time with a hidden camera in tow.

Alison questioned employees and persisted until the general manager was forced to call the bank. Lo and behold, it confirmed Alison's belief that she was being charged for something she already had. The dealership did agree to reimburse Alison $456, which it claimed was for the amount of the GAP insurance at $12 per month over the life of her loan.

Alison's complaint was instrumental in the commencement of an investigation. In November of 1996, New Jersey's Attorney General filed a civil complaint against Ramsey Nissan, alleging that for a four-month period in 1995, the dealership had engaged in improper advertising and leasing practices in violation of the New Jersey Consumer Fraud Act. The Attorney General's lawsuit requested an injunction, statutory civil penalties, and restitution for consumers. Ramsey Nissan denied the allegations, stating that the state of New Jersey was wrong on the facts and the law and that if any mistakes were made by the dealership, they were honest mistakes. In May 1998 the New Jersey Attorney General's Office confirmed that the case was still pending and was scheduled to go to trial in August 1998.

Disclosure Mandates

The lesson here is that everything for which you are being charged must be clearly *itemized* on your lease or buying agreement. In October 1997 the Federal Reserve Board introduced new regulations on the leasing industry that mandates full disclosure and requires all specifics on leases be put in writing.

But again, don't get all cozy and neglect to read your lease thoroughly before signing. Check the math. If you need more time, take it home. If the dealer balks, or claims the offer is for one day only, walk out. And while you're at it, put in a call to your local consumer reporter, consumer protection agency, district attorney, or state attorney.

WHERE DO CARS COME FROM?

A little information about how dealerships work will go a long way in helping you get the best transportation for your buck. Dealers are under pressure. They need to meet quotas set by the automaker in order to earn the biggest allotment of hot-selling cars.

Dealerships actually must purchase new automobiles from the manufacturer. So before you step onto the showroom floor, Mr. Wheeler Dealer has had to borrow the money to buy the cars . . . so he has cars available to sell to you . . . who probably will borrow the money to buy the car from him.

This means that Mr. Wheeler Dealer will make a bigger profit if he sells the cars *quickly* and pays less interest, and that the bankers of the world will be smiling no matter what happens.

Which Wheels?

So with your newfound understanding of why car salespeople are so motivated, you must begin to consider what it is you are going to buy from them. If you are buying or leasing a new car, do your research and decide what make, model, color and options you want. (Used car shopping requires a more flexible approach since availability varies.)

As we said before, don't walk into a dealership with no information or preference. If you do, the super-duper helpful salesperson of the month will make sure you drive away in the car you've always dreamed of but could never afford. And worst of all, you'll be temporarily convinced that it was only a tad extravagant!

Tricky Tidbit

While it is wise to know what make, model, color and options you want to buy or lease, it is equally unwise to be in love with one car. This can put you at a negotiating disadvantage. Most American models have "sisters" or "twins." Twins are similar cars that vary slightly in styling or price. For example, the Ford Taurus and the Mercury Sable are considered twins. And even if you are infatuated with a one-of-a-kind import, do your best to come up with a second choice.

It's particularly easy to get emotional over a used car purchase—with all the lemons out there, you may feel that if you don't "Get It Before It's Too Late!" you'll never find another "gem" just like it. Perhaps. But keep this story in mind. An office worker at a car dealership spotted the used car that was perfect for her the minute it came in. She came to work the next morning, checkbook in hand, and was devastated to learn the car had been sold overnight! From her own dealership! The crusty old sales manager had these words of wisdom: "Babe, I've been in this business so long I remember when it was okay to call you babe. And there is one thing I've learned. A car ain't nothing but some steel and rubber. Steel and rubber! And there is always another hunk of steel and rubber out there to fall in love with."

Tips for Getting the Perfect Salesperson
Have you ever walked away from a purchase or stopped browsing in a store because you didn't feel comfortable with the salesperson who approached you? We hate that! And we hate having to do business with people who are incompetent or difficult. When it comes to large purchases—cars, houses, boats, computers, or cappuccino—the salesperson is key in the transaction.

The general rule in the car biz is that you must work with whoever attacks you first. Step onto a showroom floor and you are likely to be face to face with what is delicately referred to in the business as a "floor whore." These are hungry salespeople who figure that success is a function of pouncing more times than the other guy.

In the best of situations, you have been referred to a salesperson by a friend or family member who has done business there before. But this isn't always possible. Dear old Dad may have a great Oldsmobile salesman, but you have your sights set on a Range Rover. But don't discount Dad's contact too quickly either. It might be worth a call to Dad's buddy to see if he knows someone reputable over at Range Rovers-R-Us.

If you have no referral, pick up the phone and call the sales manager at the dealership where you intend to shop. Introduce yourself and say you'd like him or her to recommend a salesperson. Be specific. Maybe you do or don't want the newest salesperson. Maybe you hate the idea of working with Carl "never met a customer I couldn't con." Say you are particular and are calling in advance for the top recommendation. One sales manager told us that he often gets calls from customers who ask to work with a woman, and he appreciates the opportunity to get things started off on the right foot.

THE SALES PROCESS
The sales process at most dealerships has these steps or elements: Greeting, qualification, presentation, test drive, negotiation, close, deal signing, delivery. These are pretty self-explanatory. What is not self-explanatory is the secret language spoken at the

dealership. Some of our inside-the-business buddies clued us in on what the sales staff calls you, the paying customer, behind closed doors.

Terms They Use to Talk About You

- *Bad Pays:* See Buyers damaged or bad credit.
- *Buyers Are Liars:* Refers to customers who hold back information in order to hold on to their wallet.
- *Get Me Dones:* Buyers with damaged or bad credit.
- *The Grind:* Lengthy negotiations during which buyers get ground down.
- *The Hero:* The person brought in to do the negotiating or dirty work for the buyer. (Historically a male negotiating for a female, but these days The Hero is often a woman!)
- *Laydown:* See *Sally.*
- *Rolled and Sold:* A buyer who "caves in" during negotiations.
- *Sally:* A buyer who offers little or no resistance to paying full price or being "sold" as in "Lay Down Sally," a song recorded by Eric Clapton.
- *Spot:* A buyer who caves in and takes spot (immediate) delivery.

A Salesperson's Bag of Tricks

So now you know a little about the secret lingo used during the sales process, but don't get too distracted by such silliness. Your job is to make a great deal for yourself. And the easiest way to accomplish this is to keep the transaction simple. Dealerships don't want things simple. They want lots of profit sources found only in complicated deals. Watch out for these tricks and tactics.

- The salesperson will talk to you only about your monthly payment. This gets your mind off what the overall cost of the car or lease will be.

•The salesperson will talk to you about every purchase or lease variable under the sun, including trade-ins, financing, insurance, and extended warranties. This makes comprehending the equation impossible.

•The salesperson will try to convince you to lease a new car rather than to buy a used car. This is easy to fall for because those new cars are so much sexier than the used ones. Some dealers pay cash bonuses, called "spiffs," to salespeople who can convince you to make the switch! *Even if* you have decided to lease, keep this information to yourself. Negotiate for the car as if you were buying it. Then, when you have agreed on a purchase price, discuss leasing the vehicle based on that figure.

•The salesperson will try to rush or intimidate you or make you feel guilty. Do not put up with this under any circumstances, even if the intimidation is subtle. This is where calling ahead to request a salesperson comes in handy. Say "Your sales manager recommended you to me. Obviously he made a mistake. I'm not comfortable dealing with you." Give the salesperson one chance to apologize and change his or her tune. Otherwise walk into the sales managers office or walk out.

•The salesperson will insist that you fill out a credit application or agree to a credit check before or during negotiations. He or she is trying to establish your ability to buy and get information about you that will give him or her an edge. Refuse. You are not applying for credit and will not consider your financing options until you have a deal on a car and price.

THE BUYER'S BAG OF TRICKS
While an experienced salesperson's bag of tricks can be likened to a Gucci attaché—stylish and impressive—your bag of tricks is a paper bag. A paper bag is all you need because you have only one trick. Your trick is to know your numbers. Find out what the dealer paid for the car.

The $64,000 Question: What Did the Dealer Pay for the Car? (Not $64,000, We Hope!)

Once upon a time this was very difficult. A dealer could show you an invoice, but you would never be let in on the real numbers because why in the world would dealers be dumb enough to tell you what they paid? They've got "dealer holdbacks" and "factory-to-dealer incentives" and "factory rebates on fish bait" for all we know. There are new names for these things every year, and they don't always appear on the invoice you're shown.

But fortunately for you, this is the information age and almost all information is gettable. You can find it yourself through guidebooks (although these are outdated quickly), magazines, or on the World Wide Web. There are also services, some are for profit and some are not, that will sell it to you. We'll give you the sources later in the chapter.

Doing Your Deal

So you take the dealer's cost and add a reasonable (meaning small) profit and make your offer. *Consumer Reports Buying Guide* suggests that 2 to 5 percent over invoice is reasonable, although you'll have to add a few percentage points for new and popular models that are in demand.

Dealers will try to get you for 7 to 10 percent. Statistics show that on average, they are able to get nearly 7 percent. They accomplish this by trying to get you to negotiate down from the sticker price (MSRP). But you should only negotiate up from the dealer's cost!

You are not interested in the sticker price. That sticker may have the meaning of life written on it, and you don't care. You also are not interested in discussing your trade-in, financing, insurance needs, or picks for the World Series until you have a deal on the purchase or lease.

When your offer is not accepted in a short amount of time, leave. Explain that you will take the same offer to another dealership. Name that dealership. Then leave and go do it. Ploys will be used to convince you to stay, but pay no attention. Talk very little. Your only parting words should be "Thank you for your time. You have turned down my offer. Think it over and call me at home with the lowest amount over invoice that your dealership will accept. I'm on a schedule and will accept only one phone call from each dealer. The lowest bid will get my business. I expect to wrap up this deal by tomorrow night."

You will have a deal very quickly unless you have made a mistake on your figures. To avoid using incorrect figures, check two or three of the sources listed against each other. The fax/mail services are particularly reliable for reflecting daily changes.

Know Your Numbers
Here are some guides, magazines, Web sites, and services that will help you find those elusive "what did the dealer pay for the car" numbers.

New Car Prices
The Complete Car Cost Guide, Intellichoice, Inc.
Edmund's New Car Price Guide, Edmund's Publishing

Used Car Prices
The Kelley Blue Book Auto Market Report, Publishers Group West
The NADA Official Used Car Price Guide, National Automotive Dealer Association
The National Auto Research Black Book, Random House

Edmund's also has a popular Web site, http://www.edmunds.com., which has more up-to-the-minute information about dealer costs, holdbacks, and factory-to-dealer incentives. A great source for information, but we found it to be heavy on the advertising.

OR . . . *Consumer Reports* magazine is published by the not-for-profit Consumers Union and does not accept advertising. This is an excellent source for everything from pricing information to terminology. This is a good place to go if you don't know your MSRP from your WD-40.

OR . . . several services will mail or fax you a complete package of daily, up-to-date buying and leasing information for a fee (between $7 and $25).

Car Price Network, 800-227-3295

Center for the Study of Services, 202-347-7283

Consumer Reports New Car Price Service, 800-933-5555

Fighting Chance, 800-288-1134

Intellichoice, 800-227-2665

The Other Ways They Get Ya

So you've made a deal. Congratulations. If you've done well, the dealership staff is upset. And they will be super-motivated to find a way to make some back-end profit. (Dealers call add-ons "back-end profit.") Front-end profit is the money dealers make off the base vehicle and factory options that they sell you. But there are as many dealer profit sources as there are treads on a tire. We haven't even touched on how much money they make off their parts and service departments, but we'll talk about that later.

You will now be offered financing, extended warranties, insurance, and dealer "packs"—paint sealing, rustproofing, pinstriping, upholstery preservatives, theft protection devices, and so on. Perhaps they even know of a good deal on vinyl siding. And you'll be made to think that you need these things. You are remiss and irresponsible not to protect your investment by buying them. Don't believe it!

Consumer Reports Buying Guide, 1998 advises that with the occasional exception of financing, all these other products are "unnecessary and overpriced." One former car salesman from California told us that the "paint sealant" sold at his dealership as an expensive extra was actually Mop 'N Glo.

So skip these extras entirely or shop around and purchase them elsewhere. A dealer may offer a good deal on financing, but need we say it again? Shop around before signing up! Our sources tell us that by the time customers get to the F&I department (finance and insurance), their resistance is worn down and they are often vulnerable enough to agree to high interest rates and costly or hidden extras. A comparison call to your own bank or credit union is always in order.

AUCTIONS AND BUYING SERVICES

A Word About Auctions

Auctions are events. Dramatic events. Dozens of people lined up to get in first. The prospect of scooping up vehicles for next to nothing. Fast-talking auctioneers whizzing through the bids. But can you really get a good car for next to nothing?

Consider this undercover investigation that we reported on for NBC's *Today* show a few years ago. A New York City auction had been cited twice by the local consumer affairs department for deceptive business practices. We wanted to find out if it was still bending the rules. We discovered that this particular auction was selling cars without allowing bidders to start the engines. And a New Jersey auction we investigated was denying bidders the chance to sit in the car or look under the hood! Many of these automobiles had more than 100,000 miles on them!

Is Air Included?

Perhaps the worst deception was at the New York City auction, where our undercover representative discovered that the auctioneer was driving up the prices with "air bids." Air bids refer to trickery used to make bidders believe that the bidding has gone higher than it actually has. The auctioneer points into the crowd and calls out a bid. In a crowded room it's hard to tell who is raising a hand. And in this case no one had. We used three spotters to verify that many of the bids were fictitious. But in ten to twenty seconds the car is sold.

Auctions attract those who can least afford hefty repair bills. One couple we interviewed, Charles and Jeanne Finne, had spend most of their cash to purchase a $2,800 Mercury Mercur. They needed transportation because they were working three jobs between them. They drove off the lot and quickly found out the car needed more than $4,000 in repairs.

Bill Landau, a third-generation auctioneer, says he's seen some colleagues in the industry do just about anything to sell a car. "There are all kinds of tricks. There's sawdust in the transmission, which will keep it going for a couple of more hours before it grinds to a halt."

In our opinion, auctions are comparable to a roll of the dice. Both are games of chance, although with the former one tries to avoid getting crap while with the latter it is desirable. All in all, the odds are greatly stacked against you coming out a winner.

Bob Elliston, president of Automotive Consumer Information Services, Inc., and author of *What Car Dealers Won't Tell You,* sums it up. "Most industry auctions are restricted to dealers. Those that are open to the public are best suited to people who truly know cars, know how to fix them, or have access to a low-cost maintenance facility. In most cases, full payment is required at the time of purchase and all sales are final. No guarantees and no warranty."

CAR-BUYING SERVICES AND OTHER NO-HAGGLE OPTIONS

Saturns

If you want a stress-free way to get mobile, you have a couple of options. One is to buy a Saturn, made by GM. Saturn dealerships advertise what is referred to as "no-haggle prices" and "no-dicker stickers." The price they ask is the price you pay. So if you really want a Saturn, then your life is simple. Get on over there and write a check. According to some of their television ads, you will not only get a new car, you will get a new best friend and a warm cup of tea. Apparently, the Saturn factory workers (who never smoke or have tattoos) care so much about your special needs that they keep a framed picture of you on the dashboard while they install your drive shaft.

Okay, so we are poking fun at the Saturn ad campaign. But

Saturn isn't stupid. The company understands that people abhor the car-buying experience and it recognizes that this touchy-feely approach works. Other car companies, such as Ford, Chevrolet, Volvo, Buick, and Oldsmobile, are giving this method a try on some of their models. Imagine knowing that you will get treated well when buying or leasing a car—not hoping you will get treated well, but actually *knowing* it in advance. Pretty appealing. But there is one downside to buying a Saturn: You probably will pay more than you would for a comparable car. Industry estimates show that the Saturn dealership profit is on average about 13 percent above dealer cost, while the profit for other dealerships is between 6 and 7 percent. Is a cup of tea worth 6 to 7 percent? You decide.

Car-Buying Services

Also in the no-hassle department are car-buying services. The term "car-buying service" is used generically to describe firms that offer a variety of services. Our research into this area taught us this: You can hire out your hassle. If you don't have the time, energy, inclination, or guts to go it alone in the car-buying battle, there are plenty of people who will do it for you. For a fee.

The size and services of these firms vary. Some are large, national chains and others consist of one person, who is in business for him- or herself. Solo consultants probably focus on buying and leasing in one geographic area, where they have the most expertise and contacts.

Brokers and Buyers

A main point to understand is the difference between brokers and buying services. Car brokers buy the car from a dealer (supposedly at a low price), add a small markup, and then sell the car to you at a price that will still add up to a savings compared to what you could have gotten yourself.

Car-buying services negotiate a car purchase or lease for you. But they are not selling you the car. When you pay for the car, you pay the dealer. These services claim that they can get the car either slightly over or sometimes slightly under dealer invoice. Some will charge you a flat fee and some are free. Those that are in the business on a flat-fee basis charge anywhere from $50 to $500.

Two words about the free ones: Nothing's free. Unless you should find one that is operated by missionaries, it is *not* free. Dealerships pay the fees of these "free" ones. While that may sound great, it certainly will be reflected in the cost you pay for the car. It's a blatant conflict of interest.

Some services do everything from negotiating the price, to getting the car insured, to checking the paperwork, to delivering it to your home or office. Others only get you lower price quotes and then send you to the dealer yourself to do the deal. Basically, you get what you pay for. The more you pay, the more service you'll get.

Services have a variety of ways of getting the cars cheaply. Sometimes it's a function of doing the most looking. Other times they deal with industry managers who are more interested in moving numbers of cars and therefore not as concerned with the markup. On occasion dealerships have accepted slow-selling models from the manufacturer in exchange for getting more of the hottest-selling models in their allotment. So if the service can find a client who wants the slow-selling car, then that client will get it at a super-cheap price. A variety of other opportunities and favor exchanges can occur because the car-buying service knows the inside of the industry.

The upside of using a service is that there is a good chance that you will save more money on the car than you would pay on their fee. However, the downside is that it is difficult to know what you have saved. Often you must take the firm's word for it. Services appeal to people who don't want or don't know how to do their own legwork. And these customers are the ones most likely to be gullible. On the other hand, if you take the time to double-check all the facts, figures, and claims that the buying service makes, you might as well have negotiated for the car yourself.

One of our producer friends used one such service with mixed results. "My husband and I were living in New York City, car-free, but were about to move to the suburbs. So we needed a car. The Manhattan dealerships were intimidating. You always pay more in the big city. So we were forced to rent a car on weekends in order to car shop. It was a big waste of money. Eventually we hired a car broker for $150. She suggested a certain model, negotiated the lease, and delivered the car to us. We felt we got a decent but not great deal. Still, the convenience was worth it. When our lease was a few months away from being up, we called her again. She promised to start searching for us, and we figured we'd get an even better deal this time because we were repeat customers and we were giving her more lead time. But she never came through. She left us hanging until the last minute, promising to get back to us shortly with some choices. But she never did and we had to run out to a dealership with only two days left on our current lease and grab something."

So if you want to go this route, do at least enough legwork to get referred to a reliable company, and good luck!

THE TRADE WARS
When it's time to trade in your car, you must consider the tricks of the "trade wars." It is time to switch hats. You are no longer thinking like a sharp-minded consumer, analyzing every aspect of a purchase. In a snap of the fingers you have become the seller. You own something and you must sell it for the best price possible.

You can sell your used car in a variety of ways. We'll focus on the three most common avenues. You can sell it privately, to a wholesaler, or to a dealer. Many people sell their car to the dealer as part or all of a down payment on a new purchase or lease.

Private Buyers
Selling your car privately offers you the opportunity to make the most money. Unlike a dealer or wholesaler, you have no over-

head costs or commissions to pay. You are in business for your-self, baby. Your mother would be so proud. But selling it your-self opens you up to the hassle disadvantage. You must get the car cleaned and up to date on maintenance (although you should do this no matter where you choose to sell the car), you must ad-vertise, put up with phone call inquiries, and spend time show-ing it. Driving around with strangers, after all, is rarely fun and could be dangerous. Our friends at *America's Most Wanted* would strongly advise you not to go for test drives alone.

Wholesaler Buyers

Selling your car to a wholesaler is pretty straightforward. You determine the value of your car (See "Know Your Numbers." listed earlier), present the car to a wholesaler, and start negoti-ating. The wholesaler is going to try to knock you down on things like mileage, condition, and wear and tear. But the math here is pretty obvious. Wholesalers have to be able to make a profit when they resell your car, so you are going to get less than it's worth. Some wholesalers will buy your vehicle with the in-tention of auctioning it off in an area where it might be in more demand. And some wholesalers will buy your "dog of a car" for the purpose of selling the parts. The upside here is that whole-salers will probably pay you cash on the barrel head. No wait-ing for a private buyer to get financing arranged.

Dealer as Buyer

Selling your car to a dealer, either as a trade-in against another car or alone, can be both complicated and simple. It's simple in that you are doing all of your business in one place. You can ditch your old car and snag a new ride in one fell swoop. If you are not selling it to the dealer against a car purchase, then you are dealing with the same math as above. Your job will be to get the dealer to offer as close to wholesale value as possible . . . keeping in mind that he or she must make a profit.

Stealing the Trade

If dealers succeed in convincing you that your car is worth less, then they make out big time. Dealers call this "stealing the trade."

Trade-in Trickery

If you are selling your car to the dealer against the purchase or lease of another car, the dealer will do his or her darndest to turn your car into a bigger and better profit source for him- or herself. And as a seller, you should remember that the less said, the better. Many people make the mistake of revealing information that will devalue their trade-in, even when the car has no notable problems. While evaluating your trade-in, dealers will attempt to exaggerate any imperfections they can see. Do not comment on a dealer's observations. He or she is trying to get a reaction out of you, and it usually works. People tend to get emotional about their cars and blab on: "Well, my brother-in-law did the body work himself! Yeah, he's the Picasso of the county! You've probably heard of him." The dealer did not hear of him. The dealer heard only two words, "body work."

Earlier in the chapter we advised you not to discuss your trade-in while negotiating the price of your new car. Here is why: The salesperson will attempt to determine if you can be greatly swayed by how much you get for your trade-in. If you can be swayed, you'll be quoted a large "allowance" or "credit" for your trade in as part of the new car purchase deal.

This is a psychological trick. The salesperson is looking to see if your eyes light up when you're quoted a figure $1,500 more than you had hoped to get. And it works. People's egos get pumped up when they think they've made a score! And consider for a moment how much less likely you are to walk out of the dealership if you feel you've done so well in the first half of the deal. So watch out for words like "allowance" and "credit." You should be quoted the actual trade-in value of your car. These "allowance" and "credit" figures apply only if it's part of the bigger deal, and the dealership can make up the money and then some on the price of the car you're buying.

AUTOMOTIVE
MAINTENANCE AND REPAIR

Automotive repair is a multibillion-dollar industry and a complex craft. Most drivers (including men) don't have the knowledge required to properly diagnose and repair their vehicles. *That's why we pay someone else to do it!* And we pay dearly.

Before we pay dearly, we usually pray loudly! "Please let me find a good mechanic! Please let me find an honest garage. Please, please don't let my warranty expire the day before I need new ball bearings and gasket thingamajigs!" And adding to our anxiety is the ever-increasing sophistication of the automobile.

THE COST OF FRAUD AND INEPTITUDE

Americans spent approximately $90 billion on automotive repair and maintenance last year. But take a look under the hood of the repair industry and you'll find a lot of dirty work. According to a study by the Department of Transportation, 40 percent of auto repairs are fraudulently or ineptly performed.

That's a waste of more than $30 billion a year! And we all pay for it. We pay at the dealership, the repair garage, and the gas pump. We pay at tax time and via our insurance premiums. Nondriving city slickers pay via the ever rising cost of cab fares, bus tickets, and subway tokens.

So this is a huge problem. Wow. Guess you weren't planning to deal with a national crisis when you bought this book. But don't worry. We'll stick to simple advice about what you can do to save money and avoid getting scammed when your car starts sounding funnier than Fran Drescher!

The Repair Jungle: Grease Monkeys and Other Slick Animals

There are honest mechanics. And they are worshiped more fervently than rock stars. Of course, it is not fair to imply that mechanics are out to take you for a ride. But that figure of 40 percent of repair bills being a waste of money did not come from us TV types. It came from the Department of Transportation.

THE MODUS OPERANDI OF FRAUD

If almost half of the national repair bill is a rip-off, then is it safe to say that every mechanic and garage in operation is getting a piece of the $30 billion pie? It seems so criminal! How can it be? No one knows for sure. But consider the following schemes that can cause repair bills to go through the roof.

- A mechanic/garage is honest with most customers but keeps an eye open for those who can obviously be cheated.
- The mechanic/garage skims by using cheap parts or pumps up profit by padding the labor bill.
- The mechanic/garage is motivated to sell you products and services you don't need because of sales incentives.*

---

*In 1992 the California Department of Consumer Affairs performed an undercover investigation of the Sears Auto Centers, which claimed that Sears "oversold" customers 90 percent of the time . . . with the average oversell amounting to more than $200 per customer. State investigators alleged that the fraud was a result of employees being instructed to sell a certain number of repairs and services during every shift. This turned out to be the first of similar allegations throughout the industry, with charges being filed against other retailers, including Transmission Kingdom in Florida and a franchise of five Big O Tire Stores in Orange County, California. Sears and Big O Tire settled the claims, and Transmission Kingdom was shut down by Florida officials..

Mechanical Ineptitude

Check your shocks . . . 'cause here comes a shocker. In forty-eight states, it is legal for someone to work as a mechanic with *no* training or certification. Talk about dangerous! Can you imagine knowing that the guy working on your car isn't trained or experienced but enjoys tinkering?

And garages are sometimes held to no higher a standard. In New York state there is a registration process for automotive repair businesses. According to Mike Porcelli, second-generation owner of Central Avenue Collision Work, Inc., in Queens, New York, the registration process is something of a joke. "You simply pay a registration fee and, wham, you're in business as a repair shop! No credentials required. Customers see the state registration posted and get the impression that it represents more than it does."

Tips for Choosing a Garage

You can't throw a tire iron without hitting a service station, garage, tire superstore, or oil change joint. But who does what best? And if accreditation is such a rarity, how can I find someone qualified?

- Look for mechanics who have Automotive Service Excellence (ASE) certification. This indicates proper training and extensive experience. Beware, though; garages will post the certification when as few as one mechanic in their employ has actually earned it.
- Referrals, referrals, referrals. Ask everyone you know. If you know someone who drives the same make automobile as yours, he or she may know the right mechanic for you.
- Check with the Better Business Bureau (BBB). Unhappy customers are very likely to call the BBB with automotive repair gripes so a call to them will be worthwhile.
- If your car trouble is covered under warranty, then by all means go to the service department at the dealership that sold you the car. *However,* the service department is the biggest profit center at most dealerships. The markup on parts and service is huge. They make more money fixing lemons than selling them. It is very likely that it will cost you more here.

Dealerships and Retail Chains

Large car dealership service departments have the reputation of being costly. And, on average, they are quite a bit more expensive than privately owned shops. Part of the reason for this may be to your benefit, as they employ the most highly trained and highly paid mechanics in the industry. (Although these top-notch wrench wranglers are often so highly paid because they are receiving big sales incentives!) But is it worth it? Especially with imported cars, they may be the only place that can get the parts needed to repair a certain vehicle. But not all the costs are justifiable.

We spoke to a former service manager from the Atlanta area who told us that he was hired as service manager not because of mechanical expertise but because he was a "producer"—because he could produce profit. "I implemented the practice of charging for shop supplies. A lot of dealerships do this. We added 5 percent to the service bill for repairs under $150. If the repair was over $150 we added a flat $20. Shop supplies were supposed to be anything from paper floor mats, to toilet paper, to the pencil behind my ear!"

On the upside, dealerships and retail chains have the reputation of being more reliable. The logic is that if you have a continuing problem, you can seek recourse via the national office or the manufacturer that the dealer represents. And in most cases you are much more protected when you do business with a large corporation. However, there are two downsides to doing business with the big guys. One is that the "run-around" you get pursuing your complaint might drive you to hang yourself with red tape. The other risk is that you'll call the national office expecting to express your dismay directly to the present-day incarnation of Henry Ford only to be connected to a recording informing you that the dealership/shop is (surprise!) *independently owned and operated.*

SYSTEMATIC SCAMS

The repair shop is so daunting. We sweat it out in our slimy waiting room chair, pretending to read *Popular Mechanics* while praying for the least-costly prognosis. And slick shops understand that our intimidation is to their advantage. But once you get a little information about how most rip-offs work, you'll be a step ahead of the game. Watch out for these favorite frauds.

•*Low-price come ons:* No secret here. Repair shops advertise unbelievable low prices, get you in, get your car up on the lift, and then convince you that they've just discovered (lucky for you, poor slob) that you need additional (expensive) work.

•*Lengthening the labor:* This is often referred to as the "flat-rate billing scam." The labor time is charged to you based on "repair manual estimates." The repair manuals estimate that it takes two hours to install new brakes. Your mechanic completes the job in an hour and a half but still bills you for the two full hours. Many a mechanic is billing one hundred hours a week . . . at garages that are open for business only sixty hours a week! How can this be?

•*Unreal repairs:* Shops charge you for repairs that were never made. A typical example is getting charged for a new alternator, when only the inexpensive alternator belt was replaced. After all, who could recognize "their" alternator in a line-up?

•*Fixing what ain't broke:* This encompasses a lot of areas. Unscrupulous mechanics convince you that you need major repairs or parts, when a minor part replacement or adjustment was all that actually was necessary. Common examples:
—Bogus Brake Jobs: You get a full brake job instead of the new pads or linings you needed.
—Transmission Trickery: Transmission trouble is every motorist's nightmare. Scare tactics are used to convince drivers that the glop in the transmission pan (which is probably normal) is an indicator that a breakdown is imminent.
—Too Many Tune-ups: Half the time you need an oil and fluid change, not a full-blown tune-up.
—Short Sticking: Mechanics wipe off the dipstick to check oil or transmission fluid, but when they reinsert the clean dipstick

they put it in only partway—which makes it look like you're low on oil.

—Much Too Much Maintenance: In the name of prevention, you are advised to replace parts and have costly and rigorous "checkwork" done.

—Frivolous Fuel Injector Work: You need only to switch gasolines, but you pay for a cleaning or injector flushing.

—Silly Steering Repair: You are sold shocks and struts to fix steering vibration, when you need only front end alignment.

—Charging for Freebies: Manufacturers pay dealers to fix problems that were discovered after the fact. But the dealers don't do the work for free unless you ask.

•*Out of state sabotage:* Travelers beware. The elderly and those traveling alone are particularly vulnerable to this highway robbery. Roadside service stations sabotage your vehicle when you stop to fill up. They sell you parts and services (at outrageous rates) after they've punctured your tire or squirted oil on your engine to simulate a leak or problem. You are from another galaxy, far far away. They figure it's unlikely that you'll come back to pursue them even if you suspect foul play.

Body Shop–Insurance Company Combat

The auto body industry and the insurance industry have a love/hate relationship. The romance centers around the fact that auto insurance claims account for a large portion of the business flowing into auto body shops. The disharmony revolves around the fact that (on occasion) both parties claim that the other is a big fat cheater!

Body work artisans say it's difficult to fix a car perfectly for what the insurance company will pay and that the shops that are in cahoots with insurers use cheap "crash" parts that tend to rust or don't fit properly. Insurance companies claim that they only refer policy holders to shops that do quality work at a competitive rate.

Mike Porcelli feels that the insurance industry is shortchanging policyholders. "You pay your premiums, and the insurer has a moral and contractual obligation to pay your claim. That means that the vehicle should be restored to as close to 'pre-crash' condition as possible. But the insurance companies encourage shops to do the least possible work, so long as it appears to be fixed."

Car Kinks

And while all this battling is going on, how can you avoid getting the shaft? Avoid shops that offer to refund your deductible. They accomplish this by inflating the work estimate and splitting the difference with you. One shop owner told us that some insurance adjusters take kickbacks to approve such claims. If they'll cheat the insurance company, they'll certainly cheat you too! And insist that your insurance company pays to have your car restored to precrash condition. Get your own estimates. If the car is fixed up with slapped-together parts and shoddy paint work, it will come out of your pocket . . . at trade-in time.

I GET CONFUSED WHEN I FILL UP THE TANK! SO HOW CAN I TALK TO A MECHANIC?

So now that you are up to speed, so to speak, it's time to deal with getting the work estimated and performed. You are now educated about the most common scams. These simple steps will tell the mechanic that you know what you are doing (even if you don't).

- •Speak directly to the mechanic who will work on your car. Let him know that you want a written estimate and that you intend to get a second and third opinion. You don't have to take your car to three shops unless you come across a major discrepancy. Just call the other shops and get a phone estimate on what they would charge for the same work.
- •Have the estimate itemized. Each charge, from diagnostics, to parts, to labor, to taxes, should appear on the estimate.
- •Insist on getting all used parts when the work is complete.

- Test drive the car before you pay the bill.
- Pay by credit card. This gives you protection in case of a dispute.

It Still Sounds Funny

There is nothing funny about paying to have your car fixed, only to discover that you have the same or even worse problems down the road. This can be an extremely frustrating situation because you've lost time, money, and transport.

So what can you do? You can complain to a consumer protection agency, to the automotive licensing authority (if applicable), or to the press. And, of course, if you're the hardball type, you can file a lawsuit. But these options are not your first resort. Your first resort should be to try to resolve your complaint and get satisfaction.

Our advice is to assume the best. Assume it was an honest mistake on the part of the mechanic or shop. It is entirely possible that this is the case. If you start out by making angry accusations, you'll be met with hostility and defensiveness. No one likes to be told that they've screwed up . . . especially when it's true!

Tips for Complaint Resolution

- Call the garage. Let them know you have a problem and tell them when you'll be bringing your car back in. Be considerate, but let them know that you expect your problem to take priority.
- Document the "before-and-after" trouble. Example: "Before the work was done the steering pulled to the left. After the work was done the steering vibrates instead of pulls." As you go through the complaint resolution process, it is important to document the results each time someone works on your vehicle. This gives the garage information needed to correct the problem but it also provides you with records that you'll need if you have to take your complaint to a higher authority.

•Speak directly to someone in authority, like the service manager or owner. If the work was done by a chain or franchise,
and you can't get satisfaction, call or fax a letter to the national office. If it is a new car warranty dispute, and you are
unhappy, call the automobile manufacturer's district service
representative. The number will be in your owner's manual.
•Bring your original work order, receipt, and warranty, if applicable.
•Accompany the mechanic on a test drive before and after the
additional work is performed.

WHERE TO TURN FOR HELP

Sometimes you have to pursue your dispute through legal channels. No one wants to end up spending time and (more) money
in court, but there are times when you have no choice.

Arthur P. Glickman and the editors of Consumer Reports
books have compiled an excellent list of agencies that enforce
auto repair laws and regulations in their book *Avoiding Auto
Repair Rip-offs*. The information is very helpful because it's organized by state. If your state is not listed you can start by contacting the Federal Trade Commission, 6th and Pennsylvania
Avenue, NW, Washington DC, 20580.

Or call one of these organizations for information on what to
do if you feel you've been victimized:

The Better Business Bureau Autoline: 800-955-5100
AUTOCAP, the Automotive Consumer Action Program: 800-
252-6232
Center for Auto Safety: 202-328-7700
Motor Voters: 916-920-5465

Happy trails!

▶ Top Ten Tips

If saving money is the first and *only* item on your priority list,
take a look at the following tips. We've summarized the most
important bits of money-saving information presented in this

chapter. Note of caution: These tips are only for the seriously cheap. In the great supermarket of steel and rubber, those concerned with luxury and convenience always pay more!

1. *Buy used.* When it comes to the question of leasing or buying a new or used car, you should buy a (good-condition) used car. New cars depreciate rapidly and leasing leaves you with nothing to show for your money.

2. *Love ain't cheap.* Don't fall in love with one make or model. Have a second and third choice. Setting your sights on one particular vehicle puts you at a negotiating disadvantage.

3. *Don't talk payment.* When negotiating a car purchase, keep your mind on the overall cost of the purchase. Getting distracted by the affordability of the monthly payment can lead to financing the car over a longer period than you should.

4. *Get ready for the pain: Pay cash.* Ouch. The truly frugal consumer borrows money only to pay for purchases that appreciate in value, like a home or an education, and never finances items that depreciate, as a car certainly will. If you aspire to total financial fitness, you'll save your money until you can pay cash and save yourself the cost of interest.

5. *Reading, writing, and arithmetic.* Do your homework and find out what the dealer paid for the car. Negotiate up from the dealer cost, not down from the sticker price.

6. *Skip all extras.* Your car does not need paint sealant with an SPF of 35. There is nothing that a car dealer will offer you after you've agreed on a purchase price that you can't get elsewhere for less.

7. *Don't be a trader.* You'll make the most money if you sell your trade-in yourself. Dealers and wholesalers have to allow for commissions and overhead. Your love of the almighty dollar will make the hassle of advertising and showing your car to potential buyers seem like fun!

8. *Maintain the thing.* When it comes to saving money on

auto repair, you'll save if you need as few repairs as possible. Keep up on regular fluid changes and don't drive like a maniac.

9. *Watch the clock.* Repair shops bill for labor by the hour. But flat-rate billing systems allow mechanics to bill you based on the estimated amount of repair time rather than actual time.

10. *Don't part with your parts.* Request that your repair shop save all parts replaced on your vehicle and return them to you. This can save you from being duped into paying for a repair that wasn't performed while communicating to the mechanic that you are a smart and skeptical consumer.

Suggested Reading

Consumer Reports 1998 Buying Guide, Yonkers, N.Y.: Consumer Reports Books.

Bob Elliston, *What Car Dealers Won't Tell You,* New York: Plume/Penguin Books, 1996.

Arthur P. Glickman and the editors of Consumer Reports Books, *How to Protect Against Auto Repair Rip-offs,* Yonkers, N.Y.: Consumer Reports Books, 1995.

Remar Sutton, *Don't Get Taken Every Time,* New York: Viking/Penguin Books, 1991.

CHAPTER 2
COSMETICS

Every year Americans spend $30 billion on makeup. That's billions! All to make our faces look beautiful and to restore our youthful image. We know most of what's available on the market will do nothing to stop the aging process or turn us into the Cindy Crawfords of the world. Still, we buy into the premise that cosmetics will make us sexy and youthful forever. It's no wonder that the makeup mystique is alive and well. Cosmetics giants spend millions on clever advertising, packaging, and pitches to keep us buying. And it works. We keep hoping the next jar of cream will erase the years, the next lipstick will help us land the job or get the guy.

As you will see in this chapter, it's tough not to get caught up in all this hype. The tricks used against us are outrageous, the deceit used to sell us is rampant. Women who are known to be notoriously tough consumers, checking prices and ingredients on almost anything else they buy, turn to mush at the cosmetics counter. We hope the tricks and tactics we expose in this chapter will at least make you think before you shell out $500 on a bag of creams or blushes you probably don't need.

BLAME IT ON OUR FOREMOTHERS
We come from a long history of believing in makeup magic. It's really not all our fault. Women have passed the myth along throughout the generations. In a speech delivered by cosmetics chemist Karl Laden, Ph.D., he reveals the formulas used by women two to four thousand years ago. Check out this hair care recipe:

To prevent hair from turning white, "anoint the hair with the blood of a black calf that had been boiled in oil." Hair that's falling out can be renewed with six kinds of fat—fat of the lion, hippopotamus, crocodile, cat, snake, and ibex—worked together into a pomade. To strengthen hair, crush the tooth of a donkey in honey.

And if you think fights between men and women over how much is spent on cosmetics is a modern problem, think again. How's this for a prenuptial agreement? "A Babylonian Ketuboth [marriage contract] from the Second Temple period states that a husband is obligated to give his wife 10 Dinais for her cosmetic needs." And the Roman Lucian wrote: "Women squander their entire husband's good fortune of Arabia to emit fragrance from their hair." And all through the ages, women have been trying to convince men that it was all done for them!

CALL IT WOMEN'S INTUITION
There had to be a story here. All this money spent on cosmetics, hundreds of different lines out there ready to take our money, and claims of looking young and sexy to sell the product. It had all the makings of a great TV spot.

We pitched the idea to our producers. They bought it. So Jason and I set out to do an investigation for NBC's *Today* show on cosmetics claims. Jason is a nervous producer. He anticipates the worst and always ends up with blockbusters. He had his doubts about how easy it would be to catch cosmetic salespeople exaggerating claims to us. This is one exposé I knew would not be a problem! Much to Jason's surprise, by the end of our investigation, he was actually counseling female coworkers on what was truth and what was fiction.

THE STING
The plan was to head out to the mall with our hidden cameras and randomly approach cosmetics counters. I had my camera hidden in my purse. Jason and our camera technician stood just a few feet away from me, shooting me at the counter with a camera hidden in a book.

Jason, who could not hear what the salespeople were telling

me, paced nervously. We did this at several counters. Each time we met up afterward away from the counters, I would tell Jason, "Wow, you won't believe what they are telling me!" Now that you know Jason, you can guess he wasn't so sure. So he sent me out to seek at least six pitches from different companies. When we got back to view our tapes, even Jason was amazed. I wasn't. As a woman who shops for cosmetics, I am used to these pitches. But now that I was critical of what they were saying, I was mad. The salespeople told me ludicrous stories, telling me what I wanted to hear, just to sell their product.

Our next step was to show these tapes to two cosmetics experts: Paula Begoun, the self-proclaimed "Ralph Nader of Rouge" and author of *Don't Go to the Cosmetics Counter Without Me,* and Dr. Andrew Scheman, a dermatologist in Chicago, to help us evaluate the validity of these sales pitches.

The most outrageous claim was made at a Clarins counter for one the company's antiaging face creams.

Saleswoman: This is a skin firmer. It has pineapple enzyme in it. Now, they have found that the pineapple pickers no longer have fingerprints because the pineapple enzyme has wiped away their fingerprints. So this will help get rid of the superfluous—you know superficial lines. Nothing really deep. Very honestly if you had a face lift, you would not get rid of wrinkles.

Both of our experts agree that while fruity acids may have an effect on getting deep enough to rid your skin of its top layer, making superficial lines softer, there's not enough pineapple in this product to make a difference.

Giving Clarins the benefit of the doubt, because we honestly couldn't believe how far this salesperson went with the "pineapple principle," we checked a different Clarins counter.

Saleswoman: They have no fingerprints left, so it smoothed them. Then she went a step further, saying "It's like a natural face lift."

Paula Begoun was outraged and said these claims were ridiculous. "Clarins admits it's an anecdotal story. She's making it sound like it's a fact. When you are down at the end of the list of ingredients, you're talking about less than a teardrop in that product."

We spent $45 an ounce for that skin firmer. Dr. Andrew Scheman agreed with Paula. "That one I can say is unadulterated bunk." Clarins claims didn't end with the pineapple pickers. Dr. Scheman pointed out other incorrect statements.

Saleswoman: It has horsetail extracts, which is a natural silicon.

Dr. Scheman: It's a plant extract, not a silicon.

Saleswoman: Cucumber is an astringent.

Dr. Scheman: Sorry, cucumber is not an astringent.

We offered Clarins the opportunity to view our tape and comment on their sales staff's pitches. The company declined, saying our use of hidden cameras was unethical. And it wasn't just Clarins that exaggerated claims. Wait till we get to face creams!

THE TRICKS OF THE SELL

For an industry that espouses "beauty," many of the tactics used to sell cosmetics are very ugly. "Gina" (a pseudonym), a former makeup artist and sales manager for several top lines, let us in on the tricks of her trade. She begins by telling us the makeup department at a large retail store is like a war zone. The innocent woman strolling through the department is "the prey" and the cosmetic salespeople are the "attackers." Gina explained how she could size up a customer and go for the kill:

"If they were walking through the makeup department, you would just grab them and start talking to them. You feel them out as to what you think you could sell them. You get a feel for these people and you sort of prey on them a little bit, you do. It's a big game. You can get someone who wasn't planning on spending $5 to spend $500. And when they leave I think they feel bad, and you know they feel bad about it. But they wouldn't dare return it or tell you no. And the company depends on how strong and demanding you can be."

Still, how would a makeup artist know who had that kind of money and who was worth running after? Gina clued us in. "You can tell the women who have money. You have to size them up in a matter of seconds and figure that out. You have to take a good look at them and see what they are wearing. What pocketbook they are carrying. They could be dressed like crap but have an expensive pocketbook. You kind of feel after you talk to them how far you can push them. When you are done with one person, you clean up your stuff, you turn around, and start all over again."

A TOUCHY SELL

We wondered how convincing you would have to be to get someone to shell out that kind of money without really having an idea they would. What goes into the sale that would make you buy from a makeup artist instead of going to a drugstore and picking up similar items for less than half the price?

Gina says it's all about touch. You have a professional dressed in a smock or clinician's clothing touching your face and putting on products. You are being told how beautiful you are and how these products really do you justice. You feel soft brushes and cotton balls rubbed on your face and it feels good.

"It's all about touch, you have to make them feel good mentally and physically, that's a big deal. Almost every woman I have done a makeover on told me I had a soft touch. Who doesn't like to be touched?"

And there's more to the mental escape than the touch alone. The whole experience is pleasant. You are made to feel important. The attention is solely on you and your appearance. Who doesn't find that enjoyable? "You make them feel special. You write up a whole client file including what they bought. You write down a personalized beauty regimen for them to follow, when and how to use the products. You call them for special promotions to make them think you want to find out how they are and let them in on a special sale. This hooks a client and they come back to you faithfully."

Although the pressure on you as a customer is intense after a professional spends all this time on your face, educating you and writing up charts, you are allowed to say no. Or you could tell the artist you would like to achieve that same look with less product for less money. The salesperson still wants to make a sale and probably will work with you instead of risking the chance of losing you altogether. We realize it isn't an easy situation to get out of, but spending $500 for products you may never use feels worse.

REALLY SLEAZY

Gina says stealing customers away from another product line is very sleazy. But the pressure to make your sales numbers is so intense, it's done. It causes fights at times with salespeople at the other counters, but it does happen, and you may become the next victim. Gina says it works like this. If a saleswoman sees a customer at a busy counter, she "pulls" her. "You look at her and say 'Come here, I have something to show you.'" It's unprofessional and it's not nice but it happens. What's worse is when two opposing salespeople work in cahoots. Gina says sometimes she would make friends with a makeup artist selling for a competitor. Then they would work in tandem and double-sell you. 'If she was out of something, so as not to lose her, she would send her customer to me so you get pulled from both counters." It makes the original salesperson sound sincere, because she is willing to forgo a sale to help you, the customer, out. You trust her and end up buying much more than you would from just one makeup artist from one line. You may end up with a really great product from another line, or you may end up spending double. Buy only one product for your needs, don't buy two products that do a similar job. You don't need two of the same thing. If a salesperson is very pushy, tell her you will try a sample and come back and purchase it if you really like it. That should buy you some peace.

BEAUTY IS SKIN DEEP

How can you get a tab of $500 when all you wanted is a makeover? Well, that's all planned out. Gina says the trick is to start with skin care. Skin care is expensive, and you go through it and have to come back for more. Also, there is no end to skin care, from the face, to the hands, to the body.

"Cosmetic sales supervisors or managers always want you to start with the skin care line and you always pull the most expensive product and then work down. You never talk about prices. Put it on them, make them look beautiful, and then when you ring it up that's the first time you ever talk about prices."

Notice how the salesperson skirts the price issue when we shop undercover. It isn't until we bring it up that it is ever mentioned.

Janice: And how much is that one?
Saleswoman: I believe they are $58 or $60.
Janice: So it's a couple hundred dollars just to start yourself off on a good skin care treatment?
Saleswoman: Yes. Well, what I could do is skin type you if you'd like. And if you tell me a little bit about your skin. Do you have any oils down the T-zone?

Now, what do oils in my T-zone have to do with the cost of the product? The saleswoman completely turned the conversation around and never addressed my question of price at all. Most of us do know that we can get a comparable cream at the drugstore for about $10. But we still fall for the hard sell at the counter. Why don't we use reason, the way we shop for almost everything else?

Gina explains. "Every night when they use the night cream or every morning when they put it on, they get a good feeling about the product. Whether it does anything for them doesn't matter; in their mind it does. You don't get that from a drugstore product. You remember paying $50 or $60 for a jar of cream, you pull out your little note telling you how to use it, you remember the experience of being in the makeup artist's chair. It's definitely a gimmick. When you go to the drugstore and pay $5 for a generic cream, you think it's garbage and that's the feeling you take with you." If you took the time to check the ingredients list on a Dior cream and a drugstore cream, you would see few differences. The Dior cream may have a nicer fragrance and be whipped longer, which will make it feel better when applying it, but the difference isn't worth $50. Wouldn't it feel really nice to not waste your money at a department store and buy a drugstore one for a lot less? Just think, you could use your savings and treat yourself to a great facial!

Dr. Brad Jacobs of Beth Israel Medical Center in New York, suggests trying different creams to see what works for you. He advises buying small amounts of a product so you don't waste a lot of money. Jacobs agrees with most dermatologists; the only difference between expensive creams and the cheaper ones is packaging and fragrance. If you read the ingredients lists on both, you will see they are close enough.

WHEN LESS IS MORE

Skin experts agree that most women do too much to their skin. They don't necessarily need a moisturizer, toner, eye cream, throat cream, remover, and the like. Sometimes doing too much to your skin can aggravate it. Doing the wrong thing can do damage as well. Your skin changes from season to season, and it changes as you age. You need to keep changing products to accommodate your skin. Using the same oil-free cream you used as a teenager to prevent acne will not help you as you get older and face drying skin. Here's where an honest cosmetics salesperson can help you. Have the professional look at the condition of your skin and recommend a "type" of cream, for combination skin, dry skin, or oily. You don't need to buy all the skin care products in that line; a good moisturizer should be enough.

GIRLS, YOU'RE ON YOUR OWN

You should be outraged that salespeople can get away with pitching this nonsense to customers. We realize cosmetics sales-people are not chemists, and we understand it's tough to make a sale when you have hundreds of competitors offering very similar products. You would think, though, that if you exaggerated about a product at your place of business, you would be held accountable. Well, here's the deal. The cosmetic industry is self-regulated. It answers only to itself. The Food and Drug Administration (FDA) has jurisdiction over ingredients found in drugs, but it does *not* regulate ingredients used in cosmetics. No government agency does. However, if a cosmetic says it has medicinal properties—that it will change the cellular structure of your skin, for example—the FDA can check it out.

But cosmetics companies are clever. They don't come out and say the cellular structure will change, but they sure do imply it. And some products out do contain small percentages of acids that can help change the appearance of the skin. Industry insiders call these kinds of products "cosmoceuticals." "Cosmoceuticals" can best be defined as over-the-counter products that the FDA can't get its hands on. They're products that sort of make medical claims, but not really. Most "cosmoceuticals" are safe; they don't contain enough of a strong ingredient to make all that much of a difference in your skin. Having said that, there are some warnings you should know about, although the FDA has no jurisdiction to issue those warnings. Warnings like alpha hydroxy acids could cause photosensitivity and people who use them should avoid the sun as the acids could cause burning or even blistering. Even ordinary cosmetics that may cause health risks are left on the market with no warnings to the public. Take, for instance, hair spray that can catch fire, talc that may cause ovarian cancer, or mascara that can break down, dry out, and grow bacteria—a mandatory expiration date would eliminate that. Cosmetics regulation is now left to individual states to manage. And many states don't have regulations at all.

Fortunately, California has a comprehensive labeling law. Thanks to the law's provisions, consumers were told that Epil-Stop, a hair removal cream, was linked to several cases of chemical burns. We spoke with one New York woman who was not told about the risks. She ended up with a severe burn, which she says peeled several layers of skin off her leg. The formula has since been changed.

TRICKY TERMINOLOGY

Cosmetics companies want nothing to do with the FDA. They are very careful and clever about leaving out words that claim medical miracles. The Federal Trade Commission (FTC) polices false advertising claims for all products. By very carefully selecting words, marketers can use copy that makes you think a product will do something when really the ad says nothing.

Take, for instance, ad copy like this one touting a skin cream: "The cream will change the appearance of wrinkles when you sleep. It works overnight. For younger looking skin." What does any of that mean? Really, nothing. The ads get away with incredible claims like these by using the word "appearance." "Appearance" is an acceptable word to the FTC because it really means nothing. But you probably would be attracted to the ad due to the word "appearance" and the gorgeous model. And we buy into it. But think about it now: Have you ever woken up looking younger after slathering cream on your face the night before?

Not only does the FDA have very little policing power, it does not even review cosmetics tests or claims. The cosmetics companies are not even required to report adverse effects caused by the use of their products. Some "natural" ingredients used in cosmetics can actually burn your skin or cause irritation. Paula Begoun points out that lavender is used in many cosmetics. It sounds pretty, but lavender is a photosensitizer. So use a product with lavender in it and go out in the sun and you could develop a rash. I purchased a so-called natural eye makeup remover cream, rubbed it on my lids, and had a severe red burn on my eye. Thinking it might be my sensitive skin, I gave the expensive product to a friend. She had the same reaction. That product is still on store shelves. With no special testing required and no watchdog group, these cosmetics can continue to be sold. So don't assume products on the market are safe for everyone. And don't be fooled by labels touting "proven and effective" or "clinically tested." Remember, we don't know anything about those tests, and neither does the FDA.

SCIENCE FICTION?

Long-term adverse effects are not known, because this kind of research is costly and voluntary. Yet you will see plenty of ads boasting the scientific prowess of a product. Dior Svelte Perfect's ad says "Visible results after one week. 81% of women surveyed saw satisfying results—softer, smoother, firmer skin." How many people were surveyed? Who ran the survey, and were the panelists paid for their participation? Good luck finding the answers to that one. Or how about this ad for Lancôme's Renergie? "Scientifically proven in its dual ability to firm and strengthen skin while diminishing the appearance of wrinkles." Scientifically proven by whom? And what does "diminishing the appearance of wrinkles" mean? Well, you get the idea. It's scientific when it suits their needs, it's a mystery when we need the information. Now, when you take a critical look at the ad copy, you will be more educated about what is real and what is really just poetic license.

TRENDY OR TRICKY?

Flipping through a fashion magazine is relaxing, fun, and somewhat educational. It's the source to turn to when you want the latest trend in clothing, hair, and makeup. Well, that may be true, and we are not telling you to stop reading those publications. But be aware of how the editors arrive at what they include.

Magazines are in business to make money. It's just that simple. They stay afloat by revenue from their advertisers. Their advertisers, not surprisingly, are the cosmetics companies. With that in mind, can you imagine seeing an article critical of a major advertiser's product? It rarely happens. The "must-buys" included in the latest trends are also picks from the sponsors. Beauty articles almost never list lesser-known, cheaper brands. One beauty editor told us she did once write a critical article on one of a sponsor's products. That cosmetic giant threatened to pull all its ads. To get back in its good graces, the magazine had to do a series of positive articles on that company over several months.

Use the beauty editor's advice. Rip the page out, and find a similar color or look for a lesser price. Yes, it does take work, but you could spend $5 on lipstick instead of $18 and still be "in" for the season. If you want trendy, buy one item that will fit with your regular regime. Don't go out and spend hundreds on a whole new bag of trendy items for the season. You can accomplish a fresh look by adding a new lipstick color or eyeshadow. And that extra item can come from the drugstore. Chances are if it's that "trendy" it won't be "in" next season anyway. Do you honestly think lilac eyeshadow or coral lipstick is a staple? Your cheaper eyeshadow or lipstick may not be exactly the same, but trust us, it will be close enough to get you through the season.

STAR POWER
Relying on makeup artists to the stars to reveal their favorite products is also tricky. Many of them are paid by a cosmetics company to plant its products in copy whenever they can. Not all of them are, and it doesn't happen all the time, but be aware that it does happen. These same hairstylists or makeup artists often make media tours and appear on local TV stations to "show you the hottest looks for the coming year." They just happen to have the product they are promoting with them to achieve that look. Savvy TV bookers are wary of those segments and usually ask the public relations company to come up with any array of

products at various prices. But not all TV bookers are that ambitious. There's nothing wrong with learning tricks from the experts, you just don't have to run out and buy that exact product.

Ads made to look like editorial copy are really unfair. In bold print in *Glamour* magazine, for example, the headline reveals "The everyday guide to healthy skin." Underneath is a layout that resembles a standard article, complete with pictures of models or celebrities, information on products and beauty tips. In tiny print on the top of the page is the word "Advertisement." Very misleading!

THE WRINKLE

There is an ingredient out there that will actually *prevent* wrinkles. Can you believe it? It's called sunscreen. You need to be sure you are using one with an SPF of at least 15. If the moisturizer you buy doesn't contain a good percentage of sunscreen, it won't do a thing for your future wrinkles. Of course, that's not what you're told at the cosmetics counter. This is what we were told while shopping with our hidden camera.

Saleswoman: It's claim to fame is that it's a moisturizer, but it's also a firming cream. So if you are concerned with your skin starting to sag or wrinkle, what it does is kind of firms up the skin. And also prevents the skin from sagging in the future.

The saleswoman then tried to sell me a three-step Resilence skin care process for a total of $140. Although she acknowledged that nothing would take away wrinkles, she made claims that many dermatologists say are unproven, such as that the cream would repair damaged skin and prevent further breakdown. Our talk continued.

Saleswoman: It is going to restore a lot of the lost elasticity.
Janice: So this is actually going to put elastin back into my skin?
Saleswoman: Exactly, exactly.

Dermatologists tell us there is absolutely no way a skin cream can put elastin back into your skin. Unless you happen to find a hypodermic needle hidden in the cream! When you examine the salesperson's spiel, she tells us the product is designed to block the depletion of elastin through regeneration. Here's the catch: Your body is continually regenerating elastin anyway. By applying cream that blocks ultraviolet rays, you can create a stronger barrier on top of the skin barrier that protects the elastin from breaking down. That sounds great. And that's exactly what ordinary sunblock will do for you. So this woman is selling us a very expensive jar of sunscreen.

We asked people at Estée Lauder if they wanted to view our tape and comment on their saleswoman's claims. They declined. In a written statement they told NBC News that Resilience Elastin Refirming Cream "puts elastin back into your skin." Lauder also told us they have clinical tests to prove their claims but refused to share them with us. If NBC News couldn't see their scientific study, how could an ordinary customer ever have a chance to see the data!

You can definitely buy a good moisturizer with sunscreen for a lot less. Paula Begoun gave us her picks:

Almay's SPF 15 Moisturizing Lotion	$2/ounce
Neutrogena's SPF 15 Day Moisture	$5/ounce
L'Oréal Active Daily Moisture Lotion	$2/ounce

Remember, moisturizers do nothing to rid your face of wrinkles. Dry skin shows off the wrinkles, so using a moisturizer softens those lines. Once you stop using the moisturizer, the dryness and the wrinkles come back. If the salespeople told us the truth, we would all be walking around wrinkle-free. The only way for that to happen is to visit a plastic surgeon. Sorry, that's just the plain truth.

A REAL BREAKTHROUGH
Let's travel back in time for some insight into antiaging techniques. In ancient Egypt, along with the beauty ointment to

combat wrinkles, the treatment often included a mystic incanta-
tion of prayers calling on the gods to intercede and restore
beauty. As Karl Laden, Ph.D., so aptly puts it, there are women
today who recite incantations while applying cosmetics. "They
sit in front of their vanity, rubbing special night cream and saying 'I just paid $30 an ounce for this. Please Lord, make it
work.' "

And the gods may have heard them. Actually it was back to
the future when it came to fruity acids. Cleopatra's beauty secret
of fermenting grapefruits and oranges and rubbing it on her skin
is exactly what companies are doing today. Today's glycolic acid
is made from fermenting acidy fruit, and there is promise in that
solution. Lactic acid made of fermented milk also is used to get
the skin looking fresher and less aged. These acids won't remove
wrinkles, but they will freshen skin and promote new growth.
They also may help to even your skin tone by getting rid of the
brown spots.

Dr. Brad Jacobs says the acids work much like a buff puff, but
while a buff puff may take off some of the good skin, the acids
slough off the bad skin.

When you shop for an alpha hydroxy, glycolic, lactic, or
fruity acid, you need to know how much is in the product and
how pure the acid is. You want enough acid to peel off the dead
layers of skin. The key to good results is the product's skin peeling ability. Some contain as little as 2 percent, others may have
8 percent or more. Eight percent will peel off more dead skin
than 2 percent. The problem is a lot of the department store
creams don't specify the acid percentage on the label. Dermatologists usually start their patients off with 8 to 10 percent concentration, but the concentrations can go up as high as 15 to 20
percent. A chemical peel performed in the office can be as high
as 35 to 70 percent. So purchasing an antiwrinkle cream with 2
percent acid really won't do much, but it will be safe and enable
the company to avoid coming under FDA domain.

Here's a case where safety means lack of effectiveness.

We purchased an alpha hydroxy product from the department store for about $42 an ounce. It contained about 2 percent acid. You can spend a lot less at a drugstore (about $4 to $6 an ounce) for an alpha hydroxy acid level four times that amount. Look for Alpha Hydrox's Lotion or Pond's Age Defying Cream available only at the drugstore. The real bargain for buying pure, effective acids is to visit your dermatologist. Jacobs reveals he sells acids with a 10 to 15 percent concentration that contains purer ingredients than the ones cosmetics companies offer. He told us he buys it for about $8.50 a bottle and turns around and sells it for about $25. That's still a lot less than what the department stores charge, and you are getting a more effective product.

BEWARE OF WOMEN CARRYING GIFTS

Even the most educated shopper who had no intention of shopping for makeup may be caught up in this next tactic. Everyone loves a party, and everyone loves to be a part of a special event. Cosmetics companies know that. That's why they run special promotions offering so-called free gifts. They never really are free because there's always a minimum purchase. But when a beautiful woman comes up to you dressed in the theme color carrying a sparkling silver tray with samples and invites you to come over to the counter . . . be careful.

This is what the industry calls being "in gift." It's a time when freelance models are hired to launch a new product and pull in customers. Gina compares it to an army. "So now you have girls all over the store and they bring you back to the counter where you have makeup artists. So you have this whole line of people pulling them to the counter and when they get to the counter they leave and go back out there. The makeup artists have a whole line of people behind the counter handing them product. It's like an army, one person brings you there, the other sits you down and starts playing with your face."

Giving out free gifts even when we never asked for one is a persuasion technique. Social psychologist Robert Cialdini talks about free gift giving as a well-known sales tactic. He calls it:

"Reciprocation: If someone has done us a favor—given a free sample—we feel obligated to reciprocate. And so we feel the added pressure to buy something."

For the salesperson, the pressure to sell during those times is intense. The sales staff is told they need to rake in huge figures for the week. The makeup artists will sell just about anything to make the numbers. When one company is not "in gift," another one is.

And women love samples and they love gifts. Samples work. Pauline, a former makeup salesperson, said nine times out of ten if you sent someone home with a free sample, she would be back to purchase that product. And samples are helpful. Drugstores don't offer them. If you want to try a cream or even a perfume, you often can at the department store, not the drugstore.

ILLUSION OR DELUSION?

Okay, so you pass on the pushy salespeople and opt to shop at the drugstore. Why are you drawn to one brand over another? There's no one pointing you to a display, no one offering you a free gift or makeover. You find yourself heading to Revlon or L'Oréal. Why?

Well, you knew there had to be a trick somewhere here. It's called getting the shelf space you need to catch the customer. The bigger the splash, the more eye-appealing, the more likely you are to at least check out the merchandise. It's all part of a big marketing game plan.

Cosmetics consultants tell us companies will manufacture items they know won't sell well, just to keep the displays large and full. Take Revlon; the company has lots of different mascaras to choose from. It knows black sells the most and purple will sell very little. Still, it needs to keep the displays big and give the illusion it has more to offer, is hipper to the trends, and therefore must have the better product. If you could check the inventories, cosmetics consultants tell us, you would find two mascaras selling out of twelve. It's like owning real estate and it goes for department stores as well. Erno Laszlo has about 200 different skin care products in its line. Who needs 200 skin care products? But when you think of chic skin care, you think of them, and it's all because we are conditioned to think more is better.

Which brings us to the tricks in packaging. Cosmetics chemist John Kressaty clued us into how more is better when it comes to packaging. He tells us the "double-wall jar" is a standard in the industry. It's a jar that's used for skin creams that looks bigger than it is, truly a jar within a jar. A 2-ounce jar of cream looks like a lot more when it's in a double-wall jar. If you could pull the jar apart, Kressaty says, you would find a little jar inside of it. Add some folding literature and a folding carton and you have the illusion you bought a lot of product. He admits it's very unfair. When you buy a tube of toothpaste at the grocery store, you know exactly how much you are buying and you can tell from the packaging the tube really is full of product.

It takes a chemist to also point out the tricks in ingredients listings. Most shoppers are savvy enough to check ingredients lists on the back of products. It's second nature at the grocery store, where laws are now strict about making those labels clear and understandable. Checking the ingredients list on cosmetics can be deceiving. Kressaty says cosmetics must list the highest concentration of the product first, as long as it contains at least 1 percent of that ingredient; that's why water usually is listed first. But here's the catch. Once the ingredients are less than 1 percent, they can go in any order the manufacturer wants to list them in. So if a product wants to boast it has vitamin C or some great-sounding botanical, it can list it close to the top, even if it contains as little as 0.005 percent. Consumers are not told what the cut-off is for listing ingredients. The company can put just a tiny bit of let's say "pineapple extract" in the product to catch your attention and push a sale just on a teardrop of product. The chemicals and preservatives with long names that are not attractive are naturally listed toward the end.

THE MAKEUP MYSTIQUE

Expensive makeup has become a status symbol. Chic women pull out Chanel lipsticks from their purses at a fancy restaurant. A $3 Wet and Wild lipstick with a similar shade just won't do. We've bought into a crazy notion. Who are we impressing? Is it the man we are out on a date with? Do you think he would know the difference? Or are we impressing other women? Women also have been well taught that beautiful packaging and designer names make us feel better, feel richer, feel prettier. If buying those status brands does make you feel any of those things, then in our opinion it's worth it. But if you think about why you are paying $20 for a lipstick instead of $5 and you think your ego can take it, go for the cheaper stick.

Why do so many of the chi-chi lines have foreign names? Borghese's secret to lush lips is its "Crema Perfetta Perfecting Lip Conditioner and Botanico Lip Compresses with mineral-rich Acqua di Vita . . . A fountain of youth for your lips," its ad reveals! We are always impressed with the Europeans, thinking they have the more beautiful skin and that the secrets are in the Swiss Alps at some secret spa. Paula Begoun says when you buy Estée Lauder in England, you'll be told the Americans are ten years ahead of them! She also tells us how we all get swept away with "secrets." Companies use "exclusively formulated" or "specially patented" ingredients. Even the salespeople won't reveal what that secret formulation is all about; they'll just tell you no other line has their special patent. The hole in that logic is the very nature of patents means that it is *not* a secret. You must disclose all aspects of your patent in this country. Patent doesn't tell you about the efficacy. It usually just tells you about the chemical structure. The special secret or patent could mean nothing more than one product using 99.25 percent water as opposed to another using 99.35 percent. It doesn't give you any information about what the product does for the skin. But we all get sucked into those catchwords. We want to believe there is a secret out there and there's a reason to shell out $50 on a face cream.

GO TO THE PROS

When you want to know the scoop on what's good and what's not, you go to the pros who make up faces every day. Believe us, they want their job to be easy, and they want it to look good. So we snooped inside their makeup kits to see what works and what doesn't. We found professional print and TV makeup artists have a mix of product lines in their kits. They tell us they usually buy cheaper bases, mascaras, and powders. Usually they will splurge on blushes, eye shadows, and lipsticks. They also will use the higher-end lines that offer them professional discounts, such as MAC. The makeup artists we spoke to say they do find a difference in some drugstore products compared with the higher lines. They find working with some of the better lines is easier. And there is truth to that. Some of the better cosmetic lines whip their powders or creams longer, use less iridescence, or flake and crumble less. But when it comes to mascaras and pressed powders, they go for the cheap. Knowing the right mix of products is the trick, and it's very individual. You'll have to try a few cheaper brands to see if you like the way they work. Ask friends for recommendations. We've all made mistakes buying makeup that ended up in the garbage, so share your knowledge with a friend so we don't all end up with useless stuff.

HOW NATURAL IS NATURAL?

And speaking of useless, are botanicals better? Is greener healthier? These are the buzz words of the 1990s. But greener also means more "green" for the cosmetic giants. Promoters of botanicals say natural scents are better for you, more relaxing, destressing. They claim aromatherapy products that use natural plant essences will energize your body. Sure, it feels great to soak in a tub filled with delicious-smelling scents . . . but are you more energized? Do you feel better when you soak in something 100 percent natural as opposed to a fragrance made from man-made ingredients?

Joel McGowen, editor of *Green Consumer News,* tells us there are no legal definitions for the word "natural," so a company could put anything short of poison and call it "natural." Basically, he says, you are buying a feel-good image. It is strictly a marketing term. So a product really can contain very little of the natural ingredient, even if it has a cucumber, lavender, or pineapple splashed on the label. Dr. John Bailey, the director of the division of colors and cosmetics at the Food and Drug Administration says, "Some of these products are made with ingredients that just can't be considered natural." He uses Revlon's New Age Natural line as an example. While the more "natural" line does use plant extracts, its base formulations include the same chemicals that are in the company's other products. Even the Body Shop, which sells itself on "greener" products, uses preservatives. The cosmetics do have natural ingredients in them, but they also contain the same stuff every other firm uses, such as paraffins and sodiums, to balance out whatever else they are made of.

There's no way a product could be completely natural. A product containing bananas, cucumbers, and pineapple would be a moldy mess without a preservative. Cosmetics consultants do tell us that Aveda is probably the most natural line out there, as it uses the least preservatives. That's also why the cost is higher; the shelf life of the product is much shorter.

Aside from being a marketing tactic, "natural" cosmetics may in some cases actually be harmful. Dermatologists are not necessarily thrilled with the naturals. Natural does not mean non-allergenic. Many people with sensitive skin are drawn to the naturals, thinking that the mainstream lines may irritate their skin. Yet the opposite may be true. Doctors say fragrance is what many people are allergic to, and naturals contain a lot of fragrance. While fragrance itself may be natural, that doesn't mean it won't irritate your skin. As mentioned, lavender is a natural essence, but it's also a photosensitizer; some people can get a rash after using a lavender product and then going outside. Lanolin, an oil from sheep's wool, is a common allergen. Peppermint oil, menthol, and camphor are all very natural, but they are highly irritating to some skin. Paula Begoun warns "Women who complain about having irritation and dry skin run and buy a new moisturizer when all they might have needed to do is stop using the dry, irritating toner or bar soap, or avoid using something they were told was natural and wonderful for the skin but wasn't."

Until the FDA can come up with a definition for "natural," manufacturers will no doubt continue to use the marketing term at their own discretion. If you enjoy the smell of a natural product, go for it, but read the label; it probably contains some "unnatural" ingredients.

THE MAKEUP OF MAKEUP

One of the most extensively used ancient cosmetics was kohl, or black material to line the eyes. In addition to its beautifying effect, some believed it also served to prevent eye infections by repelling flies and also cut down on sun glaze. Today eye pencils are made by two major companies, the largest being Kohl, in Germany. Take a look at most pencils distributed by any cosmetics company; you usually will see "Made in Germany" on them. A cosmetics consultant told us making pencils can be tricky. Kohl is a reliable company. It has products ranging from a very hard pencil to a soft one, and the color spectrum is provided by the client. It's not worth it for cosmetics companies to make their own pencils, as the machinery is cumbersome and the process is long and tricky. So, if there are basically two eye pencil plants in the world, how different can the products be? How can one company justify charging $17 for one pencil and another $5? Our cosmetics consultants said this occurs "because customers are willing to pay it."

THE MAKEUP MARKUP

Our cosmetics consultant (who did not want to be identified, as she is still working in the industry) clued us in to the incredible amount of money that can be made in makeup. She tells us the cost of ingredients used in the industry is very low compared to what we pay retail. In other industries, she says, manufacturers "keystone" or "flip" the cost of the goods by doubling, so if a product costs $1 to produce, they will sell it for $2. In the cosmetics industry, the ratio is much, much higher. It is not unusual for a manufacturer to mark up the price by six times, so a product that costs $1 to make is sold for $6, a truly "beautiful" profit! Let's take the eye pencil as an example. The cost of the pencil to the cosmetics company may be $1, but by the time they put their scientific or specific formulations; their advertising, packaging, their administrative costs, and everything else they have on top of their goods, the price can go up to $6. After that, the retail cost has to be flipped. That's how you end up paying $12 to $17 for a pencil. Most professionals use the cheaper ones.

Mascaras should be thrown out after about three months because bacteria can grow, and eye infections can develop. So spending more than you have to makes no sense. Our consultant reveals that one color house, a plant that manufactures colors for cosmetic lines, can have up to 400 mascara accounts from different companies. Lancôme and Maybelline are two of the top sellers, and Revlon is in the top five. John Kressaty says mascara is basically a cream with black pigment. He says the variables in quality have more to do with the method of application.

We asked why some mascaras "clump" more than others. Kressaty says it has more to do with the wand than the formulation. A good brush or wand scrapes the excess mascara off in the tube, which allows less to clump on your lashes. The wand has nothing to do with how much you pay at the retail counter for the mascara.

Nail polish is a bit different. Some chip faster than others, some are thinner or thicker going on your nails. But here again, the price you pay makes little difference. There are three major nail polish manufacturers. DuPont is probably the largest. The cosmetics company gives the color specs to the manufacturer and pays a price per pound for the finished product, then the color maker fills it, gives it basic or very fancy packaging and the cosmetic company slaps its name on it, turns around and sells it.

Our consultant tells us Brucci, a $1 nail polish, is a much better product than Chanel's at $15. Brucci pays $18 a pound for its polish at the manufacturing level, where Chanel pays $13 a pound. Granted, the colors at Chanel are more current and the packaging costs are much greater.

When shopping for polish, shake it and look how fast it runs. If it's fast, it's too thin; if it's too thick, that won't work either.

Use a good base coat before applying nail polish to prevent chipping. Don't refrigerate polish; it makes it too thick to work with. Don't add nail polish remover to old polish to thin it out; doing so breaks down the chemical structure. Our consultant likes Brucci, Almay, Guerlain and Dior a lot. The price ranges are wide, but the quality is close. She says she will splurge on a higher line because of color, not quality.

Nail polishes still won't last more than a few days after a manicure, but water-base lacquer is in the development stages. It's more environmentally friendly and may be better for you.

THE KISS-OFF

How much money do you really need to spend to get that long-lasting, lip-smacking color? We plan to kiss and tell. ABC's *Good Morning America* decided it was time to put those long-lasting lipsticks to the test. For Valentine's Day, we gathered some gals and had them apply long-lasting lipsticks. The products ranged in price from less than $10 a tube to over $20. We asked the Michelangelo of makeup, Joe Blasco, a film and TV makeup artist, to judge our beauties. We headed to Venice Beach, California, and had the ladies take bites into pizza, sip soda, and then slather kisses on some hunky muscle men. After the informal tests were performed, Blasco judged the results.

Without question, the cheaper products held on better. The more expensive ones faded or came off. When we asked the expensive companies why, they told us they use more emollients, which makes the product more expensive and makes it feel better on the lips. And that's true, the cheaper ones felt dry on the women's lips. All but one woman said they would not opt for the long-lasting lipsticks, no matter what the cost. They said the lipsticks just weren't comfortable to wear.

If you are looking for the perfect lipstick, no matter how long it lasts, you are not alone. There are definitely lipstick junkies out there. Some women who must carry seven shades with them at all times. Know anyone like that? There is no way a woman could really use up all those shades, but still the search continues and the makeup bag bulges. This chapter probably will not change that addiction, but you should know what goes into the lipstick and that there really are differences. Why do some go on smooth and others tug at your lips? It has to do with the cream base the cosmetics company uses. The upper-end cosmetic lines spend most of their money on research and development. Our expert says that 60 to 70 percent of the ingredients are the same from line to line. But all is not exactly equal. Estée Lauder might add a decent amount of vitamin E to its lipstick, whereas a cheaper brand might just use a drop. Does the vitamin E really add that much? That's questionable. Kressaty says cosmetics companies ask chemists to duplicate expensive formulas for use in a lipstick that costs half the price. He says there's a lot of duplication work out there for chemists.

While the cheaper lines keep their same base formulations for years, Estée Lauder, for example, is already working on a lipstick for the year 2000. Along with costs for R&D comes the cost of packaging. That status lipstick case from Lauder comes from Italy and costs the company around $2. The Wet and Wild case may come from Korea and cost the company just 30 cents.

Lipstick texture varies widely within the same line. So it's really a product you have to experiment with to see if it works for you. You don't get the chance to do that in a drugstore. We've all been disappointed when we purchase a drugstore lipstick only to find when we get home that the true color is nothing like what was displayed at the store. Shopping at a cosmetics counter makes the choice much easier. First of all, you can try on a dozen different colors to see what works for you. But even better is asking a makeup artist you respect to narrow the choices down for you. Spending money on lipstick at the department store makes sense. It will save you a lot of time and probably money in the long run.

THE PAYOFF
When we speak to professional TV makeup artists and try to convince them that cheaper makeup is *always* as good as the higher-priced lines, they don't buy it. They do mix cheaper with the upper lines on some products, but they refuse to go completely on the cheap. The professionals say some of the cheaper eyeshadows or blushers flake or the pigment isn't strong enough. They are not wrong.

R&D departments at the major companies take that complaint seriously. They call it "payoff." That is how much of the powder once applied to the brush is actually transferred to the skin and how much just falls off the brush. Kressaty says the better brands use better pigment. The pigment load has to be strong enough so that you get the good payoff. Pigment can be expensive, so adding more of it to make a better product can raise the price.

Pressed powders as in eye shadows, face powders, or blushers can get a "glazing." That's the shiny surface that sometimes occurs with cheaper makeup. Kressaty says it happens when the product is not well made. The base could be off, the pressing time not right, or the surface too hard. The better brands spend more time and money on R&D and manufacturing to try to make sure that glaze doesn't occur. Using your fingers to apply the powders, whether expensive or not, coats the cosmetic with oils from your skin. Those oils can add a glaze to your powders and make them hard to apply. So use a brush to apply and keep your brushes clean.

SCENTS CENTS
The trickiest and most expensive ingredient in cosmetics is the fragrance. There is fragrance in everything you buy. Our sources

tell us that the smell of the raw product is horrible. The formula usually is made first and then masked to push down the raw ingredient smell. Ninety percent of the expense comes from developing the fragrance. Fragrance is made up of a combination of oils. The more pricey the oils, the more expensive the fragrance. After figuring in the cost of fragrance, the rest of the cost of the product is packaging, marketing and advertising. Fragrance is important and can draw us to one product over another, but as far as efficacy, fragrance makes no difference.

THIGH ANXIETY

Our faces aren't the only place on our bodies that deserve our attention and our money. From the neck down, women are willing to spend to make age disappear, to look smooth, silky, and sexy. Which brings us to what women young and old fight: cellulite, also known as cottage cheese or orange peels. These are all endearing names we have assigned to our dimply thighs and buttocks. Here is where even the smartest, most critical consumer may have very little willpower. We try dieting, exercising, and wishing those dimples away, and still even the thinnest among us lose a battle with a genetic giant. Creams, treatments, and surgery that promise to rid us of those unsightly bumps are hard to resist. Cosmetics companies have struck gold offering creams that lessen the "appearance" of cellulite for upward of $40 a pop.

There are no less than twenty-five different thigh creams on the market. After spending $40 or more on a tube of miracle cream, you are told to use it every day. One tube should last you about four months. That's an expensive proposition and a lot of massaging work. Sales for these thigh creams reach $100 million a year, so women are buying them. But most doctors say the creams are not much more than wallet-slimming, expensive moisturizers. Sorry, ladies, dermatologists tell us that cellulite is just about invincible. Even the current liposuction cannot fully get rid of the dimples.

Don't count on the cosmetics salesperson to tell you that. We searched the aisles asking about cellulite creams. The Estée Lauder salesperson told us their "Thigh Zone" at $45 "Thickens the outer layer of the skin so you can't see cellulite under the skin." We wondered if thick skin would be uncomfortable. The saleswoman told us: "Well, it feels like you are wearing panty hose all day." Shisedo's saleswoman told us something a little different: "The cream pulls water out of the skin, so the skin doesn't look so crumply." When we asked how the cream does that, she admitted that she didn't know how, but it did.

There just isn't enough evidence out there for dermatologists to believe in any of these creams. And scientific tests contradict each other. A well-publicized UCLA study showed that a cream with aminophylline as an active ingredient resulted in a half-inch reduction in thigh measurements among women who used it daily on one thigh and not the other. But a similar experiment was conducted at Washington University School of Medicine in St. Louis where some women rubbed on a cream with aminophylline and some rubbed on a cream with no active ingredients. The difference: none!

Even if women think their cellulite appears to be going away, they must never stop using the cream, ever! That's a wonderful market for cosmetic companies. Doctors believe if there is a difference in appearance, it's because these so-called miracle creams contain astringents, usually botanicals, such as butcher's broom and birchbark, which create a temporary tightening effect, or rely on massage to swell the skin and temporarily level its topography.

Aggressive massage may seem to work temporarily. A new procedure called "endermologie" developed in France has now arrived in the United States. It's just a mechanically assisted mega-massage that attacks the connecting tissue and breaks up the fat. The treatments are pricey. Weekly treatments can run from $80 to $125 a pop. You'll need about fifteen treatments and then one a month for maintenance. Doctors we spoke with say once you stop the treatment, the lumpiness comes back in about three months. Still, some women who are desperate to don a bathing suit for a week's vacation sans cellulite seem to be willing to spring for it.

Industry insiders predict the number of creams will only increase. Soon creams for stomachs, hips, and general body contouring will appear. As women try to stay fit at the health clubs and diet like crazy, they will continue to buy whatever promises them the end to the hereditary headache we call cellulite. It's a market cosmetics companies are dying for, one that requires faithful usage, one that costs a lot to maintain.

Cellulite creams are classified as cosmetics, not drugs, so there is no FDA approval process. Cosmetics companies are careful to say their cream "lessens the appearance of cellulite." They do not tell you their product or even mega-massage will get rid of the cellulite. As you can see, what is said behind the counter is not as carefully monitored. "It's like wearing panty hose all day!"

WHERE TO BUY YOUR COSMETICS

Infomercials

Cosmetics are so lucrative, lots of celebrities have gotten into the business. Late-night infomercials are compelling. It's intriguing to watch a beautiful star share her beauty secrets with you. We have a friend who is a brilliant attorney; she checks documents for falsehoods all day long. Yet she is convinced that the concealer she purchases from a Lori Davis infomercial is the best product she can buy. We looked at the concealer and thought it was good, and not overpriced. But we wondered how you could check the colors by watching them on a TV screen.

If you enjoy ordering from TV infomercials or shopping networks, by all means do it it. Just realize that the stars hawking their products may know nothing about the makeup they represent. It's a business, and it could be jewelry, exercise gear, or makeup. They are using their star power to sell, and star power works. We encourage you to watch infomercials to learn about products and makeup tips and then use those techniques to apply makeup at home. It's difficult to figure out texture and colors by ordering off the tube. However, return policies are usually good and the prices aren't outrageous, so if you are not happy, by all means, get your money back.

Drugstores

As you can tell, we are big fans of buying cosmetics at the drugstore. We hope we have illustrated how you can buy very similar products, with very similar ingredients, for less than half department store prices. We hope you will research your favorite products on your own, checking the claims and ingredient lists against each other. There are certain products we especially like buying at the drugstores: skin care, sunblock, mascaras, nail polish, eye and lip pencils. We admit that it is difficult to buy blushers, lipsticks, foundations, and eye shadows at the drugstore. We're big believers in being able to test the product on your skin. We also suggest that you try to stay away from shimmer; the drugstore products usually have a lot of iridescence in them to attract you to the blister pack. Matte colors are not appealing to the eye when seen through plastic. Some of the cheaper lines are tough to work with.

Remember the "payoff"? That's the amount of powder that stays on your skin. You may end up using more of the cheaper product and have to buy it more often than if you bought a more expensive product where you use less. The price could even out. You have to work the numbers for yourself. The time and money you can save by asking a professional to help you select the best color for you also may be worth the price difference.

We are thrilled that drugstores are now touting new return policies for makeup. RiteAid has a new ad campaign encouraging you to take a chance on a product and return it if you are not happy. CVS and Medic Discount Drugs are also entering the return arena. This makes life a lot easier for those who are willing to try choosing colors from painted displays or blister packs.

The color you see in a blister pack is usually darker than the true color. Since the packaging is air-tight, once you open it, the actual makeup is lighter.

Buying makeup that way can be frustrating. Return policies are nice, but standing in line to get a $5 refund is a hassle. At least now the choice is yours.

Department Stores

If you can get by all the hype and ridiculous claims made by hungry cosmetics salespeople and shop for what you really need, buying at the department store can be fun and easy. A good makeup artist truly can help you select colors that complement your look. Professionals tell us bad foundations or blush shades can age you. Many women don't update their look from season to season or even for years.

Your skin does change. What you wore ten years ago probably won't work for you today. Styles do change, and getting some updating help can't hurt. Just know when you have reached your budget and don't be intimidated to ask about price. Don't even wonder if makeup at a department store goes on sale. It never does. We overheard one customer asking a salesperson that very question; her very snobbish reply was "Of course not." And remember to be wary of women carrying "free" gifts. They can be presents you wish you never accepted.

Sometimes makeovers at the department store are free; sometimes you have to make a purchase. Getting someone who is good to do a makeover can be very helpful. Ask a lot of questions and ask for a makeup chart to take home with you. You do not have to buy everything they suggest, but even a few new products and expert advice can do wonders for a new look.

Contrary to what you may believe, cosmetics at the department store can be returned. Definitely. If you get home and think you bought too much, don't like the color, or the product irritates your face, take it back. The department store policies cover the cosmetics counters as well. Don't be intimidated by a sales-person with an attitude. It is your right, even if you used the product.

SHOPPING STRATEGY

We think you need the most help with strategy at the department stores. Drugstores and infomercials are obvious. So we went back to Gina to get the inside scoop on how to deal with pushy cosmetics salespeople. We gave her a scenario: You just want to buy a new lipstick. Sounds easy, but as we've shown you, it can be anything but.

"You have to know exactly what you want. You saw a lip-stick in a magazine and think the color might be nice. You have to be very specific about what you want. If you don't want them to do something to you, say *no*. If you do, it's a free service, don't feel pressured to buy what they have put on. If you want it, that's great, but if you don't, they are there to help you. So use it to your advantage; they are trained professionals. If you have a limited amount of money you want to spend, make sure you go to Lancôme or Estée Lauder. You will spend a lot more at Dior, La Prairie, and Chanel."

It's all about attitude. Be firm. We asked Gina how she buys makeup at the cosmetics counter. "A lot of times I will ignore what they are saying. I try not to get irritated. I am very focused about what I want, or I just stop them. It's better to sell you the product, get you out of the way, and work on someone else."

How do you pick a good makeup artist? Word of mouth is great, especially if you love the way someone looks. Or go to a cosmetics counter on a busy day. Keep stopping by to see how consistent the makeup artist's makeovers look. Some artists do beautiful work on their own faces and do terrible work on yours, and the opposite is also true. Gina says the better lines of-ten have better-quality artists because they pay more. But don't forget those artists are also under extreme pressure to make their sales figures. Some of the professional lines, like MAC and

Makeup Forever, which are now offered at many department stores, do not work on commission, so if you can't stand the pressure, you might opt for one of them.

GOOD LUCK, GIRLS

Let's end this chapter by going back to the beginning. The beginning of time, that is. No doubt cosmetics will always be important to women. In ancient times, cosmetics were invariably one of the items buried with the dead to take with them into their next life. Cosmetic products haven't been found only in the tombs of queens, princesses, or other royals. Even crude burial pits of commoners often contained the implements to prepare cosmetic products.

Not much has changed, has it? Even today there are women who wouldn't be caught dead without their makeup in place!

▶ Top Ten Tips

1. *Compare prices by reading ingredients lists.*
2. *Don't buy on impulse.*
3. *Buy staples and then add a few trendy accents.*
4. *Be firm with makeup salesperson about your budget.*
5. *Don't believe everything you read about a product.*
6. *Beware of "free" gifts.*
7. *Return makeup you aren't happy with.*
8. *Find a makeup artist you can trust.*
9. *Don't overbuy skin care products.*
10. *Throw out makeup you don't use.*

Glossary

Cosmoceutical: one step before the FDA gets it hands on it.

Cottage cheese, orange peels: Cellulite.

Payoff: The amount of product that stays on your skin, not on the brush.

Naturals: No legal definition.

Suggested Reading

Paula Begoun, *Don't Go to the Cosmetics Counter Without Me,* Seattle, Wash: Beginning Press, 1993.

Andrew Scheman, M.D., and David L. Severson, *Cosmetics Buying Guide.* Yonkers, N.Y.: Consumers Union of United States, Inc, 1993.

CHAPTER 3
ELECTRONICS

This chapter is devoted to buying consumer electronics. For the most part, we discuss audio and video equipment—televisions, video cassette recorders, compact disc players, and stereo systems. But much of our advice is relevant if you're buying any type of electronic goods, including cell phones, cameras, computers, and even appliances like washing machines and refrigerators. While some of the sales techniques used are inherent only to the electronics business, many are used by salespeople of all durable goods.

Most electronics retailers are forthright and honest. They have to be. In recent years there's been a real backlash by a public fed up with unethical sales practices. By the late 1970s unscrupulous stores with overly aggressive salespeople had alienated so many shoppers with their lawless techniques that they found they had no customers left. Many went out of business, often under a barrage of lawsuits and criminal investigations. Today dishonest salespeople won't last long at any reputable store because repeated customer complaints are bad for business. Nevertheless, there are plenty of unscrupulous salespeople working at fly-by-night operations.

In this chapter we take a look at how to get the best value for your money. We expose the secret sales tricks electronics stores use and make you aware of several illegal and unethical sales practices so you can avoid becoming a victim. Once you're aware of the pitfalls, we'll help you develop a shopping strategy and offer advice on how to pick the store and the product that's right for you.

ENTERING THE ARENA: GOOD NEWS AND BAD NEWS

So you're ready to buy a new television, VCR, or stereo system. We have some good news for you and some bad news too. First, the good news: Manufacturers are building better-quality equipment with more features and greater reliability than ever before. And while prices for most things you buy only go up, the prices for consumer electronics products continue to drop. Of course, if you're buying the newest high-tech gadget you're going to pay a premium, but once it becomes more popular its price quickly dives. For example, when Sony introduced the first Betamax recorder in 1975, it cost $2,400. Two years later, as other companies introduced their own models, you could buy a VCR for around $1,000. By 1987 the average price had dropped to about $300. Today you can buy a good-quality VCR for less than $200. And today's products are vastly superior to those of yesterday. As a result, smart shoppers can get greater value for their dollar.

Now the bad news. While the intense competition between stores can result in excellent bargains for consumers, that same competition is cutthroat—and it may be *your* throat they're after. Some retailers will do anything—lie, cheat, or steal—to separate you from your hard-earned cash. Don't be a victim.

ILLEGAL AND UNETHICAL PRACTICES

It's the stuff that gives the electronics industry a bad name: the dirty tricks, the appalling lies, the unlawful activities. Don't be taken by unscrupulous stores and dishonest salespeople. If you come across any of these sales techniques, run, don't walk, to the nearest exit.

Gone Fishing: The Classic Bait and Switch

The majority of complaints against electronics stores concern the bait and switch. You've probably heard the phrase before but might not quite understand how it works. Let's start with the classic bait and switch. For bait, an unscrupulous store will advertise an unbelievable deal on a specific item. This is what lures you to the store. But once you're there, well, you're like a fish out of water. When you ask a salesperson for the advertised item, lo and behold, it's not available. "Sorry, we just sold the last one," you're told. Sometimes the salesperson actually will go through the sham of writing out a sales slip until the stock room calls with the "bad news." Now the salesperson hits you with the switch: "We do have this unadvertised sale. Actually it's a much better bargain." It's not the item you wanted. It costs more than you wanted to spend, but the pressure to buy is overwhelming. "You'd be crazy not to buy it," the salesperson continues. "Sure it costs a little more, but the quality is much better." Don't buckle under the sales pressure. Stick to your guns and leave the store if it doesn't have the advertised product you wanted to buy in the first place.

As consumer reporters we've heard many variations on the bait and switch. After doing some research, you decide to buy a Yamaha stereo system. But when you get to the store, the salesperson badmouths the product. She might say, "Yeah, the price is good on that, but we've had a lot of dissatisfied customers." Then in a soft voice: "Between you and me, the quality is just not that good." Next thing you know, she's pressuring you to buy another brand that's even cheaper than the Yamaha. It isn't a brand you've heard of, but the saleswoman assures you she's just trying to prevent you from wasting your money. Unfortunately, chances are she doesn't have your best interest in mind. She's switching you to a no-name product because it has a higher markup, which means more profit for the store and more money in her pocket.

That's just what happened to Jay, who went to a camera store to buy a Nikon telephoto lens. The salesperson asked him, "Why do you want to buy that lens? It's garbage." He offered to let Jay in on a secret: "How'd you like to see a lens made by the same manufacturer that makes lenses for Nikon?" The salesman then pulled out a cheap lens made by an inferior company. Without mentioning the brand, we can tell you the salesman's claims were complete hogwash.

Consumer protection agencies have been effective in curbing bait and switch, and while stores still engage in it, they're less blatant, especially in their advertising. If you see an unbelievable advertised price, read the fine print carefully. To get around bait-and-switch accusations, some retailers still advertise fabulous deals but put an asterisk next to the price, which leads you to the fine print. After you find your magnifying glass, you'll see that great price usually comes with a few stipulations like "cash only," "only five in stock," or the classic "limited supply."

An important note: There's a fine line between legitimate sales techniques and illegal practices. Many salespeople will try to talk you into buying a more expensive product. In the industry that's called "bumping" or "stepping up." (See "Do the Bump.") It's not considered bait and switch if the product you want to buy is available, and the salesperson simply suggests a different product without undue pressure. However, many salespeople are experts at straddling this very thin line. Our advice: If you think you're being hooked, leave the store immediately.

Refurbished Goods: Getting Used

Some stores and mail-order catalogs specialize in refurbished goods. These are products that were sold as new but returned, usually because of defects. They're then rebuilt by the manufacturer or a third party and resold. Refurbished goods are also called "reconditioned," "factory-serviced," and "rebuilt."

There's nothing wrong with buying refurbished goods, as long as you realize that's what you're getting. Often you can get a generous discount when buying a rebuilt product. Legitimate mail-order catalogs such as Damark specialize in selling refurbished electronics. However, one of the fastest-growing scams, particularly in big cities, is selling used and reconditioned merchandise as new. In New York City, the Department of Consumer Affairs does occasional sweeps of electronics stores. In a recent investigation, it found almost half the stores it inspected were selling reconditioned products as new. Talk about getting "used"!

Unfortunately, often it's hard to tell if an item has been refurbished. In fact, rebuilt products often look identical and are packaged in the same way as brand-new merchandise. Barbara, of Brooklyn, New York, has a typical story of how consumers get scammed. She bought what she thought was a new Panasonic telephone and answering machine for $140, but when she got it home, it didn't work. When she tried to return it to the store, the salesperson actually admitted he had sold her a rebuilt phone but refused to give her a refund. Sean, of Ridgefield, Connecticut, has another good example. He thought he was buying a new video camera, but when he got the merchandise home he quickly realized he'd been had. "The boxes weren't sealed," says Sean. "There were no warranty cards in the box, and the accessories weren't wrapped in plastic bags."

Unfortunately, electronics manufacturers have yet to come up with a universal method to help consumers easily identify items that have been refurbished. New York City Consumer Affairs Commissioner, José Malonado, is pushing manufacturers to develop an industry-wide standard. "Customers shouldn't have to wait to get home and play detective to figure out if what they purchased is in fact new," says the commissioner. Nevertheless, consumer affairs inspectors have their own tricks of the trade to help them identify refurbished goods. Working undercover, they look for several telltale signs the average consumer normally wouldn't notice.

- An "X" engraved on the back of the product near the model and serial numbers.
- A mark or hole on the product box where the merchant has "skinned," or cut out, a manufacturer's stamp or sticker, which marks the product as refurbished.
- A manufacturer's warranty page in the instruction manual that's been ripped out or crossed out.
- A warranty issued not by the manufacturer but by a third party.

If you think you're being sold a refurbished product on the sly, consider these tips before you lay down any cash. Look at the product box carefully. Make sure it's properly sealed and is not marked "used," "rebuilt," "factory serviced," "reconditioned," or "refurbished." Open the box and verify that the model number listed on the box matches that on the product you're purchasing.

Buying refurbished items can be a good way to get a product you need while saving money, as long as you understand that what you're buying is used. A legitimately rebuilt item is inspected thoroughly by the manufacturer before it's resold. If you choose to buy a reconditioned product, make sure it comes with some kind of warranty, preferably one from the original manufacturer.

Stock Splitting: Batteries Not Included

Stock splitting is another unethical sales practice that stores use to fool consumers into thinking they're getting the best price. Take a camcorder, for example. Usually manufacturers package a camcorder with certain necessary accessories: the camera battery, battery charger, adapters, and special hook-up cables. You can't use the camcorder without this standard equipment. An unscrupulous store will open the manufacturer's box and take out these essential items, then sell them to you individually.

It happened to Sean, of Ridgefield, Connecticut, whose work as a driver for corporate executives often takes him to New York City. Sean wanted to buy a camcorder for his family and thought he could get a good deal in Manhattan. In one store he found a JVC camcorder at what he believed was a very good price. But as the clerk was ringing up the sale, Sean was told that he'd need to buy a battery and an adapter for an additional $60. When he got home, he noticed the camcorder box clearly stated that those accessories were included free. Our advice: Examine the product box carefully before you buy any accessories and certainly before you leave the store.

Real Prices and Fake Discounts

By law manufacturers cannot set prices for their products, so they've established what is called the "list price" or "manufacturer's suggested retail price." Almost everyone knows that the manufacturer's suggested retail price has absolutely no meaning because the "street price"—the price the product usually sells for in most stores—is significantly less. It would be almost impossible to buy an item at its inflated list price from a legitimate store. Expect discounts of at least 10 to 20 percent off the manufacturer's suggested retail price. You should beware of any price comparison to the manufacturer's suggested retail price, particularly when it comes to sales. Offering 10 percent off the list price, instead of the store's everyday, real-world price, is really offering a fake discount.

Taking fake discounts one step further, some unethical stores actually have the audacity to display a price that is even *higher* than the manufacturer's suggested retail price, and the manufacturer doesn't have any control over this repricing. When the salesperson sees you're interested in an item, she'll casually mention that she can make you a deal. After knocking off $100, she's still selling it to you for about the list price or higher. It happened to two of our colleagues at *Dateline NBC* who went undercover at several Manhattan electronics stores. A JVC camcorder was priced by one store at $2,000, but the salesman made them an offer they couldn't refuse. He knocked the price down to a "bargain" $1,200. However, JVC's list price for that camera is only $699.

In several states it's illegal for a store to display a price above the manufacturer's suggested retail price without making such a disclosure. What can you do to protect yourself against this retailer scam? We urge you to take the time to do a little price-comparison shopping before you make your purchase.

Buyer Beware: Gray-Market Goods

No, this doesn't refer to products that are only offered in the color gray. You've heard of the black market? Well, some con-

sumer electronics, as well as computers and photography equipment, come from the gray market. They're products that are
legally produced but distributed in unauthorized ways. We
won't bore you with a dissertation on trade law—we'll keep it
simple. You get a great deal on a Nikon camera, which turns out
to be a gray-market Nikon. This means that while your camera
looks identical to a U.S.-licensed Nikon, it wasn't made to be
sold in the United States. It was brought into the country by an
importer not authorized by the manufacturer to distribute the
camera in the United States. There's nothing illegal about buying or selling products on the gray market, as long as the consumer knows what he or she is getting.

What difference does it make to you where the camera was
supposed to be sold if you got it for a great price? The main risk
of buying gray-market goods is that the manufacturer's warranty usually isn't valid. Occasionally gray-market items come
with an international warranty, which means if the item breaks
you must send it abroad for repairs or replacement. Sometimes
the store will offer a warranty itself or a warranty through a
third party. However, as one New York City consumer investigator points out, "Would you rather have a warranty on your
Nikon camera from Joe Blow Warranty Service or from
Nikon?" Other problems with gray-market goods: The instruction manual may not be printed in English, the product may lack
certain safety standards required in the United States, and if it
was made for the European market, it might not operate on
standard 110-volt U.S. current.

Most gray-market items are sold through large mail-order
companies. In fact, those low prices you see advertised in the
back of audio, video, and photography magazines are usually for
gray-market goods. (See "Shopping by Mail or Telephone.") In
New York City, where many of these mail-order companies are
headquartered, the retailer is required by law to inform you
whether the item they're selling is not covered by a U.S. warranty.
Nevertheless, be sure to ask the salesperson, and make sure the
U.S. warranty card is in the box when you receive your shipment.

Also be aware that some manufacturers won't honor U.S. warranties for their products unless they were purchased from an authorized dealer. If you have questions about the manufacturer's warranty, we suggest you contact the manufacturer directly before you make a purchase. Most manufacturers even have a toll-free phone number.

In our opinion, buying gray-market electronics isn't worth the comparatively small amount of money you'll save. Especially with major purchases, buy a product only after ensuring it comes with a manufacturer's U.S. warranty and confirming that the manufacturer will honor it.

INDUSTRY SECRETS REVEALED

We've alerted you to the illegal and illicit, but now we want to reveal some common but little-known sales techniques you're likely to encounter when shopping for electronics. Much of the information in this section comes directly from former electronics salespeople.

Confessions of a Salesman

Steve spent five years working as a salesman at a regional electronics and appliance chain in the New York City area. He quit because he got sick of the long hours and the pressure to sell, sell, sell. Here he discloses some of the tricks of his old trade.

Steve loves consumer electronics and prided himself on knowing a lot about the equipment he sold. In fact, he was known among his fellow salespeople as the "spec guy" because he knew all the product specifications. If a customer wanted to know the "signal-to-noise ratio" of a tape deck or whether a TV had a "comb filter," Steve was the guy to ask. Getting paid solely by commission, he quickly realized that knowing this information wasn't the key to making a good living as a consumer electronics salesman. "You really didn't have to know a lot about the equipment at all, as long as you knew more than the customer," says Steve. "If the customer had a question, you just needed an answer; it didn't matter if it was the right answer."

Steve explains the first thing a salesperson does is to "qualify" a customer. With just a few questions, a salesperson can determine just how much customers know and how willing they are to buy. If the other salespeople couldn't fabricate enough information about a product to close a sale, they'd usually call in Steve. "In fact, the top salesman in the store couldn't even program his VCR," says Steve, "but he had a great rapport with the customers."

"There were a lot of honest salesmen at my store," Steve emphasizes, "but the dishonest ones would make a lot more money." While many of the techniques revealed in this section are not necessarily dishonest, you might find them quite unfair. Keep in mind that they are industry-wide selling methods used in most electronics stores. By becoming aware of these little-known techniques, you'll certainly become a smarter consumer.

Seller Incentives: The Biased Salesperson

Did you ever wonder why salespeople are often quick to recommend a certain brand? Say you're looking for a video camera, and the salesperson really talks up an RCA camcorder. He tells you, "No one makes a camcorder like RCA, it's the best value for your buck. I just bought one myself. I wouldn't have bought anything else." So what's going on here? Does this guy really love RCA? Does he think those dogs in the commercials are just too adorable to resist? Does he have an uncle who works at the factory? Or does he just think RCA makes a hell of a product? Well, certainly any or all of the above could be true, but remember, salespeople are motivated by money, and there's something that goes on behind the scenes that you probably don't know.

It's known in the industry as a "hit" or "spiff," which stands for "Sales Promotion Industry Fund." Basically, a manufacturer or the store itself will push a product by offering a cash bonus to salespeople for selling that model. In other words, if the store has an overstock of a certain model of Zenith televisions, the sales force will be notified that on top of their regular commission, they'll get a $10 spiff on that product. Even salespeople who don't get paid on commission can still receive spiffs from manufacturers.

Salespeople often get spiffs when they sell a lesser-known brand because these brands often yield a higher profit margin for the store. For instance, consumers seem to love Sony televisions. The Sony Trinitron has amazing name recognition. As a result, customers go into an electronics store and say, "I want a Sony." They won't even look at other brands. But Sony doesn't give retailers much room to mark up prices; the store's cost is often very close to the sale price. But lesser-known manufacturers or manufacturers trying to increase market share, such as Mitsubishi or Samsung, will give retailers a high profit margin, and in turn the retailer can offer its sales force a hit or spiff to push the product.

For former salesman Steve, these cash incentives were a big deal because his base commission was only 1 percent of his gross sales. "The hits had a big influence," he reveals. "It really determined how much money you took home at the end of the week. Why would I sell a customer a $299 Sharp television with no hit and make just $2.99, when I could sell them a Mitsubishi for $350 that had a $40 hit on it and take home $43.50?"

Actually, many stores offer their sales force cash incentives for more than just selling certain products. They'll give a cash bonus when a salesperson peddles an extended warranty or signs up a customer for the store's credit card. Computer stores also will offer an extra commission to their salespeople if they enroll customers in training sessions. This explains why you often still feel sales pressure even after you tell a salesperson you'll buy a product.

Surprised? While there's nothing illegal about the practice of spiffs, when we tried to get a comment from some of the big electronics retailers as well as a manufacturers' association, they all either refused to acknowledge the existence of spiffs or simply refused to comment. For instance, when we asked one superstore spokesperson to address our questions about spiffs, he told us in corporate doublespeak, "I don't know if I could get into that even if I were aware of it."

We've heard the argument that spiffs create a win-win situation for both retailer and consumer. A store moves its overstock, and consumers get good deals. Well, it's certainly a good deal if you get the spiff, but unfortunately that check goes to the salesperson while you end up with a product that might not suit your needs.

A Spiffy Holiday: Sell a Television, Win a Trip
How'd you like a free trip to the Caribbean? Maybe we should rephrase that. How would your electronics salesperson like a free trip to the Caribbean, because that's what she might be getting from your purchase. It's another type of spiff, but instead of cash, a salesperson earns points or coupons for lots of free stuff.

Steve, the ex-salesman, did pretty well with noncash incentives. Every time he sold a Mitsubishi product, he'd get points. Eventually he earned enough points to get a top-of-the-line Mitsubishi television worth $1,000 for less than $100. When he sold a GE or RCA appliance, he'd get credit at Eddie Bauer clothing stores. He earned $985 worth of credit, enough to go on a shopping spree for a brand-new wardrobe. Another manufacturer offered coupons good for cash-off travel. Steve collected enough to take two free trips, one to Jamaica and another to Puerto Rico. His hotel and airfare were completely free.

While we're happy for Steve, we think all spiffs are a misguided form of compensation because they reinforce behavior that isn't consumer friendly. Unless they're disclosed to the consumer (which just ain't going to happen), we think spiffs send a dangerous message to salespeople. They can bias them and skew their recommendations to their customers. How are salespeople supposed to help a customer make an appropriate selection when they have a shot at getting some extra bucks by recommending a product with a spiff? Even if spiffs don't bias all salespeople, now that you know this insider information, won't you be more suspicious of their recommendations?

Loss Leaders: Your Gain

"Loss leader" is the retail term for an item priced at or below a store's cost to attract shoppers. Many electronics stores will advertise loss leaders in their ads and weekly circulars. They're not so much trying to sell you the specific product advertised as they are trying to show you what low prices they have to persuade you to visit their store.

Advertised loss leaders are usually last year's versions or bare-bones models with few features, and they're often in limited supply. The bare-bones models generally lack features that you might find essential while last year's discontinued models often utilize older technology. Still, for some, loss leaders can be a good value. You get a decent product at a wholesale price. Here's a hint: If you're looking to buy last year's model at a loss-leader price, do your shopping from January to March—this is when many retailers clear their shelves to make way for new merchandise.

Actually, aggressive consumers who go into a store with the sole purpose of buying a loss leader have a name: Retailers call them "cherry pickers." Generally, stores don't worry too much about these shoppers because for every cherry picker there is a legion of consumers who are drawn in by loss-leader advertising. Stores can then battle the potential profit plunge from loss leaders by using a technique to get your dollars called the "bump."

Do the Bump

The "bump" is a sales technique used by many retailers, including electronics and appliance stores. It's also called the "step up." The goal of the bump is to convince you to buy a model that has more features, is higher priced, and has a higher mark-up than the model you planned to buy.

Take a basic 27-inch television, for example. A no-frills model retails for about $449. Step up to a model with the picture-in-picture feature, and it costs you $499. Add a few more bells and whistles, and you'll pay $549. Finally, a top-of-the-line model, which includes extras like a two-tuner picture-in-picture and an on-screen TV listings guide, sells for $599. Even if you enter a store intending to buy the basic model, an adept salesperson will push the features that "you can't possibly live without," and you'll walk out with a top-of-the-line TV and $150 less in your pocket. Evan, a former salesman who worked in Los Angeles, explains, "The common logic is that if a person comes in saying they want to spend $500, that means you could probably bump them up to the $600 or $700 level."

Sound like bait and switch? Well, it's close, but there is a difference. If the item you wanted to buy is unavailable and the salesperson pressures you to buy something more expensive or of lower quality, that's bait and switch. But many customers are happy to pay for what the industry calls "value-added features" when a salesperson can properly demonstrate the advantages. "It can be a fine line between bumping up and bait and switch, and riding that line can be an art form," says Evan. "It's all a matter of how you explain it. If a customer comes in and says, 'I want that tape deck you have advertised for $99,' and the salesperson tells him it's out of stock or a piece of crap, that's bait and switch," he explains. "But I'd tell the customer, 'Okay, we have plenty of the $99 tape decks in stock, and I'd be happy to grab one for you. Or can I show you a couple other tape decks, some of them just a few bucks more, some a lot more, so that you can look at the differences and compare the features?' I'd say 90 percent of the time I bumped the customer up to a more expensive product."

In training sessions, Steve, our former New York City salesman, was drilled again and again with the acronym FAB: Features, Advantages, Benefits. The concept is to demonstrate the features and explain the advantages and benefits so customers think they can't live without them. Then it's an easy sell.

Steve says it was easy to step up a customer to a television with the picture-in-picture feature. Picture-in-picture sounds great: It allows you to watch two programs at once. It can be the ultimate feature for a sports fan. A downside is that if you have cable, it can be very difficult to set up and might not work correctly. Plus, it's one of those features that just sounds better than it is. Have you ever tried to watch two television shows at once? Most of the people we talked to who have picture-in-picture, including diehard sports fans, admit they rarely use it.

There are times when you should consider a bump up. You shouldn't always buy the bare-bones model. Often it makes sense to invest in a more expensive piece of equipment that is of higher quality and incorporates the latest technology. If the salesperson can explain the added features, and you believe they will benefit you, by all means step up. Spending an extra $50 for a stereo that has features you know you'll use is smart shopping. If that stereo lasts ten years, it's only costing you an extra $5 a year, not a bad investment versus a bare-bones model that will quickly become outdated or obsolete. We urge you to do a little research on your own. Learn about the features and buy what you need. That same $50 is wasted if it's spent on extras you never use.

Often stores are laid out to help salespeople convince customers to step up by placing cheaper models next to ones with more features and higher mark-ups. "In our store we'd put the loss leaders next to the best products," says Steve. "That way it was easy for the sales force to point out the model with all the bells and whistles compared to the stark, basic model." An honest salesperson at a reputable store can be very helpful when explaining the benefits and advantages of certain features, while the dishonest salesperson will use confusing technical jargon to try to fool naive consumers.

WHERE TO SHOP: A PLETHORA OF CHOICES

When buying consumer electronics, you're bombarded with choices. Not only do you have dozens of manufacturers offering hundreds of different models, but a wide variety of stores sell electronics. Which store is best? Should you go to a small mom-and-pop merchant, or buy from a large chain like Circuit City? Should you shop in a specialty electronics boutique with luxurious listening rooms, or try a discount store like Wal-Mart or a warehouse shopping club like Costco or Sam's Club?

As we've mentioned, electronics shopping is much more enjoyable than it used to be. In the last decade stores have started focusing on value and service. Aggressive salespeople have had to make way for stores that call their staffs "sales counselors" or "customer advisors." This section looks at various types of stores that sell electronics and establishes their pros and cons to help pick the type of store that's best for you.

Commission or Noncommission? That's the Question

Most electronics stores don't pay their staff a salary. Instead, the salespeople work solely on commission, which is based on the products they sell. Other stores choose to pay their employees only a salary on the theory that customers don't want to be hassled by aggressive salespeople.

"A salesperson is motivated by money," says former salesman Steve, who was paid by commission. "Make your sale and make your commission." Salespeople paid by commission usually get between 2 and 4 percent of their gross sales, plus spiffs. That's about $6 for selling a $300 television, so it's easy to see why they need to move a lot of product to make decent money. That's also why selling those extras is so important to salespeople—they can make a bonus on everything. When Steve sold an extended warranty, it meant extra money in his pocket; when he signed up a customer for a store credit card, he got a $5 bounty.

It's survival of the fittest at the commission store. "The top salespeople receive bonuses," Steve explains, "while the low-earners are retrained on their selling techniques or simply fired." At Steve's store, the manager posted a list in the employee lounge of the best and worst salespeople, based on gross sales. The pressure to perform was intense, and the competition between salespeople was fierce. Steve says the veteran salesmen would do what's called "sharking." "I'd be inside dusting the televisions when there was a lull and the veterans would hang out by the front door smoking cigarettes and watching customers drive up," he says. "They'd avoid all the old ladies and keep a look out for any thirty- or forty-year-old men entering the store. They'd check out a customer's car and look at what kind of clothes he was wearing. They'd look for people with money who they knew were coming to buy." When customers entered the store, the salesman would ask them what they were looking to buy. Steve explains, "If it was a low-commission item like a Walkman or alarm clock, the salesman would simply point them in the right direction and say, 'That guy over there can help you.' But if the customer was looking for a stereo system or a big-screen television, the salesman would put out his cigarette and say 'Right this way.' "

Sharking. Aggressive salespeople. It doesn't sound very consumer friendly, does it? So why even go to a store that pays its sales force on commission? This is a tough one because it's a paradox. The commission stores have a very attentive sales force. And boy, can these salespeople be attentive. Unfortunately, they often cross the line from attentive to aggressive, high-pressure intimidation. But some consumers feel commission stores are the way to go. One shopper explained, "I love the commission stores because the employees love to sell stuff and you can get the best service."

Circuit City is one of the best-known consumer electronics and appliance chains. They pay their "sales counselors" by commission but say the commission is based not only on what they sell but on customer service as well. A Circuit City spokesperson explained, "If a sales consultant is getting a lot of returns on items, we know that individual is probably using a hard sell and not really selling the customers products they need. We can analyze their sales and then retrain that counselor. If the counselor continues to hard sell, he won't work for us."

At noncommission stores, where the sales force is paid a straight (and often low) salary, the staff is usually younger and not very skilled. (We could use the term "pimple-faced," but we won't.) Getting paid by the hour, they might not go out of their way to help you. In fact, many customers tell the old joke, "it's

Tom is a retired schoolteacher who lives in a small town in Pennsylvania. In the last few years, superstores have been popping up all over town. There's now a Circuit City and a Best Buy within driving distance of his home, but Tom refuses to shop at these stores. He prefers to buy at the same family-run business where he's bought all his electronics and appliances for the past twenty-five years. He knows it costs him more money—he'd actually save up to $100 on his bigger purchases if he drove farther down the street—but he swears by the service of the smaller merchant. "If something breaks down, I never have to worry because they'll come right to the house and fix it," Tom explains. "The store's owner gets calls from people who bought their stuff from those big stores, but he won't fix it if you didn't buy it from him." Tom has a point—most of the time you just can't beat the personal service of these smaller family-run businesses.

Department Stores, Discount Stores, and Shopping Clubs
It was the popularity of radio in the 1920s that gave the consumer electronics industry its start in the United States. Back then folks bought their radios at big department stores like Macy's. But today there's a greater choice in where to buy a TV or VCR. In fact, department stores are selling fewer and fewer consumer electronics, finding it too hard to compete with superstores. You'll find department stores don't carry as wide a variety of manufacturers and models as their megacompetitors. In general, the everyday prices are a little higher at department stores, but if you like the shopping atmosphere, you usually can get good deals during their big sales. As with superstores, manufacturers sometimes make derivative models for department stores too. So if you find, for instance, a JVC television with a different model number from an identical JVC TV you saw somewhere else, be sure to compare features.

Mass merchandisers like Wal-Mart and Kmart also carry electronics, as do warehouse clubs like Costco and Sam's Club. However, don't expect to find expert advice from the sales staff at these cavernous retailers. Keep in mind that a warehouse store that sells five-pound cans of peas and toilet paper in bulk along with VCRs and fax machines shouldn't be expected to have a sales clerk who can advise you on the finer points of your electronics purchase. These stores are strictly cash and carry. Whether it's a giant can of baked beans or a television, you're expected to simply hoist it into your oversize shopping cart and pay at the register. Don't look for high-end electronics at these retailers either. Selection is limited. They usually carry one or two brands, often the cheaper no-frills models of value brands like Goldstar. You'll find the prices comparable to those of the superstores, and occasionally you can get really good deals. For a simple and straightforward item, these mass merchandisers aren't a bad place to do some comparison shopping.

Shopping by Mail or Telephone

Mail order can be a way to get good prices on electronics, particularly if you live in an area that doesn't have a large variety of electronics stores. In fact, one of the most popular ways to buy a computer is over the phone. Consumers can save about 20 percent when they order a computer directly from companies like Gateway 2000 or Dell Computers.

But keep in mind that it can be difficult to do business with a company that's located thousands of miles away. There are many advantages to buying locally. As we said, when you find a reputable store, your local salesperson can be a big help in advising you on purchases. It's also much easier to return to a local store to complain or get service if something breaks. We've heard frustrating stories from mail-order customers who tried to reach customer service with a problem only to be put on hold indefinitely, transferred to dozens of different people, or have messages go unanswered. Needless to say, it can be frustrating if you get stuck doing business with a deceitful company that's far away.

Before you place your order with a mail-order company you've never done business with, it's essential to run their name by the Better Business Bureau or consumer protection agency in the city where the merchant is located to see if other customers have logged complaints. Here's a typical horror story: A New Hampshire man ordered a fax machine from a Manhattan mail-order retailer. Although the company billed his credit card immediately, he didn't actually receive the product until seven months later. In the interim he placed about forty calls to the company but only got excuses and pitches to buy a more expensive machine.

When you call to place an order, always ask if the item you want is available immediately and demand to be charged for the purchase on the day the company actually ships it. Some companies aren't always completely honest about product availability, but you have the law on your side. According to the Federal Trade Commission's Mail or Telephone Order Rule, a company is required to ship your merchandise within the time stated in its ads or (if no time is stated) within thirty days after you place your order. If the company is unable to deliver on time, it must send you a notice offering you the option of waiting longer or canceling your order with full refund.

You also should confirm the total price, including shipping and handling charges, of any order you place. If you don't ask, you might be surprised by a company's hefty shipping charge. Also be forewarned that some mail-order companies deal in gray-market goods, so find out if the item you want carries the manufacturer's U.S. warranty. (See "Buyer Beware: Gray-Market Goods.") Make sure to inquire about a company's return and refund policies. Some retailers have very strict policies on returns if a product isn't defective and it's simply a matter of customer dissatisfaction. Understand the allowable return period. Many companies will not pay the return shipping if you decide to send back an item. This can be quite costly if you need to return a heavy item like a computer or television. Also, ask if there is a restocking fee on returns. This fee is usually a percentage of the original purchase price that you won't get back if you decide to return a nondefective item. A typical restocking fee is 15 percent, which means if you return a $2,000 computer, you'll only get back $1,600. The reason for the high fee is that once a box is opened, the store usually can no longer sell the product as new. Often it has to be marked down as a clearance item, so you're paying for the store's loss in profit. Some mail-order companies don't charge a restocking fee, so be sure to ask.

When you're ready to place your order, use a credit card and don't pay the charge until you've received the goods in satisfactory condition. The Fair Credit Billing Act offers some protection when you use a credit card to pay for purchases. If you're charged for merchandise before you receive it or have any problems with your mail-order purchase, call your credit-card issuer immediately and contest the charges. While the bill is being disputed and investigated, you shouldn't have to pay the amount in dispute.

Keep track of your order by taking good notes. Write down the date you placed it and the name of the salesperson. Note the total amount you'll be billed and confirm you'll be charged only upon shipment of the product. Jot down the brand, model number, and color of the products you ordered as well as the expected delivery date. Keep a copy of the ad or catalog you ordered from. When the product arrives, open it immediately and check it out thoroughly. If there are any problems, contact customer service at once. Save all your receipts, mailing labels, and original boxes for as long as possible.

Considering the risks involved in buying products over the phone, we suggest you do some comparison shopping at local stores. Compare the local price with sales tax to the mail-order price with all shipping and handling charges. If the prices are within 5 to 10 percent, do yourself a favor and buy it from the store near you. You can even ask if the local store is willing to match the mail-order price. However, if the mail-order price just can't be beat and you've checked out the company, by all means order by phone.

Order by Internet: Cybershopping
Today many retail stores and mail-order houses have set up sites on the Internet. This enables consumers to browse, compare features and prices, and even place orders all with a few keystrokes

and mouse clicks. It sounds great, but when buying via the Internet you should take the same precautions you would when ordering by phone or mail. In cyberspace, you might be doing business with a company that's thousands of miles away, or even in a different country, so if something goes wrong, it could be hard to get the matter resolved. In addition, it's difficult to confirm just who you're dealing with because anyone can set up an Internet "home page" and start collecting money. Because it's easier to start an Internet site than it is to get an 800 number, the Internet has become like the Wild West, opening up a whole new frontier to con artists. Also, don't judge a company solely by its slick Web site. Make sure you know who they are and where they're physically located.

When placing your order, pay close attention to the order form before you transmit your data. For instance, with an extra keystroke you might mistakenly order eleven VCRs instead of one. Also make sure you know the shipping and handling charges, and double-check that everything adds up correctly. Print out a copy of your order before you submit it.

When sending personal information over the Internet, it pays to be paranoid. Don't provide a company with information that isn't necessary to make a purchase because information over the Internet can be intercepted. You should use a secure Web browser and give personal information only on "secure" sites— sites that will "encrypt," or scramble, sensitive data like your name, address, and credit card number. If you're unsure if your information is encrypted, plan your purchase by computer, but when it's time to place the order, call the company and pay by phone with your credit card.

New York, New York: If You Can Buy It There, You Can Buy It Anywhere

New York City is the nation's electronics retail capital. Unfortunately, it's also the electronics rip-off capital. Folks from out of town flock to its gaudy midtown stores or call toll-free ads they see in magazines. And while all this intense competition can offer some great deals, we think it's fair to say your chances of being ripped off in New York are pretty high. Why are there so many flashy electronics stores in the heart of the Big Apple? Because gullible tourists from Pittsburgh to Pakistan flock to them in search of bargains. Because of the high volume of transitory customers, some of these stores have honed their deceitful sales techniques into an art.

How bad is it? Each year the New York City Department of Consumer Affairs responds to approximately 700 complaints about electronics stores and issues some 1,000 violations. In a 1997 investigation, the department went undercover to thirty electronics stores. Of the thirty businesses, twenty-eight were cited for 926 consumer-protection violations ranging from selling products for more than the manufacturer's suggested retail price without notifying the customer to trying to pass off used items as new.

There are countless news reports of tourists being ripped off by these stores. For example, a South African tourist purchased a $1,000 "satellite" phone that he was told could operate at distances of up to 186 miles, only to learn he'd bought a regular cordless phone that came without an instruction manual or warranty and was valued at less than $100. The Department of Consumer Affairs recently brought suit in State Supreme Court against eight stores and three distributors accused of similar scams. Even hardened, street-smart New Yorkers are overcome by the high-pressure, fast-talking sales techniques of these fly-by-night stores. When shopping in New York City, keep the following tips in mind.

•*Beware of salespeople who ask where you're from or how long you're going to be in town.* They might simply be making small talk, but chances are they're setting you up for a scam on the premise that you won't be around long enough to complain.

•*Inspect before you buy.* It's not uncommon to get stuck with off-brand merchandise. For instance, that great price on a Pentax 35mm camera isn't so wonderful when you learn that while the camera body is Pentax, the lens is a cheap, no-name brand. Even worse, some stores will sell what appears to be a Panasonic product, but a close look at the box reveals it's spelled "Pana-soanic." That's not a typo—it's a counterfeit fraud. Obviously these practices upset manufacturers as much as they do consumers.

•*Beware of instant inflation.* A common scam is for a salesperson to quote one price, but when you go to the register the clerk rings up a higher one.

•*Protect yourself from charge-card scams.* Check your charge slip carefully to make sure the store hasn't added digits to the total price. Always save your receipt in case the store decides to add a few numbers after you're gone.

Being paranoid, apprehensive, and anxiety-ridden is certainly no way to live your life, but it is the way to go electronics shopping in New York City.

Summary: Picking the Right Store for You

Shop where you're comfortable. If you get a bad vibe from a store—or the pressure seems too great—don't be intimidated. Just say "thank you" and head out the door. Also, base where you shop on what you want to buy. If it's a cheap Walkman or clock radio, you can purchase it anywhere. If you're looking to set up a home theater with a Dolby Pro Logic surround sound audio/video receiver, five speakers, a subwoofer, and a digital video disc player—and you don't have a subscription to *Video* magazine—you might want to at least start with a high-end specialty store.

Find knowledgeable salespeople you can trust for objective advice. If you're still narrowing down your choices, get their expert advice. Tell them how you'll use the product, who will use it, what features you want, and your price range. Allow them to guide you, but do your own evaluation and make the final decision yourself. And if you're lucky enough to find a store and a salesperson you like, by all means keep going back to him or her for future purchases.

SHOPPING STRATEGY

Research, Research, Research

Before you start shopping, it's imperative to determine the kind of product you need and learn a few details about it. Evan, our former salesman, explains, "If you go in blind, the salesperson is going to have you by the nose and lead you where he wants." We're not asking you to become an electronics expert, but gaining some knowledge will go a long way toward making you a smart and confident shopper. If you're buying a television, for example, learn the basic features. With technical jargon like PIP, comb filters, active channel scan, MTS Stereo, and Invar shadow masks, we realize it can be intimidating and confusing. Look for features you know you'll use, and don't pay for features you know you won't.

Talk to your friends and read reviews in electronics magazines. Many people start with *Consumer Reports*. Published by the Consumers Union, *Consumer Reports* is a nonprofit independent magazine that doesn't accept advertising. Every March it publishes an issue that reviews and rates home electronics, including televisions, CD players, cassette recorders, camcorders, receivers, VCRs, and speakers. Discuss *Consumer Reports* magazine with a serious audio/video hobbyist and you're bound to hear some criticism. Alex, an electronic engineer in California, likes the magazine's unbiased reviews but feels its rankings are based on criteria the editors think will satisfy the needs of the majority of consumers. "Their 'Joe-six-pack' approach to evaluating audio, video, and computer equipment can be annoying sometimes," Alex says. "In most cases, my criteria would be totally different, as would my rankings." Therefore, Alex would never base his decisions solely on the magazine, but he uses it to give him better insight into products and their shortcomings before he visits stores to do his own comparison shopping. Another complaint is that with model numbers changing so frequently, by the time the magazine hits the stands the models reviewed are outdated. Our opinion: *Consumer Reports* is a valuable resource and a great place to start your research, but you should always check out all the resources available to you, no matter what you're buying.

If you like to surf the Internet, you'll find it a useful research tool in planning your purchases. Many consumer electronics magazines are now online, which makes it easy to search for recent product evaluations. Also, it's simple to compare different models and features since most major manufacturers have sites, as do the big retailers, so you can comparison shop and even make purchases from the comfort of your own home. You can also log on to Usenet newsgroups or Internet discussion groups where you can request and trade buying advice with other consumers as well as professionals. Some of the best newsgroups for consumer electronics are misc.consumer, alt.consumers.experiences, rec.video, and rec.audio.

If you're dealing with a retailer you don't know, always check the store's customer experience record with the Better Business Bureau and with your state's Department of Consumer Affairs.

Getting the Best Price: Dickering for a Deal

Some people will look at the price tag on a television and assume that's the price they have to pay, but in many consumer electronics and appliance stores, price is quite negotiable. The real price is whatever a buyer is willing to pay and a seller is willing to accept.

Prices are most often flexible at stores where the salespeople get paid on commission since commissions are based partially on the price at which a salesperson sells a product. At ex-salesman Steve's store, the more he sold an item for, the more money he got to keep for himself. All the information he needed was at his fingertips on a nearby computer terminal. If a customer asked about a certain product, Steve would say, "Okay, let me see what we have in stock." The computer not only told him if the item was available but also what the cost price was for the store, the normal selling price, and the lowest price he could less it for and still make a commission. He knew immediately that even if he had to drop the price by $20 to close the sale, he could still get a $50 spiff to make up for it. And it didn't matter if the customer was right over his shoulder reading the computer screen, because it was all in an alphanumeric code that only the sales staff knew how to decipher.

Steve says salespeople want to lower the price only as a last resort. "You never want to drop your pants too soon," he explains. "Often we'd wait till the customer was walking out the door, and then chase after them." Evan, the former electronics salesman who worked in Los Angeles, says customers who like to bargain are called "grinders." And the best grinders know rule number one in negotiating. "If you're working a salesman on the price and the salesman won't budge, don't be afraid to tell him you're going to look around at other stores," Evan says. "You have nothing to lose. The salesperson will probably run after you because they are taught that once a customer leaves the store, they're probably not coming back to make their purchase."

Be aware that once a salesperson starts lowering the price, he's going to apply some pressure to close the sale. You're sure to hear "What do I have to do to make you happy? If I knock off twenty bucks are you willing to buy today?" Don't feel that you have to give in to sales pressure.

If you hate to haggle, then we urge you to shop around and compare prices to be assured you're getting a good deal. Because of the intense competition between stores, there can be more room to negotiate, particularly if you can prove that you can buy the product cheaper somewhere else. Many retailers will match or beat a competitor's sale price, making the whole haggling process a little more civilized. Don't be afraid to bring in a competitor's ad or ask the store to call a competitor directly to verify a lower price.

More and more stores are starting to tout a low-price guarantee. They'll tell you "Buy the product today, and if you find it at another store for less, we'll pay you the difference." Some stores even offer the difference plus 10 percent. We think these guarantees sounds a lot better than they really are. Since salespeople know that customers want to be assured they're getting a great price, they can use a price guarantee to close the sale. "What do you have to lose?" they'll ask. "Buy it today, and you'll have it in your home immediately. If you find it for a lower price later, we'll refund the difference." It's a good pitch, but it's unrealistic. The stores know most consumers aren't going to go through the trouble to collect on this guarantee. Let's face it: Once you have a new television set in your living room, are you really going to trudge to other stores to check prices?

DARE TO COMPARE: Investigating a Good Deal
Comparison shopping is the only way to ensure you're getting the best deal on your purchase. You may feel a little self-conscious going to a store with a pad and paper, and you may even sense some hostility from the sales staff. This is partly because they might think you're a spy. The Cold War is over, but undercover agents are everywhere in the electronics and appliance business. With the intense competition to have the "best price," most retailers send shopping spies to scout rival stores' prices. Pricing espionage helps give a store a competitive edge. Often price information is sent to a retailer's headquarters, where they can decide to lower their own prices in response. Sometimes a store will drop its price by just pennies to ensure that it has an edge over the competition.

Stores will do whatever they can to prevent infiltration by a competitor's secret agents. This might explain why Ronald Kahlow got arrested. Kahlow was in the market for a big-screen TV, so he went to a Best Buy store near his home in Reston, Virginia. With a laptop slung around his waist he proceeded down the aisles, logging model numbers and prices. That's when the sales staff, thinking he was a spy, demanded he stop. Kahlow assured them he wasn't from the competition, but when he refused to leave the store manager called the police. He was handcuffed, taken to jail, and booked on trespassing charges. After posting bail, Kahlow wasn't about to give up. He went back to the same store the next day armed with only pencil and pad. He was promptly arrested again.

Kahlow's story doesn't say much about Best Buy's treatment of potential customers, but the chain has changed its policy to allow shoppers to take notes as long as they do it discreetly. (The charges were dropped against Kahlow. Kahlow sued Best Buy, but he lost the case.) Be aware that some stores, trying to make it harder on spies, do have policies that prohibit customers from taking down prices.

We urge you to comparison shop. We think customers have a right to take notes to help them compare prices, but our advice is to be somewhat discreet. It might be best to leave the computer or big clipboard at home. Take a small pad or ask the salesperson to write down the prices on his business card.

Instead of going from store to store, you can try to save some time by having your fingers do the walking. But don't be surprised if you call up a retailer to ask the price of a product, only to be told "I'm sorry, but by law we're not allowed to quote prices over the phone." Guess what? There is no law. The truth is the store just wants to discourage easy comparison shopping. It wants you to drag yourself into the store because the salespeople can't use their selling techniques if you don't enter their lair. Just tell the store you want the price over the phone before you decide if you're going to pay a visit.

So how many stores should you go to? Well, that depends how important it is to you to get the lowest price. Some folks don't care how much they spend, they just want to buy quickly and get on with their lives. Others will visit a dozen stores if they think they'll be able to save a few bucks. We recommend that you shop and compare prices at a minimum of three different stores. Base your purchase not only on price but on the service you receive. It's the best way to ensure you're not being ripped off.

A Word About Warranties

Always consider a product's warranty before you make a purchase. There's a difference between a manufacturer's warranty and an extended warranty, which we discuss later. Most consumer electronics come with a manufacturer's limited warranty, but the terms vary. Don't be surprised if one VCR has a one-year warranty, while another company's VCR is covered only for 90 days. Before you buy, make sure you compare and understand the terms of the warranty. Also make sure it's a valid U.S. warranty. (See "Refurbished Goods: Getting Used" and "Buyer Beware: Gray-Market Goods"). Stick with manufacturers that stand by their products by offering lengthy and comprehensive coverage.

It's not necessary to mail in that little registration card that accompanies your purchase (and asks for all kinds of personal information) to be eligible for the warranty. Just make sure you save your sales receipt to prove the date of purchase. (Mailing in the registration is, however, the best way to ensure that you'll receive any important safety notices, such as product recalls.) Most warranties are limited strictly to defects in manufacturing. If your item breaks, and the manufacturer finds it wasn't a defective product or determines that you were somehow at fault, you might have to pay to have it repaired.

Written warranties aren't required by law, but most states do require an "implied" warranty on the sale of all products. The most common type of implied warranty is the "warranty of merchantability." What this means is that the product must do what the seller says it's supposed to do. A VCR should be able to play and record onto videotapes, for instance. Implied warranty coverage can last up to four years, but length varies from state to state, so check with your local consumer protection office.

Extended Warranties—A Great Deal, But for Whom?

There's nothing like a little insurance, right? After you've spent your hard-earned money on an expensive piece of electronics or a large appliance, you certainly don't want it to break down. Wouldn't it be nice to have a little peace of mind? That's how the extended warranty was born.

After a salesperson sells you a product, she'll immediately start her pitch for the extended warranty. It's been called the consumer electronics equivalent to "Do you want fries with that?" Although they're called extended warranties, they're not warranties at all. According to the Federal Trade Commission, warranties are included in the price of a product. What the electronics stores are actually selling are service contracts, which are similar to the service contracts that are available when you buy a car, house, hot water heater, or just about any major appliance. A service contract, like a warranty, will provide repair if the product breaks down within the contracted time period.

Each store has a different name for these contracts; some in use are: extended service protection, service guarantees, and performance service plans. And do you know what some salespeople call extended warranties when they're talking to each other? They call them "cheese," and selling a product with cheese on top is big business.

Here's how extended warranties work. For anywhere from twenty to several hundred dollars, you can buy a policy that promises to make free repairs if the item breaks. There are a wide variety of plans. Some just offer repair service, while others include things like routine maintenance or at-home service for large items. Typically, you can buy coverage that lasts from one to five years.

It's a gamble really. If the product does break down and you bought the service plan, well, great. But like at any casino, the odds are with the house. Stores wouldn't offer the service if they didn't make money selling it. Consider this: Only about 15 percent of consumers ever use the warranties they buy.

The increased competition in the electronics industry has led to some very low profit margins for stores, so selling extended warranties has become their new cash cow. In fact, many stores, and many salespeople, make more money peddling "cheese" than they do selling product. It's been estimated that for every dollar a store takes in from selling the plans, it spends only 4 cents to 15 cents on service and repair. Most stores wouldn't make ends meet if they didn't make such a huge profit on these plans. Some even impose quotas on their sales force, pressuring them to sell a certain number of service contacts a month. And many salespeople don't mind—the better you are at selling "cheese," the more money you're going to make.

"The extended warranties are a little tricky to sell," says former salesman Steve. "After a customer buys something, you don't want to imply the product they just spent money on is liable to break, but you want to plant a seed. The thought: What will happen if it breaks after the manufacturer's warranty expires?"

Because extended warranties are so profitable for both the store and the salesperson, you may experience some high-pressure techniques. Steve says much of the corporate sales training he got was "in how to sell the cheese."

You'll frequently hear salespeople try a scare tactic: "What are you going to do if this breaks down after the ninety-day warranty is up? Have you seen what it costs to get something repaired—it's like $50 just to look at it. If you need to fix it, it's going to cost you a mint. It would be foolish to spend $400 and then not spend another $100 to protect yourself." Or they'll try this tactic: "It's worth the $100 just to know that if anything ever happens you're protected."

Steve says at his store, some salespeople were extremely aggressive with customers. One unethical technique is actually to berate the customer. Steve recalls, "They'd say things like 'You've just spent all this money on new stuff, you'd have to be crazy not to buy the extended protection.' " In fact, some salespeople would take it one step further and threaten not to sell the customer the product. "They'd say things like 'I don't even want to sell you this television set because you're just so stupid not to get the insurance.' "

Steve says a proud moment for one salesman at his store was when he sold a video cassette player for $195 and then got the customer to buy the service plan for an additional $200. While it seems unbelievable that someone would buy a service plan that costs more than the product it protects, the way the salesman explained it to the customer seemed to make perfect sense. And later, the salesman actually hung the sales receipt in the employee lounge for everyone else to see.

If a store isn't selling enough extended warranties, often the store manager is pressured by corporate headquarters to improve the numbers. Salespeople who aren't successful at selling a plan to a customer then will have to call a manager over to try to close the deal. It's called the turnover, or T.O., and it works just as you might have experienced at a car dealership. Any salesperson who can't sell the service contract will be forced to T.O. to the manager. Since the manager is usually the best salesperson in the store, he or she then tries to sign you up.

The pressure is so great to sell these plans that salespeople often will do a "forced buy" and "backload" the service plan into the purchase price. This industry lingo means that when they write up the invoice, they'll add on the extended warranty plan and subtract the cost of the plan from the cost of the item. It's not costing the consumer any more money, but the salesperson sells the plan, makes a larger commission, and everyone's happy. We think this is unethical—the consumer should always have the choice. If the salesperson wants to lower the price of the product, you shouldn't be forced to buy the warranty.

Solid state products, such as stereo receivers and televisions, have very few moving parts and are highly reliable. But with products like fax machines, VCRs, camcorders, and CD players, all those gears and motors mean there's a lot more that can go wrong. As you might guess, the service plans charge much more to cover these fragile products. "It's ironic," says Steve. "There are certain products where it does make sense to buy an extended warranty, but for those products the plans are just too expensive to buy."

Often the service contract duplicates the regular warranty coverage because most service contacts take effect the day of your purchase. Therefore, if you buy a TV that's covered by the manufacturer's warranty for six months and you purchase a one-year service contract, you're actually paying for six months of overlapping coverage. Look for service plans that kick in only after the manufacturer's warranty has expired.

There are also many complaints from consumers who bought warranties from companies that subsequently went out of business. For example, when big chains like Crazy Eddies and Newmark & Lewis went bankrupt, thousands of their customers were left with worthless contracts. Some states have begun instituting laws that offer some protection to folks who find themselves in this situation, but the Federal Trade Commission acknowledges that "there is little recourse available to these consumers."

If you're going to buy an extended warranty, look at the contract to see what company will provide the service. Many electronics retailers don't cover the warranties themselves, they only act as a middlemen. In these cases, the repairs are covered by a third-party insurer. If the third party goes out of business, once again, your product won't be covered. Also, stick with reputable companies, although, let's face it, it's hard to predict if a company will declare bankruptcy in the future. Think about it: Probably several electronics stores, including some big chains, recently went out of business in your town. If you're holding a contract with a company that went bankrupt, contact your local consumer protection agency for help.

Our Advice: Just Say No

That's our advice: Just say no to service plans. Buy quality products that are built well and come with a good manufacturer's warranty. Then take good care of the products you buy.

If you like the idea of an extended warranty, consider using a bank-issued credit card that offers a built-in extended warranty that automatically doubles the manufacturer's warranty. Keep in mind that making a claim can involve a lot of paperwork, and since many electronics products only have thirty- or sixty-day warranties, doubling them isn't quite like buying a one- or two-year service plan, but it's certainly a lot cheaper. Give your credit card company a call; it might already be offering this free service.

Another alternative to buying a service plan: Every time you buy a product and say no to the extended warranty, put the money you would have spent on the plan into a coffee can. When something breaks, chances are you'll have enough money in the can either to cover the repairs or to buy yourself a new piece of equipment.

If You Can't Say No: Some More Advice

If you're really nervous and you think it's worth the extra expense, consider a service plan only for products that have a lot of moving parts or you think may get some abuse: VCRs, camcorders, and portable CD and cassette recorders.

If you're going to go with a service plan, read the contract carefully and make sure you understand everything before you sign. There are many different types of plans. Some won't cover you if the product is broken by your negligence. (You dropped your camcorder, for instance.) Some cover only labor, others cover only parts. Some plans may have you pay for each service call. Beware: Often salespeople exaggerate or embellish coverage. Don't just take them at their word. Most salespeople have never read the fine print on service contacts themselves, so make sure you do. If the salesperson doesn't have a written contract for you to look at, don't buy it. Reputable stores won't force you to make a decision about an extended warranty on the spot but will give you a few days to mull it over. Take advantage of this; it will give you time to evaluate the contract before you sign on the dotted line.

Like most everything in this world, the price of a warranty is often negotiable. If you want the warranty, you might try a little haggling. Also know that extended warranties vary immensely in price and coverage from store to store. If you know you'll want to buy the service plan, we urge you to take the time to comparison shop. Here are some crucial questions you should ask as you're looking over a contract.

- If you decide to return the product, will you get a refund on the warranty?
- Exactly what is and what is not covered?
- Is damage from "abuse" covered, and if not, who determines whether the product has been broken by abuse?
- What's the name of the company legally responsible for the service, and where is it located?
- Where will the product be serviced: In my home? At the retail shop? In a manufacturer's service center?
- Does the contract begin when my warranty ends so I don't pay twice for the same coverage?
- Is the warranty good only at the local store? What happens if I move?
- Is the service contract transferable if I sell the product?
- What happens if the product can't be repaired?
- If I have repeated problems, can the product be replaced with a new one?

Credit Traps

Many stores will try to issue you their own store credit card. Think twice before accepting. Salespeople try to push you into applying for a card because often they get a bonus if you sign up. At Steve's former store, for example, the salespeople got $5 for every person they signed up. If they hooked more than fifty people, they got $10 each.

Store credit cards are usually bad deals for consumers. They have outrageous interest rates, often around 23 percent annually, which is much higher than most bank credit cards like VISA or MasterCard.

Stores push the cards as instant credit, and salespeople use it as a tool to close or enhance a sale. "We'd have a customer come in who wanted to buy a basic 20-inch television," says Steve. "Maybe he only has $400 in his pocket, but you tell him he can get a store credit card with $1,000 of instant credit, so why buy a 20-inch television when you can walk out with a 35-inch set?" Steve's advice: "People need to make their own credit decisions, and they shouldn't let the salesperson talk them into overextending themselves."

To entice you even more, electronics stores often have special financing deals. Beware of deferred payment plans. These plans are most popular around the Christmas holiday, as consumers find themselves buying more than they can afford and stores try to maximize their holiday revenues. The pitch sounds great. For example, around Christmas you see promotions like "Make no payment until spring." What they don't tell you is that while you don't have to make a payment for three months, the interest will start kicking in from your date of purchase, at a very high rate.

Slightly better deals call for no payment and no interest. For instance, if you're on a six-month no-payment and no-interest finance plan and you pay up in full before the six months are up, you'll actually do okay for yourself. The savvy customer can keep her money in the bank gathering interest until it's time to make the payment. But industry observers say that 60 percent of shoppers using these deferral plans end up incurring interest fees. If you can't pay your balance in full when the time comes, most plans will assess interest from the original purchase date. That means you'd owe about $110 in interest in just six months on a $1,000 purchase. "These plans are a double-edged sword," says Steve Rhode, president of Debt Counselors of America, a not-for-profit organization that uses the Internet to help consumers get out of debt. "It's American consumerism at its finest: We want it now, we want it fast, we want it free." But Rhodes says when the deferred time comes, many consumers forget that they have a debt due and are surprised when they get hit with a high interest charge when they miss a payment. "Time never flies faster than when you have a debt due," Rhode warns. If you can't afford the product when you buy it, make sure you have the money when the debt is due. Unless you know you're getting a big raise or that you're going to win the lottery, chances are that your financial situation will be the same when it's time to pay the bill as it is now.

If you want to use a deferral plan, read the contract carefully. Investigate when the interest starts to accrue. Mark the due date on your calendar and make sure you have your money ready. Or better yet, make monthly payments to keep disciplined. If you don't think you'll be able to pay the bill when the time comes, stay away from deferred plans and consider paying for your purchase with your lower-interest bank credit card.

After You Buy Your Gear: Burn It

After you get your new equipment home, you should immediately take it out of the box, read the directions, try it out, and then burn it in. No, you don't need a blowtorch. "Burning in" is an industry term that will help make sure you're not stuck with a lemon. When you buy any piece of electronics equipment, turn it on and keep it on at least overnight. This is how manufacturers test their products for reliability. At the factory, manufacturers take a small percentage of product off the assembly line and plug it in for a day or two. Why? Because if a product is going to fail due to a manufacturing defect, such as a faulty computer chip or bad soldering, chances are it will happen during this crucial twelve- to twenty-four-hour period.

Following this same procedure at home should expose any problems quickly. If your new product fails, demand that it be *replaced,* not repaired.

SUMMARY

We hope you've learned some insider information from this chapter—things that might have surprised you. However, we don't want to make you paranoid. Plenty of electronics and appliance salespeople are true professionals and can offer terrific advice. Don't set up an adversarial relationship with them right from the start. Be respectful, and you might get a little respect in return. When shopping, give the salesperson the benefit of the doubt. Steve, our former salesman, was shocked at how hostile the relationship can be on both sides. It's not right for a salesperson to bully a customer, but neither is it fair for a customer to browbeat a salesperson.

▶ Top Ten Tips

1. *Do your research.* A little knowledge goes a long way. Dishonest salespeople can immediately spot naive shoppers and take advantage of them.

2. *Buy what you need.* Purchase products that have features you will use. Don't waste your money on features you won't.

3. *Use the salesperson, don't let him use you.* A salesperson may have good buying advice and be knowledgeable about products, but don't let him manipulate you into a purchase that's not right for you. Ask specific questions and have the salesperson help you compare features and brands.

4. *Be wary of a salesperson who pushes only one brand.* He might be getting an incentive or "spiff" for selling certain items.

5. *Beware of extremely low prices.* You've heard our mantra: "If it sounds too good to be true, it probably is." An extremely low advertised price often indicates you're in for the old bait and switch or are buying a reconditioned product.

6. *Don't give in to pressure.* Take your time and don't be bullied into buying. Never jump into a large purchase. Dare to compare prices at other stores.

7. *Check the return policy before you buy.* Once a store has your money, it can be hard to get it back.

8. *Make sure your purchase comes with the manufacturer's U.S. warranty.* If it doesn't, be aware of the dangers of buying gray-market goods.

9. *Pay by credit card.* Think twice about signing up for a store credit card. Consider using a bank credit card that doubles the manufacturer's warranty. Save your receipt.

10. *Inspect your purchase.* Before you leave the store, make sure the model number on the box matches the product you intended to buy. As soon as you get home, make sure the product works. Save the box and packing materials for as long as possible.

Glossary

Bait and switch: When an advertised product isn't available and the salesperson pressures you to buy a more expensive or inferior item.

Bump: See "step up."

Cheese: A salesperson's term for selling extended warranties.

Cherry picker: Shoppers who go to stores only to buy loss leaders.

Derivative models: Models built by a manufacturer exclusively for a retailer. A different model number on an almost identical product seen at other stores makes it harder for the consumer to comparison shop.

Gray-Market goods: Equipment manufactured for sale outside the country, which is brought into the country by an unauthorized importer.

Grinder: A customer who haggles for a better price.

Hit: See "spiff."

Loss leader: An item priced at or below store cost to attract shoppers to the store.

Refurbished: Equipment that has been returned or was defective, which is serviced and then resold.

Sharking: A term used by a salesperson to mean seeking out only those customers who look like they'll make a big-ticket purchase.

Spiff   An incentive for a salesperson to push a certain product.

Step up: The process of convincing a customer to buy a more expensive product with more features.

Stock splitting: Breaking up products a manufacturer has packaged together and then selling the pieces separately for profit.

T.O. (turnover):   A term used by a salesperson who can't close a deal and must have the store manager try to convince the customer to buy.

CHAPTER 4
GROCERIES

Most consumers agree that grocery shopping isn't the most exciting way to spend their time. In fact, an *Adweek* survey found that 53 percent of Americans dislike buying groceries and 14 percent actually hate it. But grocery shopping is a fact of life. While you probably buy a car, television, or mattress only every few years, you buy groceries every week. According to the Food Marketing Institute, the trade association of the supermarket industry, the average American visits a supermarket 2.2 times per week and spends 8.7 percent of his or her weekly income on food. Add it all together and Americans are spending a whopping $425 billion at the supermarket each year.

There is good news for supermarket consumers. Grocery shopping generally doesn't involve high-pressure sales techniques or unethical salespeople stalking you around the store. And unlike the electronics or automobile industry, which don't count on repeat business, it's very important for supermarkets to build customer loyalty. Since a supermarket's average profit margin is very low—it makes only about a penny for every dollar you spend—a store prospers on volume. In fact, the average store needs about 20,000 shoppers a week to realize a profit. How do stores meet this goal and keep consumers coming back for more week after week? Read on and find out.

TRICKS OF THE SUPERMARKET TRADE: MARKETING MANIPULATION

Grocery shopping—how hard can it be? It's something you've been doing for years. The biggest challenge is finding a cart with four working wheels, right? After that, it's simply a matter of throwing in the items you need and praying the checkout line is short. Maybe this is your view, but those in the supermarket industry don't take your shopping experience so lightly. Millions of dollars and years of experimentation in marketing research have told the industry exactly what makes consumers buy. This research has turned your neighborhood supermarket into a well-organized machine aimed at separating you from your hard-earned cash. By utilizing clever marketing and consumer-buying psychology, a supermarket can easily quadruple its product sales. By learning how to outsmart some of these industry tricks of the trade, you'll be able to shave money off your grocery bill, get more bang for your buck each week, and maybe even start enjoying your trips to the supermarket.

Setting the Mood

Atmosphere plays a large part in the supermarket shopping experience. From the moment you enter a store, you're bombarded with a plethora of enticing sights, sounds, and smells: fresh-cut flowers by the entrance, produce displayed in appealing wooden crates, calming music flowing from the sound system, and the smell of fresh bread and pastries wafting from the bakery. Although you may not realize it, these little touches are appealing to your subconscious. They put you in a good mood, and as the supermarket industry has learned, a happy shopper spends more money than an unhappy one. "It's about building relationships, so when you walk in the store you'll feel more at home," says Phil Lempert, a leading food-industry expert and the author of *Phil Lempert's Supermarket Shopping and Value Guide*. Some stores take this to an extreme. Lempert particularly likes the unique approach of Byerly's supermarkets in Minnesota. "Their supermarkets are carpeted and have crystal chandeliers," he says. "Shopping an hour or more in these stores is more comfortable on our legs and eyes."

While making shoppers comfortable may seem simple, stores actually employ very calculated techniques to attain the desired effect. For example, flowers and an abundance of well-displayed produce at the front of a store ensures a good first impression and conveys a feeling of straight-from-the-farm freshness. Warm bakery smells often are a supermarket's version of aromatherapy and are projected intentionally at unsuspecting shoppers' noses via fans. And music is carefully selected to put consumers at ease. Even more sophisticated are the lighting techniques used by some stores. The average person blinks thirty-two times a minute, but with carefully planned lighting, a supermarket can have you blinking only fourteen times a minute. Experts say this serves to relax you, putting you into an almost trance-like state. While we're certainly not saying that these techniques cause you to lose all control of your faculties once you enter your neighborhood supermarket, they are in place to make you feel good, and studies have shown that happy shoppers shop longer.

Shop Till You Drop: Your Time Is Their Money

Most of us would like our grocery-shopping trips to be quick and painless. The Food Marketing Institute estimates that the typical shopper spends an average of twenty-four minutes going up and down the aisles. The stores, on the other hand, want you to spend as much time shopping as possible. It's estimated that every additional minute you're in a supermarket equals an extra dollar spent. That's one reason today's stores offer the consumer a lot more than just groceries. Some supermarkets now feature gourmet coffee bars, fast-food outlets, pharmacies, dry-cleaning shops, bank branches, and lottery machines. While these added services offer one-stop shopping convenience, they also give you more reasons to go to the supermarket and then linger there.

Even the layout of today's supermarkets is intricately designed to increase profits by keeping you in the store longer. You probably already realize that milk—one of the most frequently purchased staples—is always located about as far from the front door as possible, forcing you to walk by a lot of other enticing products to get to it. And if you also need bread, another staple, it's probably nowhere near the milk. But this concept goes a lot farther than wheat and dairy. In fact, a supermarket is a marketing maze, an obstacle course that the consumer must traverse to get from the door through the checkout line.

For example, the width of supermarket aisles is carefully planned to make you spend more time roaming them. A wide aisle forces you to zigzag and scan to find the products you need. Doing this slows you down and forces you to glance at other items that you might impulsively throw into your cart. Navigating these aisles becomes even more of a challenge with point-of-purchases displays—you know, those big cardboard boxes that showcase special items. You have to slow down to avoid hitting them with your cart, and they also call your attention to the product, enticing you to buy. "Hmm, maybe I could use one of those things," you muse. It's the same reason stores have those waist-high frozen-food displays smack dab in the middle of the freezer section. They're just another obstacle to slow you down and force you to browse.

Impulse Purchases: Seducing Shoppers
Supermarkets might have a hard time turning a profit if it wasn't for humankind's impulsive nature. Indeed, according to Phil Lempert, up to two-thirds of what consumers put into their grocery carts are impulse purchases. It happens to all of us. You go into the market to buy a few staples and come out loaded down with a newfangled spot remover, the latest, super-rich, three-layer frozen carrot cake, and the *National Enquirer.* Who threw all this junk in your cart when you weren't looking? Some may claim the devil made them do it. In fact, part of the responsibility lies in the marketing methods the industry uses to make consumers buy, buy, buy.

The modern-day supermarket is set up to entice customers to impulse buy in a variety of ways. "If you're aware of these environmental motivators," Lempert says, "you can reduce your impulse purchases and focus on the items you really want." One of the most common methods utilized is what the industry calls "integrated merchandising" or "adjacencies." By placing related items together, the store encourages its customers to buy more than planned. For instance, while picking up a pound of peaches, you happen to notice pastry shells and whipped cream displayed right next door. "Hmm, why don't I make a pie?" you say as you throw two extra items into your basket. Similarly, when you pick up your favorite potato chips, you spy a neighboring display of onion dip. "Yummy," you think as you toss it in. Maybe there's barbecue sauce conveniently displayed in the meat section. You have some sauce at home, but this brand looks interesting. "Why not, it's right here." While integrated items may seem convenient, realize that they're preying on your impulse to buy. Something else to note: Manufacturers often pay supermarkets to display their products next to complementary ones. This isn't illegal, but you probably can find competing brands of the same product elsewhere in the store, sometimes for less money.

End-of-aisle displays are also meant to seduce shoppers into buying on a whim. You certainly can't miss these mammoth displays situated at the end of each supermarket aisle. The product that is being pushed usually is stacked to the ceiling, accompanied by signs that suggest it's on sale. Beware. While these items might be discounted, it's just as possible that the price displayed is the everyday price. Often end-of-aisle displays are used to sell high-profit items simply by virtue of grabbing your attention. Grocers also will showcase products that are near their expiration date at the end of the aisle. While the price for such items is usually reduced, be careful to check the expiration date. Don't consider buying the product unless you know you can use it before it expires.

While end-of-aisle displays may not always offer a good deal, surely bins filled with a jumble of soaps, canned soups, or spices will give you a bang for your buck. Don't count on it. Called "dump displays" in industry lingo, these bins are purposely made to look disorganized so consumers will assume the products are on sale. Sometimes they are, but this isn't always the case. You might find the same products only a few aisles away, neatly stacked and selling for the same everyday price as the ones in the dump bin.

Our tendency to buy on impulse is also why supermarkets stack up goodies in their checkout lanes. Along with candy, gum, and tabloids, you'll see everything from little booklets that reveal your horoscope to phone cards and batteries. Grocers love consumers who grab these last-minute, high-profit purchases. A recent addition to the list of checkout impulse items is refrigerator displays filled with 20-ounce bottles of soda. They may only cost a buck, but you could buy a 2-liter bottle of the same soda in the same store (albeit warm) for about the same price. Think before you grab.

Certainly we're not telling you to totally avoid impulse buys. Food shopping should be fun, and you should experiment with new products. But by understanding the marketing at work behind the supermarket scene, you'll have a clearer understanding of why you often spend more money than planned. Later in this chapter, when we outline some money-saving shopping strategies, we'll show you ways to make your shopping trip enjoyable while curbing your impulse spending at the same time.

More Manipulative Marketing Madness

Supermarkets constantly rearrange shelves in an attempt to keep you shopping longer and to bait you into buying more than you'd planned. That's why, after much searching, you might find your favorite iced tea mix in aisle seven, instead of aisle six, where it had been for months. In its old spot is a brand-new product the store is hoping you'll see during your iced tea search and impulsively decide to buy.

For another trick, take a look at your soup aisle. Wouldn't it be easier if all those cans were arranged alphabetically? You could jump directly from chicken noodle to vegetable in no time flat. But this isn't what your grocer wants you to do. Stores have discovered that they can increase sales by not alphabetizing cans. If you have to scan past tomato, cream of mushroom, and minestrone, you just might be tempted to throw a few extra varieties into your basket.

Product Placement: Pumping Up Profits

You might think stocking shelves is a no-brainer, but product placement actually has become a marketing science. Studies have shown that we see things best when they are fifty-one to fifty-three inches above the ground. That's eye level for most people. Thus eye-level shelf space is the most coveted real estate in any store. It's the Beverly Hills and Fifth Avenue of your local supermarket, and it's where you'll find the products a store most wants to sell. Often impulse items are placed here along with high-profit store brands. There's actually sophisticated computer software that helps retailers determine where to place products for maximum profits.

The cereal aisle offers a good example of shelf-placement maneuvering. Sugary children's cereals usually are placed at a child's eye level, not yours. If you have kids, you already know it's tough to roll past the cereal aisle without hearing pleas for a fun breakfast treat. In fact, just about every food aimed at children is placed at their eye level and within easy grabbing distance. Meanwhile, you have to do some bending to reach staples. Things like flour, salt, and sugar often are located on the bottom shelf, where you'll have to stoop to get them. Since stores know these are products almost everyone buys, they know consumers will search them out.

Product placement is so important in the supermarket game that manufacturers actually pay stores to ensure their products get desired positions. As we said, eye level is a coveted spot, but every location in a supermarket has a different value. For example, while all the spaghetti sauces at your local supermarket might be located on a bottom shelf, a manufacturer will pay the store to place its sauce in the center of all the other spaghetti sauce brands. End-of-aisle displays, which we mentioned earlier, are another location popular with manufacturers, who pay an average of $2500 per store to get their product placed here.

Product placement is a sensitive topic within the industry, something retailers and manufacturers don't like to talk about. However, it's estimated that manufacturers pay around $8 billion a year to get their products on supermarket shelves. In addition to product placement, product manufacturers pay supermarket retailers a plethora of other fees. For example, companies coming out with a new product may pay a slotting fee to ensure their product gets space both in the warehouse and on the shelf. A one-time slotting fee can range from $1,000 to $10,000 per store. When a supermarket changes hands, manufacturers might pay the new owner a pay-to-stay fee to keep their products on the store's shelves. A facing fee helps ensure a product gets a better shelf placement than it has currently.

These fees are not illegal, as long as they aren't abused. However, opponents of the fee system call it commercial bribery. Since smaller companies can't afford the extra expense, their products are either never seen or are quickly pushed out of the market. Also, manufacturers have to recoup the cost of paying big fees, and critics charge this tab is picked up by the customer in the form of higher prices. However, defenders in the grocery industry claim that fees help cover the cost of failure so stores can afford to take chances on new products and thus offer their customers greater variety. They say fees also serve to hold down prices.

Not all manufacturers pay fees. Supermarkets will always carry established, name-brand products like Tide laundry detergent or Ivory soap. Such popular products are always assured shelf space. Likewise, not all stores charge fees. In particular, smaller stores with very limited shelf space can afford to carry only those products they are confident will sell. Nevertheless, paying for placement continues to be a secretive and controversial practice in the industry.

The Color of Money: How Packaging Affects What You Buy

Power packaging, the industry notion that consumers can be made to buy almost anything based solely on packaging appeal, was actually born in the supermarket. Prior to the 1950s, most consumer goods came in functional but dull wrapping. With the advent of the supermarket and its capacity to hold tens of thousands of items all vying for the same consumer dollar, that changed. It didn't take manufacturers long to realize that with 35,000 different items on supermarket shelves, their products needed to reach out and grab shoppers before their competitors did. These days, with a full 70 percent of all purchase decisions made right at the store shelf, experts say that a package has only a fraction of a second to attract a consumer's attention. It's easy to see why packaging has become big business.

Package designers in the grocery industry have spent years figuring out what captures consumers' attention and motivates them to buy. Before a new package debuts on supermarket shelves, it's tested and retested with focus groups, through individual consumer reaction, and even complex eye-tracking studies that analyze how shoppers read labels. All those bold colors and eye-catching letters are designed to do one thing: make you buy. In fact, the duller the product, the bolder its packaging. That's why items like laundry detergent, dish soap, and paper towels practically scream at you from their perches on supermarket shelves. "A product has one purpose in life," says Michael Coleman of Source Inc., one of the leading package design companies in the United States. "It wants to get noticed so it can get off that shelf and into your home."

Packaging is an ever-changing business. "It used to be that we would redesign a package and it would be good for five to eight years," says Howard Alport of Lipson, Alport, Glass & Associates, another large package design and consulting firm. "But now the life span of a design is only two or three years." These days, if a company doesn't continually update its packaging designs, its products will look outdated next to competing brands.

"It's been proven that when a company doesn't keep up, sales will suffer," Alport says.

A good food-package design must meet many criteria. Since the key to success for any grocery package is to catch shoppers' eyes as they roll down the aisle, designers consider the fact that most consumers approach products at an angle. As you near a certain food section—your store's selection of salsa, for example—a good package will grab your attention from fifteen feet away. As you move closer, your eyes will start scanning the various brands. At this point, a successful product must stand out, and its label must clearly display the information shoppers want to know about the product.

Color is one of the biggest factors in determining the success or failure of a product's packaging. Designers know that different colors affect people in different ways. Although it's subliminal, people have emotional and even physiological responses to certain colors. Here are some of the subtle messages various colors can send to your subconscious.

•*Red:* The most popular color used in product packaging. Experts say a bold red makes the heart beat faster and increases adrenaline. Many shades of red are used to grab shoppers' attention. Well-established brands like Campbell's soup and Coca-Cola have come to be associated with red.

•*Blue:* Invokes thoughts of sky and water. Not surprisingly, blue often is used on seafood products, like fish sticks, and on many bottled-water labels. Depending on the shade, blue can be bold or soothing, or remind shoppers of the cool in Cool Whip dessert topping. Consumers also associate blue with royalty and class.

•*Green:* Twenty years ago designers never used green. They feared consumers would associate the color with spoiled or moldy food. But this old wives' tale of the packaging profession was thrown out when green became the main color for both

Healthy Choice and Snackwell's brands. Green is now so closely associated with healthful or low-cal foods that you'll see it used on most products trying to compete in this market. In addition, many brands use a green banner to highlight health claims such as "no-fat" and "low in calories."

•*Yellow:* One of the most visible packaging colors, yellow can grab a shopper's attention quickly. It also makes a product appear bigger on the shelf. A golden hue evokes images of the sun and feelings of warmth, happiness, and quality. On the other hand, a bold shade is said to send a cut-rate, cheap image. One packaging designer told us that over the years Oscar Mayer has turned the familiar yellow of its product packaging into a warmer, more golden shade.

•*White:* Suggests freshness and purity. It's often used on the packaging of low-fat or diet foods—Lean Cuisine frozen dinners, for example. When a brand has a lite version of a product, often white is used on the packaging.

•*Black:* Implies luxury and premium. Have you ever seen a lime-green limousine? Consumers often think of products packaged in black as classy, sophisticated, and elegant. Many gourmet products come in black packaging.

Packaging can be more influential than you realize. Studies have shown that if the same food or drink is placed in two different packages, consumers will swear the two taste different. Everyone is influenced by well-designed packaging. Think about it. Would so many shoppers buy bottled water if it weren't for the French names and images of cool mountain breezes and gurgling brooks? What if all toothpaste came in plain aluminum tubes or cake mix just sat on the shelf in clear plastic bags? Now that you know some packaging tricks, we hope you'll better understand why you're drawn to certain brands and can scrutinize the reasons you're throwing them into your grocery cart.

Light, Lo-cal, and Lean: The Labeling Laws

Few supermarket shoppers can honestly say they've never bought a product because of an impressive health or nutritional claim emblazoned on the package. Low fat, light (or "lite"), reduced calorie, and extra lean are examples of prominent health claims that try to appeal to your sense of good health and make you buy. In the past, companies touted these nutritional assertions with little or no regulation. Many of these claims were nothing more than marketing hype used to sell a product with little thought to truth in advertising. Take the term "light," for example. When consumers saw this descriptive term, most assumed the product was low in calories or fat. But that wasn't always the case. Light olive oil could have simply meant it was lighter in color. A light cake may have had a fluffy texture. And even if a food was lower in calories or fat, there were no guidelines in place to let consumers know how much lower or lower than what.

Because nutritional claims had lost all credibility and in many cases were misleading consumers, the federal government stepped in during the early 1990s to regulate and standardize them. Here are some of the terms used to describe the amount of fat, saturated fat, cholesterol, sodium, sugars, and calories in the foods we buy.

•*Free, zero, no, without:* These terms can be used to describe a product that is completely without the nutrient in question, or if the nutrient is present, the amount must be insignificant. For example, a food advertised as fat free must have less than 0.5 grams of fat. Similarly, a claim of zero calories means less than 5 calories per serving. In addition, foods that are naturally without certain nutrients must say so. All applesauce is free of fat, for example. Therefore, one brand can't simply claim to be fat free, implying that other brands are not. The claim would have to read something like "applesauce is a fat-free food" or "naturally fat free." Read claims carefully. "No sugar added" literally

ground beef with up to 22.5 percent fat can be labeled lean. So if you're trying to keep those arteries clear, be careful. We hope the government will continue to expand the labeling laws so consumers have a better understanding of what is in the foods they buy.

Fresh from the Farm, or Not? The Dating Game

Most food items in the supermarket are marked with some sort of freshness date. These dates, accompanied by phrases like "sell by," "use by," and "best if used by," are seen all over today's supermarkets. You might be surprised to learn, however, that these dates actually say very little about a food product's life span. Unfortunately, the Federal Food and Drug Administration doesn't require manufacturers to date food products. Many companies voluntarily provide dates for their products, but these dates are usually meant for the supermarket retailer, not the consumer. And because of lack of regulation and general guidelines, even these dates can mean different things depending on the product or manufacturer. Product dates say little about what consumers care about: namely, how long a product will last once you get it home. Here are some commonly used terms that accompany freshness dates and what they really mean.

•*Sell-by date:* This tells the supermarket how long a product should be displayed for sale. Often referred to as the "pull date," it's usually found on highly perishable foods with short shelf lives, such as meat, milk, and bread. As long as the food is safe to eat, it's not illegal for a store to sell a product after its sell-by date. If stored well, most foods are safe to eat up to a week past their sell-by date, although fresh meats should be used within a day or two.

•*Best-if-used-by date:* This is not a purchase or safety date but indicates how long a product will retain its best flavor or quality. Often this date is found on products such as baked goods, cereals, snack foods, and some canned foods. It's still safe to eat a product after its best-if-used-by date, but it won't be at peak freshness.

•*Use-by, Expiration, or Use-before dates:* These dates usually appear on foods that require refrigeration, including eggs and yogurt. A product past this date should not be eaten.

Besides use-by, expiration, and use-before dates, all the other freshness indicators just outlined really apply to the product's shelf life, not its life after you take it home and open it up. For example, a jar of salsa might have a best-if-used-by date of March 2000. However, once that jar is opened, the salsa will be at peak quality only for about thirty days. Same thing with pickles or canned cake frosting. Each may have a listed shelf life of months or even years from the date of purchase, but once pickles are opened they should be eaten within a month or two, while frosting starts turning in one or two days. After mayonnaise is opened, it will last only two months in the fridge; cream cheese is at peak freshness for two weeks. And whole wheat flour, even unopened, starts to go bad within a month. The Food Marketing Institute and Cornell University have produced a brochure called "The Food Keeper" to help you determine the shelf life of various foods both before and after opening. (See "Where to Turn for Help.")

You'll also find that many products in your local supermarket don't have freshness dates at all, or there will be a date with no indication of what it refers to. Most manufacturers say consumers don't need freshness dating on most products, and claim it would be too much information to fit on most food labels. However, we'd like to see dates that are geared more toward the consumer; dates that tell us how long a product will last after we take it home. But for now, remember, when it doubt, throw it out.

WHERE TO SHOP: SO MANY CHOICES, SO LITTLE TIME

Back when our grandparents went food shopping, their choice of stores was limited. They bought fresh meats at the butcher, vegetables and fruits at the fresh-produce stand, and dry goods at the local grocer. In 1930 things began to change in the food-shopping biz when Michael Cullen of Long Island, New York, opened his King Cullen food store, the world's first supermarket. In the decades following World War II, tens of thousands of small, independent grocers were driven out of business as the one-stop convenience of supermarkets changed the way America shopped. Today things are changing again as supermarkets find themselves competing with a variety of different types of stores. These days you can buy groceries at convenience stores, drugstores, and gas station minimarts. Supercenters and warehouse clubs also have gotten into the action, and some community co-ops are still going strong. You can even shop from the comfort of your own home over the Internet. This increased competition can mean great deals for consumers as stores compete for your loyalty and shopping dollars with a variety of services and incentives. Here we take a look at current supermarket alternatives that can offer some great deals.

Supercenters: Is Bigger Better?

Supercenters are mammoth retailers, generally over 150,000 square feet, that offer a large variety of food and drug items as well as just about any other merchandise you can think of, from automotive parts, to electronics, to intimate apparel. Devoting up to 40 percent of its space to food items, supercenters can rival traditional supermarkets in the number and variety of products available. Wal-Mart Supercenter, Super Kmart, and SuperTarget are three of the country's most popular supercenter stores. The sheer size of this type of store is both a strength and a weakness. In a store this large, you can easily find thirty types of pasta, dozens of varieties of spaghetti sauce, and a deluge of laundry detergents. At the same time, shopping supercenters can be exhausting and overwhelming. Forgot to pick up some milk before you hit the checkout lanes? You'll need a road map and a sturdy pair of hiking shoes to get back to the dairy section. Nevertheless, these stores use aggressive pricing, particularly on their food items, to draw shoppers in. While it might take twice as long to do your shopping at a supercenter as compared to a supermarket, you'll often save up to 10 percent on your grocery bill.

Warehouse Shopping: Join the Club

Member-only warehouse clubs (currently 24 million shoppers strong) charge an annual membership fee of about $20 to $35 but offer some terrific bargains. Like supercenters, warehouse clubs are humongous in size, although they typically devote less floor space to food items. Sam's Club, BJs Wholesale Club, and Costco are three of the country's most popular warehouse clubs. The name of the game at these stores, particularly for groceries, is bulk-size items. You'll feel like a Lilliputian straight out of *Gulliver's Travels* as you hoist a gigantic box of laundry detergent or a 40-count bag of frozen chicken breasts into an oversize shopping cart. It's definitely not the place to buy your average 12-ounce jar of pickles, but you can find gherkins by the gallon and smaller jars sold in six-packs.

Because of all this bulk buying, there are a lot of great deals to be had at warehouse clubs. A gallon of French's Mustard might cost only twice as much as a small, 9-ounce jar from your local supermarket. Spaghetti sauce that usually goes for $2.19 per 26-ounce jar might cost $2.79 for a 4-pound jug at a shopping club. Warehouse stores, however, can't totally replace your local market. Most don't carry fresh produce and meats, and because they have limited space for food, they stock only the most popular brands. Also, like a supercenter, a warehouse club's sheer size can be daunting and inconvenient as you traverse a quarter mile of aisles in search of toilet paper. And warehouses look like, well, warehouses. They have a no-frills atmosphere and usually provide little service help on the shopping floor.

Then again, this doesn't bother most consumers since they don't go warehouse shopping for the ambiance or convenience, but to save money.

Buying food at warehouses isn't for everyone. A large family can certainly do well shopping at a club, but for a small family or single person, buying canned yams by the gallon simply isn't practical. Open up a bulk-size can of tuna fish and you'll either have to eat it three times a day for a week or watch it go bad. To avoid this dilemma, you might consider shopping with a friend and then splitting your bulk purchases down to more manageable sizes. And everyone can take advantage of cheap warehouse prices for nonperishables and frozen foods, provided you have the storage space. (Otherwise, you'll be making an end table out of that 4-gallon can of baked beans.) At warehouses it's easy to get caught up in buying a lot of food at cheap prices, and those oversize carts just cry out to be filled up with impulse purchases. Resist the urge. Purchase only what you can store and use. If something you buy goes bad, it's money wasted.

Co-ops: You're the Boss

Food co-ops offer consumers yet another alternative to traditional supermarkets. Instead of merely being a customer, cooperatives encourage shoppers to get involved in the store. They operate on the principle that customers should also be owners, and as a member you have a voice in how your co-op functions. In the United States, co-ops have been around in one form or another since the early 1900s and are responsible for introducing many innovations on the food front. "Old-wave" co-ops (those begun in the first half of the century) are responsible for unit pricing (signs that help consumers compare prices on similar products), express lanes, and consumer-oriented product labeling, among other things. More recently, a second wave of co-ops emerged with the peace and love generation of the 1960s and its penchant for natural foods. Today most neighborhood co-ops still have a strong bent toward organic food products and are a good place to find top-quality items in this category.

Financially, co-ops can be a good deal. Since they usually buy in bulk, their prices can be very competitive. Although each co-op store operates a bit differently, to become a member you're usually required either to pay a membership fee when you join or buy shares in the co-op. Many require its members to work at the store (as little as a few hours a month), and that labor usually translates into discounts for purchases you make. Even if you're not a member of a co-op, most are open to the general public. Down sides of co-ops include limited selection and, in many cases, cramped quarters. Also, they may not be practical for people who don't have the time to work at a store.

Shopping Online: The Cyber-Supermarket

Since most people say they hate trips to the supermarket, it's only natural that companies are trying to make the shopping experience more convenient. With more and more families buying personal computers, several companies are using the technology of the Internet to let you shop from the comfort of your own home. Let's face it, shopping in your pajamas in front of a computer screen sounds a lot more relaxing than wrestling with a shopping cart, weaving up and down supermarket aisles, and waiting in long checkout lines. And in most cases you can place an Internet order twenty-four hours a day, seven days a week.

Food shopping from cyberspace is relatively new. However, industry analysts claim that while less than 1 percent of shoppers are using online grocery shopping today, this figure is expected to jump to 15 percent by the year 2005 as people become more comfortable with the Internet and shopping services become more established.

Internet supermarkets typically work in one of two ways. Some offer national service, so no matter where you live you can have nonperishable goods shipped to you from a central warehouse. Other services team up with local supermarkets and use "professional shoppers" to fill your order at a store. This means you can buy any product that's available in your supermarket, from fresh produce to filet mignon. This type of service is available only in some regions of the country.

The online shopping experience for both types of service is similar. You browse through virtual supermarket aisles on your computer, picking products. Most have graphics that let you see an item and then pull up its nutritional information. Many also take into account your personal preferences, allowing you to specify things like how ripe you like your bananas. While it may seem strange to have someone else picking out your produce, many companies offer satisfaction guarantees. They'll also redeem coupons and offer weekly specials, just like your neighborhood supermarket. After you place an order, it's delivered right to your doorstep, or, if you prefer, some services will bag it for pick up at your convenience (on your way home from work, for example). If you still haven't made it onto the information superhighway, or if you're uncomfortable buying by computer, some services allow you to place orders by phone or fax. Two of the most popular cyber-supermarkets currently available are Peapod (www.peapod.com), and Netgrocer (www.netgrocer.com).

Online shopping is convenient for people who just can't find the time to get to the supermarket. It also gives those who can't easily leave their homes (like the sick or elderly) a chance to buy the things they need. The best services have easy-to-use computer programs that allow you to set up shopping lists of frequently purchased items so you can order everything you need in a few minutes. Some online shoppers even say they spend less on groceries because they no longer buy impulse items.

There are down sides to online food shopping. If you're picky about your produce, it might be hard to have a stranger selecting your tomatoes. It also can be challenging to choose the correct sizes. For instance, at the supermarket it's easy to see how big a 28-ounce can of corn is; it's a little harder to visualize over the computer. You'll also pay extra for the convenience. But, as more and more supermarkets go online, prices are bound to become more competitive.

SHOPPING STRATEGY

Now that you've learned a few insider secrets and shopping alternatives, we'll show you additional ways you can save money each week and get better value for your buck.

The Shopping List: Your Key to Savings

Making a list may seem like tedious work that just adds to the chore of food shopping, but it can be a great money- and time-saving tool. By planning your shopping trip in advance, experts say you can save up to 15 percent off your total grocery bill. With a list, you can shop more efficiently; you don't have to wander the supermarket aisles trying to figure out what you need for the week. With a list in hand, you won't be as swayed by the many marketing tricks that encourage shoppers to make impulse purchases. And a list can prevent you from buying products you already have plenty of at home.

Industry expert Phil Lempert suggests using the register receipt from your last typical shopping trip to create a shopping list. With today's scanning technology, most receipts record the items you've bought along with their prices. "If you're like most shoppers, each week 80 percent of the products you buy are similar to what you bought the week before," he says. Thus you'll be able to use an old receipt as a blueprint for your next shopping trip. Keep the receipt in your kitchen, adding any products you use up during the week. Before you head to the supermarket, give your pantry and refrigerator a last look for any items you still have and cross these items off your receipt. Also, flip through your coupons and scan weekly circulars. Place a check mark next to any product on your list for which you have a coupon or that you know is on sale.

When you hit the aisles you'll be organized and ready to shop. But remember, shopping should be fun, not tedious. There's nothing wrong with deviating a bit from your list. "For me, a big part of enjoying a supermarket is finding new products," says Lempert. "I can't resist buying something that's not on my list. I always permit myself three impulse items. These are products that I didn't even think about before I walked into the store." Lempert suggests setting your own limit for impulse purchases but reminds you to set it *before* you enter the store. By shopping from a list and restricting purchases made on a whim, Lempert guarantees you'll save time and money each week.

Picking a Store That's Right for You

With increased competition from superstores and other retailers, supermarkets are going out of their way to offer great values. Along with low prices, stores are offering wider selection, extended shopping hours, and more personalized service. As a smart shopper, you should take advantage of the industry's push to please and search out stores that best satisfy your specific needs.

As when buying anything, from a car to a CD player, we encourage you to shop around and try out different stores. The best way to comparison shop is to make a list of the prices of the products you buy most frequently at your current supermarket. Take this list to a competing market and note the differences. While prices are very important, you also need to look at the services different supermarkets offer. With so many stores vying for your business, there's no reason to settle for second best. Following are some questions to ask yourself.

- Are department managers available to answer my questions?
- How long are the checkout lines?
- Besides cash, what other forms of payment are accepted?
- Are the shelves usually well stocked?
- Are sale items readily available?
- Does the store have a preferred-shopping program, and does it offer double off manufacturers' coupons?
- Does it offer a good selection of brands, including store brands?
- Does the store offer other services? An ATM? Video rental? Pharmacy?
- Are the shopping carts, display cases, and aisles clean?

The Hunt for Savings

Supermarkets, like most retailers, offer loss leaders—heavily advertised items sold at very low prices. Stores make little or no profit off loss leader items, but that's not the point. The goal is simply to lure you into the store. Loss leaders are actually quite profitable because once they draw you into a supermarket, you're probably going to buy more than just the loss leader item. However, not everyone falls for this trick of the trade. In fact, the bane of many a supermarket is the "cherry picker." This is the industry's name for truly thrifty shoppers who carefully study weekly circulars and then head out to several supermarkets, purchasing only the loss leaders at each store. If you have the time and energy, there's nothing wrong with hunting for the best deals, as long as you're not guzzling a dollar's worth of gas driving to another supermarket just to save 50 cents on a box of cereal.

While most consumers don't have the time or inclination to become cherry pickers, reading your supermarket's weekly circular is always a good idea. Look for sales on items you use regularly and can stock up on. Often you'll find good deals on cereal, soda, paper goods, and meats. But buy only products you need, and make sure you'll be able to use them up before they go bad. (See "Fresh From the Farm, or Not? The Dating Game.")

Advertised specials are great, as long as they're in stock. How many times have you eagerly gone to the market, ready to stock up on a certain sale item, only to find the shelf bare? If this happens, you do have some rights. The Federal Trade Commission's "Unavailable Rule" states that if an advertised item is not available, the store must issue a "rain check," which allows you to buy the item later at the sale price. If a rain check isn't available, the store must offer you a substitute item of comparable value at the same price as the sale item, or give you some kind of compensation that is at least equal in value to the advertised item. However, stores are exempt from this rule if their ad clearly states that "quantities are limited."

Comparing Prices: You Better Shop Around

Unit prices are a great way to find out how much you're getting for your money. While the package price tells you how much the entire item costs, the unit price shows you how much you're actually paying for each ounce, pound, quart, square foot, or individual piece of a product. You can use unit prices to compare different brands of the same item or to compare the prices of different size packages to determine which one is the most economical. Unit prices usually are displayed on information tags found on the shelf under the product. For example, if you have two different size jars of marinara sauce, a quick glance at their unit prices will tell you which is actually the better deal. The smaller jar is probably less expensive, but the bigger jar might be the better bargain because it costs less per ounce. Most of us know that buying in bulk can save money. However, be careful. While this is generally true, there are exceptions, especially when sales are involved. Again, the unit price will indicate the best buy.

Unit prices also can help determine if your favorite products have fallen victim to a very common manufacturing trick of the trade, downsizing. A downsized product looks and costs the same as before, but there's less inside the package. Don't be surprised if you discover that your favorite cereal, drink mix, snack food, is suddenly giving you less for your money. Just be informed by checking out the unit price and then decide for yourself if it's a product you want to continue to buy.

Watch out for similar foods being sold at different prices in different parts of your supermarket. This often happens with cheese. For example, you might find cheddar cheese for sale in three different places in your supermarket—prepackaged in the dairy case, sliced by the pound at the deli, and nesting next to the brie and gouda in the gourmet cheese display. Prices for the same hunk of cheddar can vary widely depending on where you pick it up in your store. It usually costs the least from the dairy case and the most from the those fancy gourmet cheese islands. In most cases there's no difference in the product itself.

Prepared foods is one of the fastest-growing and most profitable areas in the supermarket industry. Things like rotisserie chickens, ready-made sandwiches, and prepackaged salads are all popular as busy families try to cut down their time in the kitchen. But make no mistake, you pay for the convenience at the cash register. It's important to weigh the cost versus the convenience. If you're looking to save money, consider doing some of the work yourself. Boneless chicken breasts can cost twice as much as buying chicken on the bone. Peeling and cutting carrots yourself can be a lot cheaper than buying a pack that's already been prepared. Of course, if buying a precooked meatloaf means you can make it to your child's Little League game, it might be worth the price. Only you can decide how much your time is worth.

Finally, beware of buying nonfood items at the supermarket. Things like shampoo, toothpaste, aspirin, and shaving cream are generally less expensive at your neighborhood drug store or discount store.

Beyond Name Brands: Putting Store Brands to the Test

There was a time when most consumers thought of supermarket brands (generally called store brands or private labels) as cheap but inferior imitations of their favorite national-brand products. Indeed, during the recession of the 1970s, many shoppers considered store brands, with their plain, generic packaging and less-than-top-notch quality, as more of a necessary money-saving evil than a tasty bargain. When the economy turned around, consumers returned to their favorite national brands.

Well, times have changed, and so too have the look, quality, and reputation of store-brand food products. Today private-label brands account for about 20 percent of a supermarket's total sales, which, as industry expert Phil Lempert points out, makes them the number-one selling brand on store shelves. "More of us are relying on store brands than ever before," he says. In fact, according to a 1996 Gallup study, 83 percent of consumers say they regularly buy store brands while 72 percent feel store brands are now equal in quality to national-brand products. It's that commitment to quality that many in the industry credit with the continuing growth of store-brand sales. To succeed in today's market, educated consumers are demanding that store brands offer both savings *and* quality.

Certainly private labels offer good deals for anyone trying to trim their grocery bill; the Gallup study found that 61 percent of consumers still buy store brands to save money. Lempert estimates that by substituting private labels for national brands, you can save over $2,000 a year. In our research, we found private-label products costing up to 40 percent less than their national-brand counterparts. A trip to a Los Angeles–area Ralphs supermarket, one of the largest chains in southern California, offers a few examples: A 10-packet box of Quaker Instant Oatmeal Maple & Brown Sugar cost $3.09, compared to the equivalent Ralphs store brand, which rang up at $2.39, a savings of 30 percent. A 22-count pack of Huggies Supreme Diapers cost $6.99 while a 24-count pack of Ralphs Ultrafit Supreme diapers cost only $4.99, a savings of more than 40 percent. Finally, a 28-ounce jar of Skippy Creamy peanut butter cost $3.69 while the same-size Ralphs Creamy Style cost $3.17, a savings of about 15 percent. Clearly, buying store brands is a great way to shave dollars off your weekly shopping bill.

Private labels can offer these big savings since they don't have all of the expenses that name-brand manufacturers do. The cost of advertising, promotion, and product placement can account for up to 40 percent of a product's price. That's why stores can afford to offer their private-label products at such reasonable prices. But as the quality of store brands continues to improve, price is no longer the only reason to buy. The winning combination of high quality and reasonable prices is leading shoppers to form allegiances to store brands. For example, in their Oakland, California, store, Safeway's brand of soft drink often outsells both Coke and Pepsi.

According to Lempert, the early 1980s saw a push by stores to expand their private-label lines to offer shoppers more variety and value. Today you might find up to three different types of store brands of the same product in your supermarket. These different store-brand types are called "tiers" in the industry. The first tier is the one we all remember from earlier days, when the only concern was low cost. These products are still inexpensive and generic, with less-than-exciting packaging. On the second tier, store brands compete directly with brand-name products, stepping up both quality and packaging design. We've already discussed how important the look of a package is in selling a product, and store brands are using those tricks of the trade to compete with the big boys. (See "The Color of Money: How Packaging Affects What You Buy.") In your local supermarket you've probably noticed that many store brands are placed right next to competing national brands. Many times the store brand's packaging uses the same colors and designs of the brand-name product as well as similar descriptions. At the Ralphs we visited, they even had small shelf tags next to their private-label products stating they were of "National Brand Quality." The third tier is the crème de la crème of private labels. Here stores strive to distinguish their product by making it a brand of its own. According to *Supermarket News,* an industry publication, about 10 percent of the big chains offer premium third-tier private labels, and the list is growing. You might recognize Nature's Best, Master's Choice, President's Choice, and American Premier as examples of top-of-the-line store brands.

While the range of quality and price options store brands offer today is great for consumers, it's important to know what you're buying and why you're buying it. If saving money is your main goal, store brands are a good way to go. But smart shoppers will always strive for value, and value is the combination of cost and quality. As we've said, most store brands have vastly improved their quality. In fact, some private labels are manufactured by the same companies that produce national brands. However, store brands won't always hold up against their national competitors. Be careful of buying a store brand to save money only to see it spoil in your refrigerator because you and your family find it doesn't taste as good as your favorite national brand. Obviously, a bargain isn't a bargain if you end up throwing half of it away.

We suggest buying the smallest size of a store brand—say, the smallest bottle of ketchup or container of yogurt—and giving it a try. If you like it, you can buy bigger on your next trip to the supermarket. If you hate it, at least you spent the least amount of money to give it a try. Lempert suggests comparing the ingredients of private labels to your favorite brand as a way of predicting how a product will stack up. For example, if your favorite national-brand spaghetti sauce lists crushed tomatoes as its first ingredient, a store brand with water as its first ingredient might not make the grade. When trying out different private labels, be aware that some stores stand behind their brands with money-back guarantees. So experiment, have fun, and save money. These days, store brands can be a great aid in the fight against rising grocery bills.

Coupons: Clipping Your Way to Savings

One of the first consumer stories your coauthor Jason produced for television was about a coupon-clipping queen. He watched in amazement as this housewife charged into a supermarket armed with a gigantic file of coupons and rebates and then proceeded to buy almost $200 worth of groceries for a little over ten bucks. Now, most of us don't have the time necessary to reap such big savings from coupon clipping, but according to supermarket expert Phil Lempert, even the average shopper can trim up to 15 percent off his or her weekly shopping bill. "For a family of four that can translate into a yearly savings of over $700," he points out.

Coupons have been with us for about one hundred years, ever since a pharmacist in Atlanta offered 5 cents off a glass of Coca-Cola at his soda fountain. From this humble beginning the industry has grown into a $6.5 billion business that churns out 280 billion coupons each year. The average American home receives over 3,000 coupons yearly. That's a lot of potential saving floating around. However, while 75 percent of consumers do use coupons at least occasionally, the overall redemption rate is a measly 2 percent. This means that 98 percent of all coupons produced never make it to the checkout line. Because of this low redemption rate, many manufacturers say producing coupons is a huge waste of money. They claim savings could better be passed on to consumers by eliminating the cost of the coupon system and simply lowering prices on all their products accordingly.

Back in 1996, Procter & Gamble tried out this idea and stopped distributing coupons in upstate New York. Consumer reaction was swift and clear. Shoppers in this test market showed their displeasure by writing letters to local newspapers, signing petitions, and boycotting Procter & Gamble products. So loud was the outcry that the state attorney general actually stepped in to investigate if the no-coupon experiment violated antitrust laws. While Procter & Gamble admitted no wrongdoing, it agreed to settle the investigation by reinstating its coupon program, and we all got a taste of how strongly American shoppers feel about their right to clip. However, somewhat lost in all the brouhaha was the fact that during their fourteen-month experiment, Procter & Gamble also reduced its list prices. As it turns out, coupon clippers in the test area ended up paying about the same for Procter & Gamble items during the no-coupon experiment as they had the previous year with their coupons. While companies probably won't make the mistake of eliminating coupons cold turkey in the future, most are quietly reducing the number of coupons they print as well as the face value of the coupons they do offer.

Even with the downsizing of coupon programs, there is still plenty of clipping to be done. These days you'll find most manufacturers issue coupons to promote new products or to lure you into trying their brand. Also, in a bid to get your business, supermarkets are offering to double and even triple the value of manufacturers' coupons as well as offering coupons of their own. The following are a few ways to put your scissors to best use.

•*Clip coupons only for products you would buy anyway.* Don't buy a product just because you have a coupon for it. Coupons actually can encourage you to spend more money by enticing you to buy products you don't need. While 75 cents off a bag of double-dipped chocolate chip cookies might sound like a good deal, if they weren't on your list in the first place, you're spending money on impulse. Also, don't immediately jump at coupons that require you to buy multiple products. For example, a coupon for $1 off six yogurts is a good deal for someone who's a big yogurt fan. However, if two or three end up spoiling in the fridge, it was no bargain.

•*Clip but compare.* Even though you have a coupon for a certain brand, another brand (including store brands) still might be less expensive. Look around and compare before you buy.

•*Organize your way to savings.* A coupon does no good if it's sitting at home in a drawer while you're at the supermarket. Keep all your coupons in one place—an envelope or wallet organizer—and sort them by product type or supermarket aisle. Discard expired coupons immediately so they don't clog up the works.

•*Don't forget rebates.* Rebates seem like a lot of work. You might ask yourself if cutting out proof-of-purchase labels, saving receipts, digging around for postage, and waiting four to six weeks for your rebate check is worth it. Lempert says that many times it is. The cash value of a rebate is almost always at least $1, and often higher. If you organize your rebates as you do your coupons, they shouldn't take up too much extra time. You'll find rebate offers at your store's customer-service counter, on its bulletin board, and on the products themselves. Mail rebates in immediately so you don't forget.

What's the new trend in supermarket coupons? Well, a more personal approach. Manufacturers are moving away from traditional mass coupon distribution in newspapers and are using to-day's technology to target coupons only to the consumers who will actually use them. For instance, why waste money distributing diaper coupons to everyone? And doesn't it make sense that coupons for dog food only go to dog owners? Supermarket scanners now allow the industry to analyze what you've purchased on any given shopping trip and immediately print out coupons tailored just for you. For example, if you've just purchased a jar of Jif peanut butter, you might receive coupons for a larger size jar of Jif, a competing brand like Skippy, or a complementary product like Smuckers jelly. These "purchase-activated" coupons can be used on subsequent visits to the supermarket (which also promotes store loyalty). The redemption rate for this type of coupon is over four times higher than for traditional coupons. Companies also are using the Internet to distribute coupons. Usually in exchange for personal demographic information, manufacturers will offer coupons you can print directly from your home computer.

Frequent-Shopper Programs: The Wave of the Future?
New technology also has sparked one of the hottest trends in the supermarket industry: preferred-shopper programs. These programs—also called discount- or frequent-shopper programs—offer automatic savings on certain products without clipping store coupons, along with a growing list of other benefits. Used correctly, they can offer a convenient way to save time and money.

To join, consumers usually are required to complete an application that asks for basics like name, address, and phone number as well as other demographic information. After you complete the form, you're given a preferred-shopper card. Each time you check out, the cashier will swipe your card (which has a bar code) over the register's scanner to give you instant discounts on certain products that are earmarked as sale items.

In some cases, shoppers can almost feel forced to join their supermarket's frequent-shopper program since it offers savings that are hard to refuse. In a typical example, program members at one store were charged 99 cents per pound for ground beef, while nonmembers had to pay the regular $2.19 price. While saving money is the ultimate goal of consumers, supermarkets originally started frequent-shopper programs to increase customer loyalty. And it seems to be working. A 1996 study by the Food Marketing Institute found that preferred shoppers spent 33 percent more a week than other shoppers and were less likely to defect to other stores. But as more and more supermarket chains start their own programs, industry expert Lempert says stores will have to take their programs one step further. "When I talk to consumers, what I'm hearing is that many have cards for three or four different stores," he says. "This does nothing to improve customer loyalty." To be successful, Lempert says stores need to take their frequent-shopper programs to the next level and start offering more rewards to the customers who spend the most—much like the airline industry's frequent-flyer programs.

Stores are offering bigger incentives to shoppers in an attempt to increase customer allegiance. For example, one supermarket offers 10 percent off your next shopping trip after you've spent $250 in the store. At some stores you can collect points for every dollar you spend, then redeem them for gift certificates, free Thanksgiving turkeys, air-fare discounts, and the like. And following in the footsteps of credit card companies and airlines, some supermarkets are now issuing "gold" cards that award their best customers special benefits including exclusive discounts, free delivery, and even private shopping hours.

So how can you use your supermarket's frequent-shopper program to get maximum savings?

•*Do your research*. Make sure you know which products are being offered to club members at sale prices before you hit the supermarket aisles. Weekly circulars will let you know.

•*Double dip*. Don't forget about manufacturers' coupons. Using them in conjunction with club sales can add up to even bigger savings.

•*Stock up.* Take advantage of items that are on sale for club members by stocking up on products you know you'll need. This is especially important for foods that usually don't have regular manufacturer-coupon discounts, such as meat, produce, and dairy.

•*Avoid temptation.* As with coupons, don't buy products just because they're on sale for club members. Make sure you need what you buy.

Preferred-shopper programs certainly can help consumers save money. But there are drawbacks. By enrolling in a store's program, you're automatically revealing a treasure trove of information about your personal buying habits. From the moment you join, a supermarket can start collecting data about you: which days you usually shop, how much you spend, and what products you buy. Stores then can analyze your purchases and target you with specific promotions. For instance, if they see you're buying newborn-size diapers, they might mail you coupons for baby formula or wipes. Retailers also use data to refine their marketing techniques. For example, one store discovered that consumers who buy cold medication often buy orange juice, so they started putting O.J. in the pharmacy aisle.

Sound a little like Big Brother is watching? Well, you might think giving up a bit of personal info is worth the savings. However, this data mining has some privacy advocates concerned. What if a supermarket sold your information to your employer or insurance company? An insurer might decide you're buying too many cigarettes while your employer might not like the amount of beer you purchase. Most stores have written privacy policies and restrict access to their database, but the industry is entirely self-regulated. If you're concerned about your privacy but want to sign up for a frequent-shopper program, make sure your store has a written policy that states who has access to your information, whether it can be sold to others, and exactly how it will be used.

Checking Out Your Checkout: Don't Be Scammed by the Scanner

Laser scanners—introduced into supermarkets in 1974—have greatly reduced the time we all spend in checkout lines. Few consumers would argue that scanners have helped make grocery shopping more pleasant. However, they're not without problems. In fact, according to expert Phil Lempert, scanner errors are the number-one complaint of supermarket shoppers. A 1996 study by the California Public Interest Research Group (CALPIRG) showed that customers should be concerned. They reported that in ten of the most populated California counties, as many as one in twenty-five scanner transactions at grocery or retail stores resulted in an overcharge, costing consumers more than $250 million a year. A 1997 Federal Trade Commission study found scanning errors (both over- and undercharges) in 5 percent of all transactions. The good news for grocery shoppers is that supermarkets were found to have the least errors, overcharging only 1.9 percent of the time. However, this still adds up to a lot of money and frustration.

We're not saying that supermarkets are out to cheat you. Scanner errors are almost always unintentional, and most of the time they are the result of human error, not mechanical failure. With a typical supermarket stocking 30,000 to 50,000 items and making hundreds of prices changes each week—mostly to reflect sale items—it's easy to see how mistakes can occur as employees change and update prices in the store's computer database.

Supermarkets are working hard to improve scanner accuracy rates. They know that overcharges undermine a store's credibility and erode customer loyalty, while undercharges reduce corporate profits. But some in the industry say stores aren't doing enough. "Grocery and retail stores should be willing to do everything possible to boost consumer confidence in the accuracy of their price scanners," says a CALPIRG consumer advocate. But instead, the group charges, industry lobbyists continually block regulation that would monitor scanning systems and expand consumer pricing laws. Says CALPIRG, "The only thing worse than making mistakes is hiding them."

You can protect yourself from being overcharged by supermarket scanners by staying on your toes at the checkout counter. Most scanner errors occur on sale items, so put down that *National Enquirer* and pay close attention to the register display. Also, hold on to the store's weekly circular. This can help you verify prices and will immediately prove to a cashier that you were charged more than the advertised cost. And don't forget, since cashiers are only human, they sometimes make mistakes. Particularly at peak times, when checkout lines are long, a cashier might unintentionally scan an item twice or make other mistakes. If you see an error, speak up. Don't be embarrassed. Many stores have policies for pricing errors and may even give you the item for free if it scans at an incorrect price. Ask a manager about your store's policy. By pointing out mistakes, you'll not only save yourself money, but you'll help out your fellow shoppers as well. If you find your store routinely makes scanning errors and you feel it isn't doing anything to correct the problem, report it to your local Department of Weights and Measures

You also should carefully monitor the accuracy of your supermarket's scales. During a 1996 survey by the Citizens Affairs Department in Long Island, New York, investigators discovered weight errors at twenty-three of the forty delis, supermarkets, and convenience stores they visited. In several supermarkets we've seen scales that read higher than zero before the cashier even placed anything on them. Again, your best defense is to pay close attention. If you feel there's an error, have the store manager check the weight of your purchases on a different scale.

WHERE TO TURN FOR HELP
•For information on food safety, nutrition, and food labeling laws, contact:
Federal Drug Administration's Center for Safety and Nutrition
200 C Street, S.W.

Washington, DC 20204
(800) FDA-4010
www.fda.gov

•For a copy of "The Food Keeper," a brochure published by the
Food Marketing Institute about the shelf life of food products
before and after opening, send a self-addressed, business-size envelope with 75 cents postage to:
Consumer Affairs Department
Food Marketing Institute
800 Connecticut Avenue, N.W.
Washington, DC 20006.
(202) 452-8444
You also can order or download the brochure from the Institute's Web site:
www.fmi.org

•For meat and poultry safety questions, contact:
USDA, Food Safety and Inspection Service
Room 1180-South
14th Street & Independence Avenue, S.W.
Washington, DC 20250
(800) 535-4555

•The Center for Science in the Public Interest is a nonprofit education and advocacy organization. Their newsletter provides
health and nutrition information and tips. To subscribe or for
more information, contact:
The Center for Science in the Public Interest
1875 Connecticut Avenue, N.W.
Suite 300
Washington, DC 20009
(202) 332-9110
www.cspinet.org

▶ **Top Ten Tips**

1. *Plan ahead.* Do your research before you hit the super-market. Planning ahead will help you shop more economically and efficiently. Survey your pantry and refrigerator so you don't end up buying things you already have. Organize coupons and store circulars and prepare a thorough shopping list.

2. *Shop at stores that best suit your needs.* With so much competition out there, you don't have to settle for second best. Pick a store that offers a good selection of products, a pleasant shopping atmosphere, and services that you'll use. Also, don't forget about supermarket alternatives like superstores, warehouse clubs, and co-ops.

3. *Never shop when hungry.* With all the savory sights and enticing smells in a supermarket, a rumbling stomach only leads to impulse purchases and a ballooning grocery bill.

4. *Consider store brands.* Store brands have come a long way and today offer both savings and quality. By substituting them for national brands, you can easily shave money off each grocery bill. If you're concerned about the taste or quality of a store-brand product, buy the smallest size and test it out.

5. *Take advantage of coupons and frequent-shopper programs.* You can save hundreds of grocery dollars a year by taking advantage of coupons and frequent-shopper clubs. Stock up on items you know you'll need whenever they're on sale for club members, and don't forget to use coupons in conjunction with frequent-shopper specials. However, never buy something just because you have a coupon or it's on sale to club members.

6. *Dare to compare.* Always check out a product's unit price. It will give you the true cost of an item no matter what its brand or size. Buy in bulk. Larger sizes are almost always a better bargain. There are exceptions, so again, check the unit price.

7. *Limit impulse purchases.* A supermarket is a minefield of temptation. Don't be the hapless victim who pushes a grocery cart overflowing with goodies that aren't needed. Stick to your shopping list and set a limit on impulse purchases before you enter the store.

8. *Don't be tricked by the trade.* Marketers are experts at manipulation. Always keep their tricks in mind. Don't immediately assume that products in end-of-aisle displays or dump bins are on sale. Remember that high-cost, high-profit products are often at eye level. Think before you give in to the pastry shells and whipped cream that have been conveniently placed next to the strawberries. Did you really plan to make a pie?

9. *Read labels carefully.* Don't be swayed automatically with bold-lettered claims offering new, improved, and healthier products. New labeling laws make it easier to decipher the truth about what's in the food you buy. Check out freshness and expiration dates on products whenever possible to make sure you're purchasing food at peak quality.

10. *Scrutinize the scanner.* Checkout scanners don't always ring up the true price. Be vigilant and watch the register display carefully. With the supermarket's circular in hand, pay particular attention to sale items. The majority of scanning errors occur on these products.

Glossary

Cherry picker: A super-thrifty shopper who goes to several supermarkets and purchases only the loss leaders at each store.

Downsizing: The practice of selling products in packages that look and cost the same as before but actually contain less product.

Dump display: A bin that is purposely made to appear disorganized so shoppers will assume that the jumble of products inside is on sale.

Loss leader: A heavily advertised item that is sold at a very low price to draw consumers into the supermarket in the hopes that they will then buy more.

Private labels: Products made specifically for the store. Also called store brands.

Rain check: A voucher issued by a supermarket when a sale item is unavailable. It enables you to buy the advertised product at the sale price at a later time.

Unit price: A price that shows you how much you're paying for a product by the ounce, pound, quart, square foot, or individual piece. Helpful when comparing different product brands or sizes.

Suggested Reading

Phil Lempert. *Phil Lempert's Supermarket Shopping and Value Guide.* Chicago: Contemporary Books.

CHAPTER 5
HOME CONTRACTING

It's the American dream. Own your own home. Make it beautiful, and either live in it for eternity or make a killing when you sell it. We spend $120 billion a year on remodeling our homes. These projects are sometimes a necessity and sometimes a nicety. There are homeowners who are handy and homeowners who hire help to hang a picture. But even the most adept tool timer must hire professionals to perform the big jobs. And while there are fabulous, artistic, and magical contractors for hire, there are, unfortunately, plenty who are dishonest, disreputable, and untalented. Contractors, we believe, who lack a conscience.

HOME REPAIR RIP-OFFS
Home improvement complaints are consistently ranked among the top five complaints received by Better Business Bureaus across the country. On occasion, they are the main consumer headache in America. This is certainly an honor reputable remodelers could live without.

Home repair rip-offs are significant. Remodeling gone wrong can cost thousands of dollars and cost a homeowner's life savings. Contractor fraud is an insidious crime—a crime that can render a family homeless. Often it's the trusting elderly who are targets, but no one is exempt. A consumer investigative team could do a "dream home turns into nightmare" report every single night and not run out of material.

It is our hope that the advice offered in this chapter by experts, investigators, and reputable remodelers, as well as our own television exposés, will alert you to the scams and unscrupulous tricks contractors use to separate you from your money. We also hope that if you are the adult child or neighbor of elderly people, you will make every effort to protect them from fraudulent contractors.

Arm yourself with our information so that you will be able to choose a reputable contractor, draw up a legitimate contract, and take pride in your finished project. The time it takes to do your research is nothing compared to the endless hours you could spend pursuing restitution for rotten repairs. And as you will see, it's not just the time you will lose pursuing restitution, it's your money, your trust, and the place you call home sweet home.

SPRING—THE TIME OF ETERNAL SCAMS
Spring arrives and the world turns green! Your thoughts turn to sprucing up and spring cleaning. But the dishonest contractors' thoughts are turning to cleaning out your bank account. Spring is an evil time for home contracting scams. They almost literally come out of the woodwork. Spring is the time to beware of the guys who come to your home unsolicited and offer seasonal home improvement work. Investigators have several names for these migrant con artists whose only aim is to rip you off.

Remodeling Roadies
"Drifters," also called "travelers," or "Criminal Gypsies" are the people who drift in and out of neighborhoods going door-to-door trying to solicit business. They come into your neighborhood, collect your money, and then skip town after doing shoddy work or no work at all. The National Association of Bunco Investigators (NABI), an association of about 700 police officers who share knowledge of current cons nationwide, knows this criminal profile all too well. NABI says the criminal travelers usually drive pickup trucks, sport utility vehicles, or vans. They usually stay at a motel, trailer park, or rental apartment. Often they solicit business far from where they are living. In most cases the travelers are mobile and quick, stopping in a town only long enough to commit a crime before moving on to a new location when the pressure heats up.

Roofers' Ruse

Travelers are charming. They'll strike up a conversation with the homeowner and, if the target is a senior citizen, they'll spend extra time with him or her, asking about the family and even sitting down to join the oldster for coffee. Travelers' motive is to gain trust. They'll explain that they are doing roofing work in the area. They'll point out some spots on the roof that need repair. Then they'll offer an incredible deal on the work and produce a business card, claiming to be fully licensed and insured. The homeowner is taken in by the charm and the low, low bid. In the end, the roof is shoddily repaired (a roof that may not have needed repair in the first place) or the victim hands over cash and gets absolutely nothing. The travelers collect their loot and head to a new neighborhood to pull the same scam on a new group of unsuspecting homeowners.

It's no coincidence that these swindlers target the elderly, who are often on fixed incomes. Seniors may be more trusting and make poor witnesses in court. Travelers know the elderly have a hard time identifying suspects and an even more difficult time withstanding the pressure of a trial. Often the aged refuse to press charges because they have befriended the contractor. They are perfect victims.

Hammer-time Hucksters

An elderly Florida man recently was targeted by a phony husband-and-wife roofing team. The gentleman was quoted a price of $1,350 to repair, clean, and tile his roof. He handed over a $350 deposit. It didn't take long for the couple to return asking for an additional $2,200 deposit. The man gave them the money. With the streak of good luck running, the couple came back and demanded $2,000 more. They insisted the roof was leaking and the job would tally nearly $10,000! The police finally arrested this roofing couple who (surprise) had a record of prior arrests.

Jodi Flitton, an attorney with the Pennsylvania Attorney General's office, is suing four members of a family who, authorities claim, concocted a sinister and elaborate scheme to defraud homeowners. Several of the family members, consisting of two brothers and two cousins, were run out of town by Maryland authorities in the 1980s for bilking homeowners out of hundreds of thousands of dollars. They then resurfaced in Pennsylvania and have been accused of suckering approximately fifty more victims! The Howards currently are facing a string of lawsuits by Pennsylvania authorities.

The Howards also have an affinity for elderly clients. According to a Pennsylvania senior citizen, she was told her roof needed to be replaced. Once Howards removed the shingles from her roof. He then "discovered" that the wood needed to be replaced. The homeowner, literally without a roof over her head, was very vulnerable. The contractor told her she needed a heavier wood, which of course drove up the price of the repair work. Then, he claimed, in order to hold up the heavier wood, support bars needed to be nailed into the frame. When Pennsylvania investigators inspected the roof, they found that the workers had left the supports leaning against the roof, supporting nothing.

Watered-down Promises
Another one of the Howards' alleged victims was told squirrels were eating away at her roof. To get rid of the pests, the contractor would spray the roof with pesticides. The man went into her home and filled a jug with water. Then he went to his truck and, a short time later, returned with a tank attached to a sprayer. The homeowner claims the tank was filled with a clear liquid that had no smell. The contractor said, "Now we have to go up and spray for these animals." The homeowner told him she thought it was nothing but the water. And he said, "Well, it has an odor for animals, but not for humans."

According to the Pennsylvania investigators, not only did the Howards use fake materials, but they were great at faking evidence to convince a homeowner work needed to be done. Pennsylvania authorities say in court papers that this very same ring of rogue roofers contracted to repair a woman's roof and garage ceiling after pointing out the damages in her property. After paying $40,000 for a new roof, her problems had only begun. Her living room ceiling started to leak. The contractor then hit her up for $1,800 more to fix the ceiling. A reputable contractor who later inspected the roof concluded that the original roof never needed repair, and in fact, the ceiling leak had been caused by the bad roof repair job.

The Pennsylvania Attorney General's office has charged the traveling family with violating the state consumer law under "confusing and misleading" conduct. The Howards have denied the various allegations and have blamed their brother or cousins, or both, for all of the problems. Will these unfortunate homeowners ever be able to collect restitution? Lawmakers say it is highly unlikely.

Pass on the Leftovers

Another trick "travelers" use is the old I've-got-leftover-materials-from-a-previous-job line. They tell you they have just finished work on other homes in your area. They need to get rid of the excess and would be willing to give you a deal just because they bought too much. Homeowners fall for this false bargain and probably end up with a half-finished roof, shoddy work, or no work at all. Reputable roofers meticulously order materials for a job. They do not try to unload their excess materials on the next willing homeowner.

Shine or Slime?

When do you find out your work is shoddy or incomplete? Investigators say you might not find out until you have real problems. Clever contractors know how to make you think the job was done well, and it's all part of their bag of tricks. To make shingles glisten like new, investigators reveal that drifters have been known to spray used motor oil on wooden shingles.

Dirty Driveway Deals

Driveway contractors use the same ploy. They also tell home-owners they "just happen" to be in the neighborhood with "ex-tra" loads of asphalt and can do your driveway for less. Again, any paver worth his weight in tar could afford to hold on to a little material overrage until the next job. Investigators tell us that most contractors carefully figure the amount of material needed. And after all, do you want a contractor who can't do math to do your driveway?

Consumers who fall prey to paving rip-offs can end up with a wafer-thin layer that won't even last the season. One dirty deal the driveway contractors pull is to mix coal tar with packing peanuts. It makes the mix look black and shiny, but the layer will wash away with the first rain. By then your driveway con-tractor has driven himself out of town.

Deputy John Nicholas, of Gypsy descent himself, works to educate law enforcers about this crime culture. Of course, not all Gypsies are criminals. Most Gypsies have a strong culture with a deep, rich heritage. It is the criminal ones who worry law en-forcers and Nicholas himself. He says criminal Gypsies teach younger ones to pull these scams early on. He offers up another blacktop trick driveway Gypsies employ. "They will often mix asphalt with kerosene to dilute the more expensive materials. The driveway will look shiny and beautiful but will never dry." Nicholas says the blacktop will bubble and stay gooey; when the sun heats up, you really get stuck with a mess. He too warns people to stay away from the leftovers' line and the lure of in-credibly low prices.

John Turner, an investigator with Pasco County Consumer Affairs department in Florida, has heard of yet one more drive-way detour. He says travelers promise to pave your driveway. They then pour asphalt right over the grass and weeds; soon enough, your blacktop starts sprouting greenery. What's worse, Turner says, is that someone from that same clan comes back to your home six weeks later, telling you that your driveway has been sealed with an illegal coating. That person scares you into believing the Environmental Protection Agency will fine you, and then offers to do your driveway again.

Prepless Paint Work

Drifters dabble in the painting arts as well. Picasso they ain't. A drifter may promise a paint job for under $500. It's a hard price for homeowners to pass up, but they wish they'd done just that when it turns out the drifter did the painting but no prep work. Not only are the homeowners out $500, but they also have to pay the next guy to strip the new paint along with the layers of old paint. The bargain just turned into a major bummer.

How about this one? A roofer promises to paint your roof with a treated paint that will deflect the light. Naturally, you'll be charged more for the expensive, specially-treated paint. You pay it, but your home is painted with the regular cheaper paint and your roof is no better off. In fact, you may be worse off down the road, when the weather hits. You think your roof has been treated when, in reality, you have no added protection.

This next con is the among the sleaziest we've seen. A drifter carries a can of spray paint around, sprays a home with graffitti, and then has the gall to act as a good Samaritan by informing the homeowner of the desecration. He then offers to repaint the house for a great price. Investigators say to complete the con, the painter uses cheap, watered-down paint. All this after it was the con man who created the damage in the first place!

A Lot of Hot Air

The warm weather also brings with it the chance to zap the wallets of those who are sweating it out. Air-conditioning systems can require costly maintenance and repairs. But when you're the one sweltering, you probably aren't in the mood to shop for a reputable service person. And that's when they get you! The best approach is to do your research before the weather heats up. Look for a reputable person to have on hand when and if you need that desperate service call.

Foiled Again!

Consumer affairs investigator John Turner, of Florida, reveals a simple but lucrative trick air-conditioning con artists use—a con that will make your emotions run hot and your blood run cold! Turner says a simple piece of foil from a stick of gum can short out an air-conditioning compressor. It's done this way.

Dishonest servicemen can cause the relay to malfunction. (The relay is the part that converts the high voltage of your air conditioner to a lower voltage that is used in your home.) They place the metal gum wrapper on the ends of the relay to short out the system. And you have no way of knowing about the sabotage. All you know is your system doesn't work. But John Turner can and does inspect units for evidence of gum. He has actually found foil residue on connectors! A new relay should run you around $80. Dishonest repairpeople have been known to charge up to $1,500 when the system shorts out.

If You See a "Runner,"—Run!

Free steak knives! Free coffee cups! To get them, all you have to do is hear the pitch from a traveling contractor. Investigators say the scheme starts with the head kingpin who hires guys to survey the area. They are called "runners," and it's their job to go door-to-door offering homeowners freebies just for listening to a sales spiel. Investigators say a surprisingly large number of homeowners actually fall for the ploy. This is just another twist the travelers use to get you to let them in your home so they can come up with home improvement projects you just "need" to have done. The same results happen as we've discussed. The bid is low, the work is shoddy, you end up overpaying, and the contractor leaves town before the work falls apart.

It's hard to imagine choosing someone to fix your home, and paying thousands to do it, all for a few free steak knives. We spend hours clipping coupons to save 25 cents at the supermarket, yet we allow a smooth-talking runner to convince us to spend our savings. Freebies are not the criteria by which you should judge a potential contractor.

Gypsy Crime Families

Gypsies are blamed for pulling many contracting scams. We hate to categorize this ethnically, but many in the Gypsy culture are taught to pull cons at a young age. Deputy John Nicholas, of the Gypsy culture, now trains law enforcers about the criminal Gypsy rings and the force behind them. Nicholas says most people know very little about Gypsies. It is a culture that is meant to stay secret and stay within the family. At a very young age, those born into a criminal Gypsy family are taught how to distract and steal.

Not all Gypsies are dishonest, but the criminal Gypsies are very good at what they do as they have had years of practice. Nicholas says certain families are trained in specific crimes. Some are fortune-tellers, others are roofers or general contractors. When committing home repair fraud, they purposely confuse homeowners. They'll dispatch different family members to the home for different tasks. One will collect the deposit, the other will have you sign the contract, and still another will do the work. The members all look similar—the same height, hair color, and age; this is meant to confuse you. Identifying the crook later to police becomes very difficult, and this is all part of the criminal Gypsy's strategy.

The crime is passed down generation to generation, although the cons may take on new twists.

Home Repair, Home Robbery

Here the crime really is burglary, but the ruse begins with some kind of home contracting estimate. The criminal's strategy is to gain entrance to your home. Deputy Nicholas says oftentimes a Gypsy repairman brings along his child or wife. The repairman will distract the homeowner while the family member runs through the house collecting cash or jewelry. To find out where the person keeps cash, the contractor might offer a rebate, giving the homeowner a $100 bill and ask for change. The Gypsy carefully watches the homeowner to see where he or she keeps money. The other family member knows exactly where to go to grab the loot. Authorities say in some cases the crooks are so brazen, they actually have walked out of homes with entire safes.

Homeowners rarely suspect a woman or a child of robbery. It's a trick that has worked for decades and has become an effective tool in the criminal family's trade.

Now that you know their ploy, don't allow workers to bring family members along for the job. Or if you do, make sure your attention is on everyone in your home. Beware of any distraction meant to take your attention away from the job. You can out-con the con man!

A Pesty Ploy

Detective Jeff Bollender of the Boca Raton Police Department in Florida tells of another front for crime: burglars posing as pest control specialists. A criminal knocks on the door of elderly people. He tells them the home has bugs or termites. In Florida, it's probably true. The phony exterminator tells the homeowners he will spray the house for termites and quotes a good price. The homeowners agree. The con artist starts spraying and "accidentally" sprays the hand of one of the homeowners. Claiming the spray is very toxic and should be washed off immediately, he urges the homeowner to remove any jewelry and soak it in a detoxifying solution. While the homeowner washes his or her hands, the con artist makes off with the jewelry.

An elderly Boca Raton homeowner lost his 2-carat diamond ring to a Gypsy, a ring that was given to him by his dying father. This exterminator ploy is spreading. Complaints of the same con have been reported in different parts of Florida. The bejeweled suspects are still on the loose.

The only one who should hold your jewelry is your honey or your jeweler. Even then, as we've warned you in our gem chapter, watch the jeweler too.

A Cold Con

If air conditioning in the southern states is a problem, furnaces up north are hot with moneymaking scams. Watch out for free energy inspections or chimney checks. Again, a traveling contractor stops by and says he notices a problem with your chimney and has done work in the area. A common trick is to go down, check the furnace and, when the homeowner isn't looking, loosen an oil line or drop a rock into the blower. These minor "adjustments" made by unscrupulous repairmen can add up to costly repairs.

If an energy check is what you really need, call your public service authority. Often free checks are offered, without an ulterior motive.

Think you've heard of every possible twist on home repair rip-offs? You haven't. There is more to come. But before you boycott the industry, curse the name of Bob Vila, and let your house fall into complete disrepair, remember that a little skepticism is a good thing. And one simple tip (if it isn't already obvious) could save you from being ripped-off, gouged, cheated, and burglarized. Drumroll:

OUR #1 HOME REPAIR TIP:
Do not hire unsolicited contractors of any kind.

Don't allow anyone on your property or into your home unless you have checked him or her out in advance. The low bid is the single most effective method of getting homeowners to let their guard down and hire strangers. Don't go for it. Told you it was simple.

Smoke, No Fire!
Beware of the old "chimney shaker." The Buffalo (New York) Better Business Bureau (BBB) is well aware of this trick. With older homes, an older population, and cold weather, the chimney scam is hot for fraud. The "chimney shaker" usually lures victims in by advertisements in local papers offering gutter cleaning at cheap rates. Once the routine work is performed, the "shaker" claims the chimney is in dire need of structural repairs. Sometimes the con man literally removes bricks and mortar from the chimney, hence the name "chimney shaker." He then

uses these props to show homeowners the chimney is in a state of decay. If that doesn't shake you up, the BBB says shakers might scare you into believing carbon monoxide will seep through if it is not fixed immediately. Whenever you are told that repairs are urgently needed, stay calm. You have time to get a second opinion. Rarely must repairs must be done that very day.

Getting Zapped

Sparks may fly when you learn about the underhanded tricks dishonest electrical repairmen use to get you to spring for major rewiring. Remember the Howard family being investigated in Pennsylvania? Well, according to the Attorney General office's court papers, the Howards allegedly pulled off some really low schemes to get thousands of dollars for work that never needed to be done.

One of the family members is accused of setting off a smoke bomb in the basement of an elderly woman's home. She claimed he scared her into believing she needed to rewire the entire place or she'd be at risk of having her home go up in flames. The job cost thousands. Pennsylvania authorities claim that because of the fear and trickery the woman agreed and ended up spending a lot of money on unnecessary work.

Not to be outdone, in another case another family member apparently thought the smoke bomb was too much work. The legal papers allege that this contractor merely pulled a fuse, causing the electricity to go out. Again, a full rewiring was required. Fortunately this homeowner was suspicious and called for a second opinion. An honest inspector came out, changed the fuse, and lo and behold: There was light again.

Lights Out

We decided to expose some of these phony electrical tricks on a CNBC *Steals & Deals* report. We created our own sting, choosing an electric repair company we knew was operating under many different names in several states. Despite hundreds of complaints throughout the years, authorities did not shut them down.

For our sting, we asked a California Better Business Bureau electrical expert to create a problem. Dave Carr of the BBB loosened one screw in a home's main circuit breaker board. This would cause the power to go on and off. Carr told us, "This should require no labor other than tightening of a single screw and no material at all because nothing is damaged or out of sorts."

CNBC producer Nicole Pierce and her husband, Jim Rohrig, set up three hidden cameras and posed as homeowners. Our undercover footage revealed that the electrician did spot the loose screw, but he didn't stop there. After a series of so-called voltage tests, he announced there were three damaged breakers. After consulting his parts book, the cost of the repair quickly began to add up. When Jim protested, the repairman made a deal.

Jim: How much?
Repairman: I'm just gonna charge you half hour for my services . . . so it will be, with new breakers, $310 plus the permit.
Jim: I'll check with my wife.

An hour later the total bill was for over $431. Just to be sure, the next day the BBB expert checked the circuit breakers and concluded there was nothing wrong with them. And as for a $65 city permit? Totally unnecessary. Carr told us: "A circuit breaker, if it malfunctions and blows, you're gonna put the exact same size circuit breaker in the exact same location. You don't need a permit for that."

While a story like this is a big hit with investigative reporters, it is also discouraging. After this blatant rip-off and hundreds of complaints against the company, it took years before the government took any action. After our report aired, we noticed ads in the newspaper recruiting new electricians to work for the company. Obviously business was still very good.

Finally, a year after our report aired, the Federal Trade Commission filed a settlement with the company prohibiting it from "deceptively selling unnecessary repairs and from double billing consumers' credit cards in the future."

Our only advice to viewers was to go with an electrician who came recommended and not to wait for an emergency to spark the search.

INVESTIGATORS TURN UP THE HEAT

Rip-offs are not entirely the domain of traveling Gypsies. Some of the seemingly legitimate service companies have been found to be less than honest. The attorney general's office in Pennsylvania conducted a similar sting targeting furnace repair companies. Investigators had an elderly woman wait in her basement with a furnace that allegedly needed repair. In truth, there was nothing wrong with it. Investigators called six different repair companies as any ordinary consumer would. They took names out of the phone book or used coupons which arrived in the mail.

All advertised "clean and check" services. Six contractors were called to inspect the furnace. Only one said there was no problem. Three quoted her $3,500. The last one sabotaged the furnace. Barbara Petito of the Pennsylvania Attorney General's office says the repairman actually caused the furnace to seize and convinced the woman it was leaking carbon monoxide! He went one sleazy step further; he then ripped the name off the furnace, making it hard to call a serviceperson and describe its brand and model. He also ripped off the sticker from the previous repair company, making it difficult to call that firm back for service.

None of the furnace companies did what was promised in the ads. The homeowner's furnace was not cleaned and checked. And in all but one case the undercover agent would have been charged for unnecessary work. It was a sad commentary: consumers are more likely to be ripped off than treated honestly. These repairpeople were not chosen because they had bad records. They were chosen right out of the yellow pages or from a coupon.

The sting was all caught on hidden camera. Investigators plan to go after these servicemen for violating the state's consumer protection law.

Deceiving Discounts

When a shady contractor does find a senior citizen, he may hit paydirt. Pennsylvania investigators say one of the crime family's come-on is to advertise "senior Citizen's discounts." What a way to bait your hook! The Howard family allegedly took a seventy-four-year-old woman for a whopping $48,000, repairs the state said should have cost under $8,000. The *Baltimore Sun* reports a consultant hired by the state calls it the worst case of price gouging he'd ever seen after evaluating jobs such as the installation of a laundry washtub in the basement (value $150, price: $5,800), and the building of wooden steps to the basement (value: $500, price: $4,700).

The lesson here? Do not take ads at face value, especially ones geared toward seniors. The state alleges all of the criminal family's victims responded to their ad. Find out exactly what the company means by discounts and how it applies to your home repair job. If the bid sounds suspect, get other opinions. Your so-called discount may end up disastrous.

SELECTING A REPAIRMAN/CONTRACTOR

Don't Get Burned!

The lesson on how not to get burned when selecting a repairman is to do your homework. Mark Pacella, an investigator on the sting, offered his advice: "Know who you are dealing with, make sure he has a good reputation. Check with the Better Business Bureau for a complaint record. A coupon should not be the only criterion you use to judge the service. If you are answering a coupon, ask about the terms of the coupon. Actually say to the repairman before he pays you a visit: 'I have a coupon, how does that affect my cost?' Look at the ad carefully. You cannot always take the ad at face value, you have to understand the discount. Make sure you ask about all the requirements needed to qualify for the discount. Some requirements may be spelled out on the coupon, others may be implied. It's the unknown stipulations that can end up costing you big time." Don't forget that once you allow a serviceman into your home, it's a lot tougher to negotiate.

Confessions of a Contractor

ABC's *PrimeTime Live* was able to find a dishonest contractor who would reveal his tricks of the trade. "Gary" (a pseudonym) told Diane Sawyer he was a member of what police call a "redneck mob." Police say it's a gang that travels across the country pulling contracting scams.

In disguise, Gary agreed to tell all to Diane. He admitted to being a part of a "pack of wolves" that preyed on unsuspecting homeowners. He called himself a "door knocker," which apparently is an "inside" term for "salesman." He is what we have portrayed as the "traveler" or "drifter." His strategy was to look for a nice, clean home. This would be a tip-off that an elderly person lived there. He would then offer a free estimate for roof repair. Once he stripped off a few shingles, he would convince the homeowner that a lot of repair work was needed—work that would double the price.

Very Vulnerable

"Getting them with their pants down": According to Gary, this is that point when you can get homeowners to do whatever you want them to do. Con artists pick a repair area that is hard to reach or see. It works especially well on the elderly who cannot climb up to a roof to check out the alleged damage. Senior citizens must take Gary's word. When the shingles are stripped and he says you've got a lot of wood rotting, what are you going to

do? He's got you "with your pants down." You are vulnerable, and you will pay.

Soggy Scam

To convince the homeowner there's a water problem, Gary carries around a bag of tricks. He may choose to use a spray water gun, to show there's a leak, or wet the insulation to prove the insulation needs to be pulled out and replaced. The owner is shown the soggy area, falls for the ploy, and pays for a job that was never needed.

Seal the Deal

Remember the Pennsylvania homeowner who questioned whether there was anything more than water in the squirrel pesticide tank? Well, Gary didn't discuss the squirrel scenario but does admit using plain old H_2O to boost his bill. Gary says an expensive water seal job can easily be faked. He claims he's seen contractors use water, bleach, or nothing to complete a water seal project.

What a Worm!

This is one we haven't heard before, but Gary says he's used it. To convince a homeowner the house is rotting away, Gary admits to going to a pet store to purchase meal worms. You may wonder why, and where would you even keep the critters if you needed them. Gary swears deceitful workers hide the worms in a cigarette box, then approach the homeowner and say they found the squigglers in their attic! Gary says the usual response is "I don't want them in my house." The contractor gets the job of eliminating the worms, and the homeowner never knows the worms were imports from a pet store.

Chances are you would know if you had worm holes in your wood, and even if you didn't, please, please get a second opinion! We hope your next contractor won't bring along any unwanted pests.

Commode Con

Apparently nothing is sacred. Gary told ABC's *Primetime Live* that even the most private rooms in your home can be preyed upon.

There's no rest in the rest room. Gary tells how the commode con works. The con man asks to use the homeowner's bathroom. The homeowner naturally says yes. The phony contractor then tells the homeowner he noticed a leak in the commode and that a new seal is needed. A new seal that should run about $65 goes for the going scam rate of about a grand.

And the con doesn't end there. Gary can bilk the homeowner for more: "You go back out and basically lie to them and say to them, 'It has rotted your floor joists that caused your floor to sag.' And you don't want to be sitting on a commode and fall through."

Gary's pitch may be hard to believe, but it does work. One member of the Pennsylvania crime family actually drove his victim to the bank so that she could withdraw $6,000 for a new toilet—a repair that the state later deemed was "essentially valueless."

The bottom line here (excuse the expression) is to make sure you see the damage the contractor is describing. Don't take his word for rotting wood, or a faulty roof, or leaky ceiling. If you cannot climb up to the area that is allegedly in disrepair, ask a neighbor or one of your children to take a look at the supposed damage. Even better, get a few estimates from several different contractors. We do believe there are many honest ones out there who will tell you the truth.

The Impostor

We have stressed how important it is to choose a reputable remodeler, someone you can trust, someone who comes with references. We will say more later on how to find that honest contractor, but first we need to discuss how a contractor's credentials may not be what they seem to be.

Jon Grow of the National Association of Bunco Investigators

(NABI) has issued an alert called "Impostor Burglary." The bur-
glaries are similar and may include the Gypsy crime family
modus operandi we have already described. Here the NABI says
the suspects pose as legitimate workers and usually approach elderly homeowners. The crooks usually claim to be from the local electric company; water department; cable company;
roofing, paving, or other building trades; city inspectors; sur-
veyors; tree trimmers; or government personnel from a social
service agency. They are not. They are impostors. Their only
purpose is to get into your home, distract you, and rob you.

Usually they prey on elderly people from rural poor to mid-
dle-class neighborhoods. Investigators say they select their victims carefully. They go door-to-door, carefully questioning
homeowners to see if they have had prior home improvement
work done. The impostors have gone as far as following the
mailperson or Meals on Wheels delivery people to see if an elderly person lives in the home.

The suspects are usually criminal Gypsies or criminal travelers and typically have a history of home repair frauds, which
may include committing some kind of theft while in the homeowner's house. They are very adept at skirting the law and running out of town when the publicity heats up.

Many now carry bogus photo identification cards and wear
legitimate-looking work uniforms meant to fool their victims.
Deputy Nicholas says criminal Gypsies are accomplished in as-
suming a false identity. One of their tricks is to call a legitimate,
licensed contractor to their own home, obtain a business card
and contract, and then copy the paperwork and become that
person. When homeowners try to reach the contractor to complain, they call the number on the business card. The legitimate
contractor knows nothing about the job. The criminal with the
fake ID is nowhere to be found. The situation becomes a nightmare for deceived homeowners as well as for the honest contractor who now has to deal with irate customers. He also will
have a tough time stopping the criminal Gypsy from using his
good name—reclaiming a stolen identity is no easy feat.

Business is apparently brisk enough to warrant investing not only in phony uniforms but in vehicles made to look like government or company cars. The bogus workers often use cell phones or hand-held radios to look legit and to communicate with their partners when committing the crime. The crime may be more than a costly rip-off; police say these distraction schemes have become violent. The crooks may become agitated if the homeowner catches on to the distraction and tries to prevent the robbery.

These are serious crimes and much more heinous than a typical home repair rip-off. We'll say it again. Do not let anyone into your home you do not know or have not called for service. Legitimate service workers call for appointments first, they do not drop by unannounced. Ask for identification and if you are suspicious, tell the worker to wait outside your home. Go to your phone, and call the agency he claims to be with to make sure he in fact is employed there. Don't be misled by an official-looking uniform, ID card, or even vehicle. Bogus clothing, IDs, and vans can be purchased easily. If a worker persists that a service call has been placed, tell him to have his office call you to reschedule. Be sure to warn your elderly relatives or neighbors about these schemes and watch for suspicious-looking service callers. These impostors are good; you have to be better.

Catastrophic Con

A service worker knocks on your door offering you a free energy inspection. He checks the furnace, the siding, the insulation. Thank goodness he arrived. You are in need of a new roof, insulation, and a furnace. Immediately! Before disaster strikes. Fortunately, he can do the work today, if you have the cash. He scares you into believing the work cannot wait; you will be without heat in the dead of winter. Or he notices the wood on your deck is rotting. The deck is about to fall down. It must be fixed now. He knows someone who happens to be free and can fix it for you. You are terrified and sign the deal.

If the contractor seems so anxious to close the deal that day, come up with reasons to stall. Say you need to discuss it with your spouse, you want a second opinion, or you are about to leave on vacation. See if he is still interested in taking on your job or if he just gives up and takes off.

WHEN DISASTER STRIKES

There's not much more heartbreaking than watching homeowners on the news who have lost their homes to the wrath of Mother Nature. Floods, hurricanes, ice storms, you name it, nature has a way of picking up property and destroying it in a matter of minutes.

As if the act of nature wasn't tragic enough, opportunistic traveling contractors see a natural disaster as open season for rip-offs. We have visited the homes of those ravaged by natural disasters and then financially raped by unscrupulous remodelers. It is hard not to feel compassion for those who have handed over their insurance settlements to flimflam artists who take the money and run, homeowners who have literally given tens of thousands of dollars to phony contractors who never as much as hammered one nail into a wall. These are the stories where it's hard to remain objective and not to feel the pain of a homeowner who is about to be left homeless.

Years after Hurricane Andrew hit south Florida, homeowners still have not gotten their lives together. CNBC's *Steals & Deals* went to check on the status of Andrew's victims three years after the hurricane. Of the 5,000 contractor complaints filed with consumer advocacy offices, only 900 were resolved. The average victim's loss from Andrew-related fraud was $30,000. To add insult to those figures, insurance premiums in those high-risk areas have in some cases quadrupled.

What should you do if a disaster strikes your area? As hard as it might be to find a contractor who is not completely booked, wait. Take the time to get written estimates from several different contractors. Check with your local building department to see if you need a permit before construction begins. Insist on a complete written contract specifying what work will be done and the contractor's timetable. Never pay the full amount up front, and pay by check if possible. It is reasonable for a contractor to ask you for a 10 or 20 percent deposit, but not more, even at the time of a disaster. And as always, before you sign on the dotted line, contact your local Better Business Bureau or Home Builder's Association.

Don't hire someone who knocks on your door and offers to help. These are travelers who migrate from disaster to disaster, taking with them your insurance settlements and offering back nothing in return.

Jeanne Salvatore of the Insurance Information Institute offers this advice. "Be as organized as possible. Make a detailed list of what was damaged. Calculate an estimated cost and age of that item. The more specific you can be, the better." Take complete photographs of the damage. If you can make a videotape, do so, and narrate it as you go. Call your insurance company immediately. If your home is totaled, get a check as soon as you can for relocation expenses.

YOUR LICENSE, PLEASE

When choosing a contractor, go for a licensed one. Not all states require licenses, but many do. Unlicensed contractors can be big problems for homeowners. According to Investigator Rick Beseler of the state attorney general's office in Florida, if you hire an unlicensed contractor, you have no bite when it comes to recourse should you have a problem. The state has less power to go after unlicensed contractors. Licensed contractors can have their licenses pulled if they do not come to some settlement with the state and the homeowner. Unlicensed contractors could care less and have no reason to pay up. Beseler warns the unlicensed workers have an unproven track record for quality work and have not passed state competency tests. Having unlicensed contractors do work on your home can be unsafe as well. Poorly done wiring or structural work can create a hazardous situation. Unlicensed contractors probably don't carry insurance, which could really put you at financial risk if there is a problem. If someone is hurt on the job, *you* may end up picking up the tab. That's why it's critical to find out if a contractor carries liability insurance and worker's comp.

To stress just how critical it is to hire a licensed contractor, the Florida State Attorney General's office set up a sting called Operation Tool Time. The state invited fourteen unlicensed contractors to give estimates to an undercover investigator. She solicited quotes for building an addition onto her home. The estimates ranged in price from $2,500 to $9,500. Investigator Beseler said this was a spread way too large for reputable, licensed contractors. When the unlicensed ones were called back to collect their deposits, instead of collecting their cash, they were arrested, taken to jail, and charged with contracting without a license. Operation Tool Time was intended to be a message to both unlicensed contractors and homeowners. Choosing an unlicensed contractor just because his bid is lower may be an invitation for fraud.

To illustrate the importance of hiring a licensed contractor, ABC's *Good Morning America* went down to Florida. We were horrified to see how one homeowner had lost $4,400 to an unlicensed contractor. This hardworking family had tried desperately to save their house from being condemned and had handed over all the money they had to an unlicensed contractor. The only work the contractor did was punch a hole through the roof and drop off cheap plywood. The hole created more damage, and the contractor never came back. And while our advice has been to go with someone you trust and someone who lives in your area, the advice did not hold true this time. The contractor this unfortunate homeowner hired was a deacon from his church, which was just down the block from his home. The deacon took his parishioner's money and made no repairs—in fact, he created more damage. The homeowner had no rights when it came to going after the contractor because the deacon was not licensed. The homeowner no longer prays at that church and awaits word on the condemnation of his home.

License to Lie?
You can't believe everything you read. Unfortunately, choosing a contractor because his ad states he is licensed isn't good enough. The traveling family of Pennsylvania contractors claimed to be licensed! Their ad stated: "It's time to save $ Money $, Experienced, Reliable, Professional, Insured, and Bonded." First of all, Pennsylvania is one of the few states that does *not* license contractors. So the ad is misleading right off the bat. In the lawsuit against these contractors, the state attorney general's office states that "although advertising the business as insured, refused to provide the name of the insurance company to one of his customers." The complaint continues by saying "although advertising the business as insured, [the defendant] damaged or destroyed the personal property or fixtures, without restoration or accommodation [to several homeowners]." The ad copy meant nothing when it was time for the homeowners to fight the contractor.

So while you might be drawn to an ad or a business card that mentions licenses, insurance, and bonding, don't take it at face value. Earlier we told you how easy it is to assume the identity of a licensed contractor; even easier is just to print up business cards that say "licensed and insured." It's up to you to do some research. Ask to see a contractor's license. Confirm it with the construction industry licensing board, or whatever agency licenses contractors in your area. Some states require the license number to be displayed on advertising and work vehicles. Jot down the number, and check it out. Ask to see a copy of the company's insurance coverage; make sure it includes liability insurance and worker's compensation. Be wary of a contractor who asks you to obtain a building permit; licensed contractors don't do that. Again, not all states require licenses, If your state does, make sure you choose the licensed contractor, even if the bid comes in higher than one who is unlicensed.

Nailing the Bad Guys

If you live in a state where no license is required, it will take more work on your part to weed through the available contractors. As we have mentioned, the state of Pennsylvania does not require contractors to be licensed. But the attorney general's office has come up with an interesting proposal now before the legislature. Because there are so many elderly people in the state, and because seniors tend to be "house rich, and money poor," home contracting fraud for the elderly is the number-one complaint in Pennsylvania. The proposal is intended to force home contractors to register with the state. With that registration comes a $100 biennial fee. That fee in essence becomes a "Home Improvement Guarantee Fund," essentially a "scam fund." If it passes, the idea is to have a pot of money in the state's hands to be distributed to victims of fraud who have sued a fraudulent contractor and who cannot collect on the judgment. The bill calls for a written contract to be presented to the homeowner and stipulates that no more than one-third of the total job can be accepted as a deposit.

We think proposals like this are a step forward in fighting fraud. Honest contractors may have to foot the bill for the phony ones, but as Barbara Petito of the attorney general's office says, "It's good business to clean up bad business." We hope this bill passes and we applaud other states that already have restitution funds.

FIGHT BACK AND WIN

You've heard the horror stories, the cases where people have been left homeless or stripped of their life savings. You've heard us tell you how hard it is to reclaim money that was fraudulently taken from you. Unfortunately, bad contractors usually win. They have your money and you have little recourse.

You can attempt to go after the contractor in court. While that might sound tempting, the costs involved may be prohibitive and dwarf the size of any award you might win. Hiring a lawyer takes big bucks, and most attorneys will not take a contracting case without money up front. Most will not take your case on a contingency basis.

Once you get to court, proving that a contractor knowingly intended to defraud you is also a tough case. If a contractor as much as hammers a nail into your roof, he can claim he planned on doing the work. Shoddy work is subjective. Your word against his in court is not open and shut. The onus is on you to prove he was out to rip you off.

You can try to mediate your case through a consumer protection agency in your area. Usually there is no charge, and they will send an independent inspector to your home to come up with an objective report. Mediation works only for contractors who agree to be part of the program; if yours is truly a con man, he probably will not comply with a mediator. Of course, it is always worth a try, and there are definitely those who value their reputation and will pay up if the mediator acts in your favor.

And once in a while you do stumble on someone with true guts and determination. Donald Sztabnik of Long Island, New York, is one of those who chose to fight back to try to win. Several years ago he contracted to have a remodeling job done on his kitchen and bathroom. He paid the contractor $8,500 to do the work. He chose the contractor because he lived in the area and because he was licensed.

He later found out the remodeler was what insiders call a "stepladder artist," a term used to describe contractors who take money from one job and use it to finance others. The money collection continues and the last ones on the list get the shaft. Donald said not only was the work was a mess, but live wires hung from the ceiling. A wall was placed in the wrong location, and the drain hole was too close to his toilet.

Furious, Donald told the contractor to give him back the $4,500 he was holding and just forget about completing the job. In the meantime, the contractor went to court and pulled his own license, claiming he was going out of business. With no license, the contractor thought he was free from the law.

When Donald went to the Nassau County Consumer Affairs

office to file a complaint, he was told the agency had no power to go after the contractor, because he was not licensed. Donald tried to hire a lawyer, but most turned down his case. He finally did find one and was determined to fight the case to the end. Donald shelled out thousands of dollars in legal fees and spent hours gathering evidence and expert testimony. He appealed to the district attorney's office for help. He was told they didn't have the resources to look into the case and advised him to do his own surveillance. Donald did; he tried to follow the contractor to prove he was accepting other jobs and therefore had the money to pay the award. The contractor, in an absurd turn of events, filed a harassment complaint against Donald. While frightened, frustrated, and out of money, Donald never gave up. Fortunately, the police dismissed the harassment charge, and this determined homeowner went back to battle.

He took his civil case to court and won a judgment against the contractor. No easy victory. That was great, but it doesn't mean the contractor would pay the judgment. And he didn't. Donald did file liens against the contractor's property, but that would be of no help unless the contractor sold his home. Fortunately, Nassau County had a restitution fund, and Donald was one of the first consumers to actually collect the maximum $5,000 from the fund. The county does not hand out restitution funds easily or often. It is incumbent on you to prove you tried to collect the judgment from the defendant. The restitution award was comforting, but it cost Sztabnik $4,000 to get the $5,000.

This story has a happy ending, and one that is certainly not typical. When the contractor went to sell his own property, he discovered the liens against him. He was forced to pay back the state $5,000 and the thousands of additional dollars he owed Donald Sztabnik.

Donald hired a new contractor who came with references, but he did not break even from his initial loss and court costs. Still, we offer kudos to him for not giving up and proving that the consumer can win.

BUILDING YOUR OWN HOME

Building a Case

We've talked a lot about home remodelers and contractors but not a lot about builders. Building your own home can cost you a lot more than a remodeling job. A $100,000 home can turn into $400,000 by the time it's paid off. Watching that investment carefully and doing extensive homework is absolutely imperative.

Many states allow subcontractors to place liens against a builder if the builder doesn't pay them. That could leave a homeowner with a virtually unsellable house that has thousands of dollars of liens against it. Commander Chuck Johnson, who formerly headed the criminal investigations division at the Port St. Lucie (Florida) Police Department, warns, "If someone gives a builder a down payment and doesn't demand the money be put in an escrow account, the builder can turn around and use it to pay off a bill on someone else's house."

Johnson also advises that once you have chosen a builder you trust, the next step is to do a careful title check on the land you plan to build on. According to Johnson, one contractor built a house on a lot he didn't own. "The people who put down the money for the house were helpless because they never asked to see a clear title for the property. They just took the builder's word for it and lost the money they had invested in the house."

When setting up financing with the bank, Johnson recommends having the bank require double signatures on the checks. He describes, "One man noticed shoddy work being done on his house, so he ordered the contractor to stop construction until he could get everything straightened out. Without the owner's permission or signature, the builder went to the bank and asked it to electronically transfer $18,000 of the man's money. In that case the bank is at least partly at fault."

Joel Dramis, licensing supervisor for Port St. Lucie, warns out-of-towners who build second homes when they are far removed from the area to be especially careful. He advises getting someone you know to oversee the building process and to have the power to sign checks for the bank. Dramis says sometimes people find out later the checks were signed by the contractor, and the work was not done at all. Dramis says if you are building out of town, make sure the homes and developments the builder shows you are actually his. Oftentimes people who are not from the area and do not do research on the builder think they are getting a great price but run into problems later. Dramis says it costs his department around $3,000 to investigate each case of contractor fraud and there's a low conviction rate because it's so tough to prove. It would save you and the inspectors a lot of time, aggravation, and money if you did your homework first.

Much of the advice for picking a builder is the same as choosing a contractor. Johnson offers these tips.

- If a builder needs to be licensed in your state, check with the licensing board to see if there are any complaints registered.
- Check out how long the builder has been in business.
- Ask the builder for addresses of homes he has already completed and talk to the people living there.
- Find out if the builder was easy to work with, if he completed a "punch list" of last-minute repairs, and if the project was finished on time.
- Visit homes the contractor is currently building.
- Look for the number of workers on the job and excess debris at the site, which could indicate a sloppy crew that's also doing sloppy work.

If you are building a home out of town, make sure you enlist someone you trust to be your eyes and ears on the project. Building a home is a huge investment, probably the biggest you will ever make. Use these building blocks to make it your dream house.

WHO'S INSPECTING THE INSPECTOR?

Most home buyers rely heavily on local building inspectors to make or break the deal. If something is structurally wrong with the home, and it's major, the home buyer will either nix the offer or negotiate. While most home inspectors are honest, there are others who are not. The dishonest ones can literally cost you your home.

In a report for ABC's *20/20,* Arnold Diaz found some local building inspectors who became too "chummy with the builders." Diaz tells of a chief building inspector for a county who was collecting money on the side working for one of his area's biggest developers. Diaz says the building inspector signed off on many homes that later became nightmares for their owners. The homeowners won a lawsuit charging that the inspector would "approve inspections without leaving his truck, which is known as a 'drive-by' inspection." Among other major problems, the homeowners complained about the septic situation. The ground was apparently too wet to build on, and in many cases too wet to absorb the septic waste. One homeowner said, "The entire backyard underneath the surface is a bowl of sewage."

Diaz asked why the developer was allowed to build on such wet soil. The answer? "Because he provided the county with soil test results indicating there was no problem. Who performed those tests? In some cases, it was the county inspector who was moonlighting on the developer's payroll, collecting more than $5,000 in checks signed by the builder."

The county did find the moonlighting to be a conflict of interest, but a jury decided the builder had committed fraud and must pay the homeowners $81,000.

The lesson here? Hire your own building inspector and don't rely on the real estate agent or builder to recommend one. But as Diaz points out in his report, in most states anyone can hang a shingle and call himself a home inspector. Alan Fields, author of *Your New House,* warns people to be very wary of a real estate agent who pushes an inspector. "We want to hire the inspector who the real estate agent hates to see driving up, I mean, they just cower. They think . . . oh no, not that guy. Because they know that guy is the most thorough. I want the most obnoxious person that you can find."

Joel Dramis told us he has never been offered a bribe to okay a home for a builder, and he's been inspecting homes in Florida for decades. He tells us he has seen cases where he clears a new home inspection and finds out later that the builder made changes after his inspection was completed to cut costs or actually removed some safety items from the home after the inspection was approved. Dramis says proving in court that the home was under code when he inspected it is a tough one.

CONTRACTING THE CONTRACT
Your contract is what will give you recourse to fight any problem that may occur. It's the last thing to be drawn up once you pick your remodeler or builder. We will tell you what you need to include in the contract to best protect your assets. But first, a scheme to watch out for: Beware of the "paper contractor." "That's a contractor, quite often with a proper license, who ties everything up very nicely with a well-written contract, then sells the contract on your home to another contractor over whom he has no supervisorial contract," says California contractors' licensing board investigator Larry McNeely. "The first contractor then goes on to another homeowner to write up yet another contract, which he again sells."

To ensure you don't become a victim of that scheme or any other, draw up as complete a contract as you can. The more specific your contract is, the more chance you have of getting satisfaction if something goes awry. Start with the name, address, and license number of your contractor. Make sure you get a definite timetable of when the work is to begin and end. Set up a payment schedule. Try not to give the contractor more than 10 percent of the total job as a deposit. Be sure to include the names of subcontractors and the nature of the work they will be doing. Include brand names when it comes to building materials, appliances, and fixtures. Make sure the contractor is the one who obtains building permits so that he is responsible if something doesn't measure up to code.

While the work is going on, make sure to write down all change orders. If you, for instance, decide you want a wall placed in a different spot, saying it verbally will do you no good if it doesn't end up there. Keep a file that contains copies of the contract, change orders, canceled check, receipts, and other forms.

When you sign with the contractor, make sure you know if he is a contractor or subcontractor. Dominic Cortese of Cortese Brothers Construction in Buffalo, New York, warns that there is a big difference. A contractor does his own work and may be a specialist in, let's say, roofing. A subcontractor "subs" the work out to someone else who may not be trained in doing that kind of work. Get it all spelled out!

Cortese also believes you should get your contractor to make two price lists for you. One would contain what is included in the initial bid. The other would include possible "extras" you may decide on as the project progresses. He warns that under-bidders often try to slip in the "extras" after the project gets under way.

Make sure to include your right of cancellation in the contract before you sign. Seventy-two hours is a fair amount of time for both parties.

And if your state allows it, try to get the contractor to put your deposit into an escrow account, not into his pocket, until the materials are purchased and the work is completed. Some states require the money to be put in escrow. Make the contractor show you proof.

Shortly after the work begins, you will be mailed preliminary lien notices from the subcontractors, who work under the general contractor, and from material suppliers. These documents are called "claims of lien" and "mechanics' liens"; they alert you that these companies have worked on or supplied materials for your project and will have lien rights if the contractor doesn't pay them.

Before you pay your contractor the final amount for the job, make sure you get a lien release. According the National Association of Home Builders, "Lien releases will protect you if your remodeler defaults on the financial obligations to subcontractors and suppliers associated with your project. State law determines who is entitled to a lien. Liens cloud your title, make it difficult to sell your property, and are difficult and costly to remove. Removal of the lien requires payment of the disputed amount or a court decision." You could conceivably lose your property if liens are filed. So make sure to get a "release of lien" from your contractor. You can obtain those forms from your contractor, a stationery store, or legal form supplier.

You can contact the American Home Foundation and purchase a model contract for $8; just call 800-489-7776. Or you can call the National Association of Remodeling Industry (NARI) at 800-440-6274. Ask for the free ninety-page booklet called "NARI's Master Plan for Professional Home Building."

GOT YOU COVERED

Making sure you have ample insurance coverage is crucial. As we discussed earlier, some shady contractors may show you phony insurance forms or ID numbers. Insurance coverage cannot be taken lightly. If one contractor breaks his leg on the job, it could cost you thousands out of your own pocket. It is up to you to make sure your contractor carries both liability and worker's compensation coverage. Without that you are responsible for damage done to workers and to your property caused by the contractor.

The contractor pays for worker's compensation coverage to protect his employees. The insurance covers medical expenses and lost income when a worker is hurt on the job. Your financial risk without this insurance coverage is huge. All contractors who have more than one employee must have this insurance.

"But not all contractors keep up their policies," writes Debra Collins in *Home Mechanix* magazine. "Because the cost of worker's-compensation coverage has skyrocketed over the past decade, it's become a major cost of doing business. When times are tough, it's tempting for contractors to work without it. Although they can lose their licenses or be fined if discovered, this doesn't protect the homeowner. If your contractor's workers aren't insured while on the job, even a relatively minor accident like a broken leg can leave you with $10,000 in bills for hospital expenses and lost wages. The cost of a more serious injury can exceed the cost of your home."

When it comes to liability coverage, Collins says the amount the contractor must carry varies from state to state and city to city. Liability insurance covers damage caused to your home or your neighbor's property if a contracting problem arises. "Sometimes only a few thousand dollars is actually required. A safe amount generally ranges from $100,000 to $1 million, depending on the size of the contractor's company and the size of the job." Collins recommends consulting your insurance company to see how much liability insurance you need.

Dominic Cortese says that a good contractor is proud to issue you his liability insurance form before he starts the job. Cortese warns if the contractor doesn't furnish the certificate, he could turn around and drain your homeowner's insurance to cover his faulty work.

Once you decide on a contractor, ask to see the actual insurance certificate. Make sure you jot down the name and policy number of the carrier. Check to see if the renewal is up to date. Then call the insurance carrier to verify coverage. Remember we told you how easy it is to obtain fake documents for almost anything.

Collins says to "Consider the process of checking insurance coverage as an additional reference check. Proper insurance is a sign of a solvent small business. Since insurance companies keep tabs on the work practices and reputations of their clients, checking with them is one way to uncover a contractor's flaws. An insured contractor is often a safer contractor, as well, since a long accident record can make insurance unaffordable for careless contractors."

And finally, check with your own insurance company to see if you are covered for smaller jobs, such as painting or replacing a door or window. A quick check could prevent a drain on your checkbook down the road.

HOW ARE YOU GONNA PAY FOR IT?

If you shop diligently for a contractor, you should shop just as hard for financing. Make sure you carefully review all written documents. You should know if you are required to get a second mortgage on your home. You should know if you are paying a competitive interest rate. Figure out your monthly payment. Do you know how long you will have to pay off the loan? What will your total interest add up to by the time the loan is paid off? Are there penalties for late payments or for paying it off early if you sell or refinance your home? Is the payment due even if the work isn't completed or shoddy? These are questions only you can ask, and they are not tough ones to answer.

Losing Your Home Equity

The elderly and the poor are the most easily ripped off. Legal services groups in California tell us these are the people who lose their homes to finance mongers whose goal is to scam homeowners into high-interest loans they could never afford to pay.

Legal Assistance for Seniors out of California says the elderly often are lured by fliers or telephone solicitations. The fliers scare the elderly into taking action, often claiming "Your house is in serious need of repair." The loan officer then comes to the house with complicated loan lingo and confuses the homeowner into signing a loan that might carry an interest rate as high as 25 percent.

Bet Tzedek Legal Services in Los Angeles has done extensive

research on these loan sharks. The scams these money-hungry vultures use even have names.

> *False payoffs:* bogus brokers create false payoff statements which are paid by the escrow company. The scammer either packs on the payoff amount of existing debt or creates the debt altogether.
>
> *Identity theft loan:* A loan broker takes initial information from the homeowner and then processes the loan, forges the deed of trust, and keeps the proceeds.
>
> *No documents:* The scammers rush homeowners into signing the paperwork so they don't figure out how much they are really paying. Homeowners don't find out the monthly payments until the coupon book arrives.
>
> *Praise the Lord:* The solicitor knocks on the door of a religious senior citizen and prays with him or her. The scamster creates a spirit of trust with the religious homeowner and gets the person to sign on the dotted line.
>
> *Spiking:* The contractor makes the homeowner sign a contract that is subject to very high financing. The remodeler starts working on the home before the homeowner can decide about the financing, the three-day cancellation period is over, and the homeowner is stuck with the remodeler and the loan.

These tactics in one form or another are used to get homeowners to hand over their home to the scamster. They are foolproof crimes. The unscrupulous mortgage broker knows a home is worth, let's say, $150,000 and gets a homeowner to sign a high-interest loan for $18,000, knowing the homeowner is on a fixed income and cannot afford the monthly payments. Then the house is foreclosed. The con artist just got a $150,000 home for $18,000. Once the home is in foreclosure, it's almost impossible to reclaim; after all, the homeowner did agree to the loan.

Save Your Home

Before signing any loan agreement, check the conditions. Some home equity loans have ridiculously high interest rates and terms. Even if you think you cannot qualify for a conventional bank loan, apply anyway. You might be surprised and be accepted. Don't believe a contractor who tells you otherwise and tries to hook you up with a lender he knows. Research the rates with several lenders and do not rush into signing loan documents with your contractor before you fully understand the terms.

CHOOSING YOUR CONTRACTOR

Here's where we sum up all our advice and try to steer you clear of the scams. As we have shown you, clever con men think of almost any way to get you to trust them, to sign with them, and to put your home in their hands. We've told you about worms, and spray guns, and chimney shakers, and lots of other tricks that may stay the same and some that may get even more ingenious as the years go by. Unfortunately, home improvement fraud is here to stay. The fact that it's so lucrative, so easy, and so hard to get caught makes it a worthwhile profession for those lacking a conscience. Gary claims to have made as much as $14,000 a day pulling illegal schemes on unsuspecting homeowners.

We hope you do not become the next victim of a Gary or a Howard family. We hope you will be a smarter shopper and will enjoy your home and its improvements with an easy heart.

So here is the most important part of our chapter.

▶ Top Ten Tips for Choosing an Honest Remodeler

1. *Decide on what you want done.* Have a clear understanding of the type of work, supplies, fixtures, paint, and appliances you intend to use. Keep a detailed list to show the contractor before you get a bid. If you have plans from an architect, keep those in that same file.
2. *Keep the lines of communication open.* Find a contractor you actually get along with, someone you like. It could end

up being a pretty long working relationship with someone practically living in your house. Make sure he doesn't intimidate you. Have a "preconstruction" meeting before the work starts so everyone knows what's about to happen. Find out if you will be inconvenienced. Will your water or electricity be shut off? And for how long?

3. *Get references* from building supply stores, neighbors, friends, or contractors you have used in the past. Check out those references. Ask for names and numbers of satisfied customers. Call those homeowners and visit them. Look at the work, ask them to be honest about any problems they might have had with the contractor. What did they like and not like about the work? Ask how long the job took to complete and if it was done on schedule. Find out if the contractor was neat and cleaned up after the job was finished.

4. *Choose a contractor that specializes.* If you need electrical work, ask a lighting store for a list of recommended electricians. You need roof work done? Go to a person who knows roofs, don't contract with a general "handyman." Be careful if you hire a subcontractor. A subcontractor "subs" the work to other contractors, and may not be doing the work himself. Who are those subcontractors? And how qualified are they?

5. *Check out the contractor* with the Better Business Bureau, the licensing board, or any other consumer agency you can contact. Find out if there have been complaints, and the nature of those complaints.

6. *Check to see if they have a license* or are registered in your town.

7. *Find out if they carry insurance.* Then get evidence of that coverage. Is it enough coverage to satisfy your needs?

8. *Don't necessarily go with the lowest bidder.* All reputable contractors should be within the same price range. You can negotiate once you choose, but opting for the cheapest price may be a big mistake.

9. *Do not agree to give a huge downpayment.* Start with offering 10 percent down, and don't give a contractor more
than one-third of the cost of the job up front. Ask to see
receipts for the building materials, and check to see they
are using the quality of supplies you agreed on.

10. *Get everything in writing.* Make sure you draft a contract
that will stick if there is a problem. Be very specific about
what the job entails, the time schedule, the building materials, the financing, the cleanup, and the release of lien
at the end of the project. If it's a big project, it might be
worth your while to hire a lawyer to take a look at the
contract.

▶ Top Ten Tips to Avoid a Rip-off

1. *Don't be lured by door-to-door salesmen.* They are
probably "travelers" who will take your money and run.
Make sure they have a real office and aren't just operating out of a van. Be careful if they offer you a cell phone
number only. Many dishonest contractors use cell phones,
then disconnect them when they are through scamming
enough people. Police try to find out who the cell phone
was registered to, and find out it was a rental. So stay
with someone local, someone you can find when the job
is in progress.

2. *Don't be pressured into having the work done that day
. . . or else.* Your house won't crumble in the next hour.
You have time to have several contractors take a look at
your home. Besides, most qualified contractors have a lot
of work and probably can't fit you in right away. Be wary
of one who has hammer in hand and is ready to get to
work.

3. *If it sounds too good to be true, it probably is.* An extremely low bid and a speedy completion date are tipoffs
to a rip-off. Make sure the bids you receive compare "apples to apples"; are the materials the contractors using exactly the same? Cheaper quotes may mean the contractor

plans to skim on the higher-quality brands. Or the bid may not include all the "extras." Make sure *everything* needed for the job is spelled out, so there are no surprises.

4. *Be wary of phony documents.* Make sure business cards, licenses, and insurance documents are all legitimate. Finding out will take some checking with insurance companies and building departments, but it's well worth it.

5. *Make sure the referrals you are offered are for real.* Some referrals are just friends of the contractor or someone who feels sorry for the contractor because he is out of work.

6. *Watch out for quick financing deals.* The offer your contractor has in his pocket may be a bad deal for you. Shop for competitive interest rates at conventional institutions before you sign away your life savings. Make sure the bank requires two signatures to cash a check, the contractor's and yours. It's your money, you should have control over it.

7. *Make sure you can see any damage* a contractor inspecting your home says he has found. Remember the bag of tricks? The worms, the spray gun, the chimney shaker? If you can't climb up to see the damage, find someone you trust who can. And definitely get a few opinions before taking the contractor's word for it.

8. *Don't fall for "free inspections."* Often they are a ruse to find everything wrong with your home. Utility companies may offer a legitimate free energy inspection, which carries with it no other motive than to help you save on energy costs. Save your energy and your money by not being lured into these sometimes bogus offers.

9. *Don't fall for a contractor who begs poverty* and needs your money to complete the job. He may be a stepladder artist using your funds to complete previous jobs. Hand over your full payment once the job is completed. Make sure to get the contractor to sign a release of lien form, which frees you up from paying off subcontractors he may owe.

10. *Don't be a victim of "leftovers."* Falling for the contractor who happens to be in the area doing work and who happens to have leftover supplies from another job is foolish. Reputable contractors plan their jobs and materials very carefully. This is a scheme that can cost you shoddy work, no work or even a robbery. The door knocker also can be a criminal contractor—one who tries to distract you and steal your money.

So do a little homework, so your home does work. We are confident we have armed you with the tools you need to beat builders at their tricks of the trade. They may be surprised when you are able to drop some of the lingo used by the disreputable trade.

Glossary

Chimney shakers: Disreputable chimney workers who bring along bricks or debris and tell you it fell from your chimney. They claim your house will go up in flames if it's not fixed immediately.

Door knocker: The person who knocks on doors looking for a clean home with an elderly person to "sell" and then rip off.

Drifters, travelers, criminal Gypsies: Terms used to describe flimflam artists who travel in and out of town. They take your deposit and flee.

Drive-by inspections: Inspections done by someone who approves your home without ever getting out of his or her car.

Getting them with their pants down: Getting homeowners to do whatever the scam artists want, at whatever price they want.

The impostor: The worker who claims to be employed by the local utility company to gain access to your home; the contractor who hands you phony business cards. Really, any dishonest remodeler who fakes his or her identity.

Runners: People paid by the big-cheese contractor to go door-to-door offering free gifts to people willing to hear the scam spiel.

Stepladder artists: Contractors who take your money and use it for previous jobs.

CHAPTER 6

INSURANCE

An insurance agent has a strange job. His task is to
find people who will bet him a dollar a day that
they won't die.

—Anonymous

The preceding quotation refers, of course, to the business of *life*
insurance. Life insurance is only one of the dozens and dozens
of insurance products on the market today. Policies available include health, auto, homeowners, tenants, disability, credit, professional liability, long-term care, and on and on. And for every
insurance policy offered, there can be hundreds of permutations.
Policies may cover fires but not floods, slander but not sexual
harassment, cavities but not caps.

Insurance as a topic is (reputedly) both highly complex and
deadly dull. In order to achieve the complexity, the industry has
adopted impressive technical jargon. Actuarial, annuity, dis-
memberment, double indemnity! This reputedly boring business
has come up with some very exotic terminology. But as you'll
find when reading this chapter, the insurance industry is anything but dull. People who make bags and bags of money are always fascinating.

And make money they do. Nearly $1 in every $12 spent in
our economy goes to pay for insurance. That's $175 billion an-
nually. To keep the coffers full, insurers exert influence through
ruthless lobbying, brilliant marketing, and all the other persuasion mechanisms that money can buy.

We hope you aren't spending every dozenth dollar you earn
on insurance. But no matter what your outlay, we can clue you

in to ways to cut your costs, get good coverage, and get wise to the tricks of the trade.

Note of Clarification: The types of insurance we will discuss here fall under two categories, *personal insurance* (life/health/disability) and *property insurance* (homeowner/tenant/auto.) Many cultural references to insurance agents apply to the agent selling personal insurance. Personal insurance agents generally sell the product to consumers directly—they come to you. Property insurance is often sold through an agency, which is a franchise of the insurer (like State Farm or American Family)—you go to them.

There is some crossover between the two, but when we discuss consumer concerns about sales practices, we generally are referring to the sales of personal insurance unless otherwise noted.

FEAR OF INSURANCE

Interestingly, people in certain cultures would rather shoot themselves in the foot than purchase life or health insurance (although podiatry coverage would certainly be advisable). The Chinese, for example, historically have held the belief that if people plan for disasters, then disasters will befall them. Call it superstition, but consumer awareness about insurance products is very low in China. And we see similar attitudes in the United States among consumers who just can't bear to think about fearful events.

The irony is that hungry salespeople have learned very well how to use fear to their benefit. A former New York Life Insurance agent told us about one such tactic used in his office. When an agent was closing in on a sale (kill) but the client wanted time to "think about it," the agent would employ the *horror story close*. In an effort to close the sale, the agent retold a sincere-sounding story about a client who had taken time to "think about it" but within days was run over by a bus/lost in an avalanche, whatever. The point, of course, was that the unfortunate fellow had no insurance at the time of the accident. Our contact told us the horror stories probably were based on *some* fact . . . and some fiction.

SELLING A PIECE OF THE ROCK
What do you expect from an industry that convinced us we should pay good money for a *piece of rock?*

THE IMAGE
It is difficult to get accurate figures about just how much money is spent selling us insurance. The Metropolitan Life slogan, "Get Met, It Pays," is pretty accurate, though. It pays, all right. It pays Snoopy a fat endorsement fee. Suffice it to say that industry critics will claim the insurance companies spend *much* more on marketing than they spend on paying claims.

A former Prudential Insurance salesman points out that we are dealing with an industry that has done a stupendous job of creating an image. Ron Alford, author of numerous books on the industry including *How to Win the Insurance Claim Game*, contends that even the basic terminology of the business is subconsciously persuasive.

> *Policy:*   What is a policy? A policy is actually a contract. But "contract" is too intimidating a term. People are hesitant to sign a contract without a lawyer's advice. The term "policy" is much softer.
> *Premium:*   Only in the insurance world do you pay your bill with a premium. Most other businesses want you to pay with money.
> *Life Insurance:*   Life insurance is actually *death insurance*. Can you imagine a commercial for death insurance during the Superbowl? In all fairness, however, "death insurance" is such an altogether icky term, we'll forgive them for inventing that one.

And the terms are no slicker than those smiling salesmen.

THE SELLERS
Ever meet a shy insurance agent? Of course, it's by no means an occupation for the softspoken. Again, we got the scoop from one of our inside-the-business buddies about the typical recruitment and indoctrination of an agent selling personal insurance.

Recruitment
Large companies use their top-selling agents as recruiters. It's standard for an Armani-bedecked recruiter to target young men and women who are searching for a professional career. Some recruits have college educations, but most do not. The promise of prestige and wealth are tossed at these hopeful souls until some of them are so starry-eyed, they sign up.

Reality
The recruit shows up for work on his first day, shiny new briefcase in hand. But the honeymoon quickly ends. The new guy is pressured to sell policies to all his friends and relatives. And he has to cover many of his own operating expenses. Our contact was made to pay for his own calls, copies, and postage. Insurance companies love to throw parties to honor their top-selling agents. But at the company where this agent worked, he was required to attend frequent sales awards functions and pay anywhere from $50 to $75 admission each time.

The Mentors
The ugliest thing this agent shared with us was that mentoring amounted to older agents advising new recruits to target minorities or uneducated individuals as sales prospects because they were an easier sell. Rookies were advised to steer clear of the elderly, however, as they were known to be more skeptical and cautious.

CAMPING OUT
The early days in the career of a personal lines agent involve what is called *kitchen table sales*. This is a euphemism for doing

business with people in their home, over the kitchen table. Agents have been known to camp out at the kitchen table for as long as it took to get an application signed. Many a policy was sold due to sheer exhaustion. And when an agent made a sale, there was huge pressure to get referrals. The sales manager would tell agents not to come back to the office until they had strong-armed some referrals. Thus the agents would have to push new applicants for names and phone numbers, saying "do you know anyone who just bought a home? How about someone who has a new baby?" So naturally the attrition rate for agents is high and only the most persistent and hardy types survive.

RISKY BUSINESS

Insurance consumers can really find themselves between the proverbial rock and a hard place. It's risky business to be an insurance consumer.

- You risk getting scammed in an unscrupulous sales scheme.
- You risk paying for duplication of coverage and/or forgoing the best and broadest policies your money can buy.
- You risk positioning yourself with dangerous gaps in coverage.

But if you're looking for reassurance, don't look to the federal government.

An Unruly Business

In 1974 Ralph Nader, big business enemy and consumer advocate extraordinaire, testified before a U.S. Senate Subcommittee on the topic of unfair business practices in the life insurance industry: "For almost 70 years the life insurance industry has been a smug sacred cow feeding the public a steady line of sacred bull."

Ralph was hopping mad in 1974 and he probably still is. Unlike the banking and securities industries, the $175 billion insurance business enjoys almost total freedom from federal regulation. How do they do it? They do it via a federal antitrust exemption that has been on the books since 1945. Don't glaze over. Simply put, the federal government doesn't do much to interfere in the operations of the industry. The business of insurance actually is regulated on the state level. Each state has a department of insurance headed by a commissioner. Consumer groups claim the state regulation is too loose, while big insurance companies have lobbied passionately to keep regulation on the state rather than the federal level. Draw your own conclusions.

What Happened to the Safety Net?

With all this consumer vs. big business tension floating around, it's easy to see why most of us are apprehensive. Buying coverage can be a costly, confusing, and uncomfortable experience. The real shame here is that the concept of insurance is actually quite humanitarian. Insurance takes the risks we face as mere mortals and distributes them evenly throughout the population.

Robert N. Veres, in an editorial in *Investment Advisor* magazine, said of insurance, "When it works right, it prices risk fairly, and redistributes money from the lucky to the unlucky without making either group feel abused, patronized, or ripped off." Veres went on to reminisce about the days when insurance was a safety net and to lament that the day has come when to most people insurance is one big headache.

Figuring Your Needs

But as an insurance consumer, you have little choice, so pop an aspirin and get on with it. The first question one must ask is "What kind of safety net do I need?" Often we are completely unprepared to answer this question.

An old saying goes, "If you want to make God laugh, tell him your plans." In other words, it's impossible to know what the future holds. But when considering insurance, it seems sensible to make an educated guess about what losses we feel we are likely to suffer. Based on those assumptions, we elect to buy coverage where we will use it most often. But is this the smartest approach?

This approach works *for the insurance companies*. They have a very accurate idea of what losses you are likely to suffer. Not you specifically—but the policyholding population in general. Insurance companies employ lots and lots of statistical wizards called actuaries. Remember those kids in the prekindergarten math club? Those kids are now insurance actuaries and are trained to figure out the mathematical likelihood of all the events of life.

Suffice it to say that if you are likely to make a claim, the insurance company is unlikely to sell you a policy.

A Likely Story
When it comes to figuring the likelihood of the events of your own life, remember that actuarials are trained professionals: Do not attempt this at home!

For instance, you may decide you are *not* likely to die in a fire (or of some other unnatural cause). At the same time, you feel it is extremely likely that you will tear a contact lens or need a new TV. And you are completely correct. Most people do not meet an untimely demise—yet we've all dealt with the annoying expense of replacing contact lenses and picture tubes.

Based on that assumption, you opt for the contact lens replacement policy or the extended warranty on your TV set. These seem inexpensive and practical. The contact lens policy costs $35, while life or homeowners' coverage will run you hundreds or thousands of dollars a year.

But the small policy is a bad choice. First of all, it can be difficult to collect on. These types of coverage have just as many exclusions and limitations as big policies, sometimes more. And you could purchase dozens of these things. Coverage on minor items is extremely expensive compared to the cost of replacing the item in question. It's smarter to stash $250 to $500 in the bank as a mini-emergency fund than to spend $75 insuring a $300 television set.

Tips on What to Skip

So think in terms of insuring yourself against catastrophic financial disaster. Spend all those dollars in a few important areas. If you do it right, occasionally you may be inconvenienced by small losses, but you'll never be wiped out. The following coverages are too small or too narrow to be worth buying.

•*Credit insurance:* This pays off your credit card balance or outstanding loan in the event you die, become disabled, or lose your income. Better to put the money toward a comprehensive life or disability policy. The exception is if you are in ill health. This coverage is usually available without a medical exam and sometimes is the only coverage an ill person can get.

•*Cancer insurance:* Life and health insurance should be broad. Cancer insurance is coverage that is much too narrow. This has notoriously been marketed to older people who have a great fear of getting the Big C.

•*Extended warranties and repair plans:* Do your homework and buy reliable products instead. Your buck is better spent on a copy of *Consumer Reports* magazine.

•*Contact Lens/Eyeglass Replacement Policies:* This is much too small an item to consider insuring. Pay for this kind of thing out of pocket. If you have recurring difficulty, your optometrist should reevaluate your prescription for free.

•*Private dental:* If you get dental coverage through a group or employer, you'll be all smiles. But buying it privately usually results in trading dollars with the insurance company. You probably won't come out ahead. Plus, lots of dental procedures are excluded.

•*Shipping/postal insurance:* The U.S. Postal Service is more efficient than it gets credit for, and FedEx, UPS, and most of the other private shipping services have excellent tracking systems. Keep your shipping receipt in case of trouble and don't mail diamonds!

•*Tanning insurance:* This is so silly we had to include it! A salon offered a guaranteed golden tan (at a price) to clients who were preparing for travel or a special occasion. If your tan started to fade before the big night, your insurance bought you bonus sessions. Talk about security!

BUY BIG AND BROAD/NEVER GO NARROW
Financial planners seem to agree that the best approach to insurance is to get "big and broad" coverage.

Insure yourself against big-daddy disasters and purchase policies that are broad in scope. With disability policies, for example, the definition of what makes one unable to work can be very subjective. That's why you have to shop around for coverage without a lot of limitations and exclusions. Buying coverage that's too narrow opens you up to the risk of having a claim denied.

Dying in a plane crash is a big disaster and for your dependents, it could be emotionally and financially devastating. But buying extra flight insurance when you pass through the airport is impulsive and narrowminded. Suppose the plane trip is successful (which is overwhelmingly the case) but you are killed in a taxicab accident on your way to your hotel? Better to have spent your insurance dollars on a comprehensive life policy. It's not pleasant to consider losing your life or ability to work, but if you're smart about getting the best and broadest coverage, you can quickly go back to happily living your life!

According to Sir Cecil Beaton, "Americans have an abiding belief in their ability to control reality by purely material means . . . airline insurance replaces the fear of death with the comforting prospect of cash."

Needs Analysis

Let us be boring for a moment and repeat ourselves—insurance is complex. No single purchasing plan is right for everyone. Our intent is to open your eyes to hidden scams and costly consumer mistakes . . . and expose you to the features of the most common types of coverage. When it comes to the question of how much coverage is appropriate, you would be smarter than the average bear if you consulted a credentialed financial advisor who could work up a personalized insurance *needs analysis*. Or if you're a do-it-yourself type, check out Dave Ramsey's book, *The Financial Peace Planner,* which does a great job of simplifying all the worksheets and equations.

THE TRICKS OF THE INSURANCE GAME

Once you've embraced the advisability of getting big and broad coverage, you must then take on the task of avoiding insurance rip-offs. Perhaps the biggest black mark on the record of the industry falls under the category of personal insurance, particularly life insurance. Scams and rip-offs related to the sales of personal insurance have rocked the industry. Property insurance issues seem mild in comparison. Consumer complaints in the property area deal more with claims disputes, rate hikes, and policy cancellations.

Protection for You and Your Assets

Consumers often are overwhelmed by the sheer number of policies available. But you can simplify your life by thinking in terms of "me and my stuff." You have only two things to insure: yourself and your assets.

Insurance on Me
- Life
- Health
- Disability

Life, health, and disability policies are considered personal insurance. But you need to decide if they are a necessity in your life.

HEALTH INSURANCE

Do You Need Health Insurance?
You need it. No matter how young and strong you are, you need health coverage. Medical care costs are astronomical these days, and major surgery or lengthy hospital stays could deplete the estate of all but the ultra-wealthy. The Bankruptcy Institute reports that approximately 52 percent of consumers who declare bankruptcy go broke because of medical bills.

Do You Need Disability Insurance?
If you work, you need it. Comprehensive disability insurance provides you with an income if you are unable to work in the field in which you are trained or educated. This is an often-overlooked bit of coverage—but younger working people are four times more likely to become disabled than they are to die.

Do You Need Life Insurance?
You need life insurance if you have dependents—a spouse, children, or others who rely on you and/or your income. This goes for the stay-at-home spouse who cares for children as well.

Families tend to insure the breadwinner only, which can be a devastating financial mistake. The most recent study done by LIMRA, a life insurance trade group, found that 80 percent of husbands have life insurance coverage while only 67 percent of wives do.

ABC's *Good Morning America* did a story on one such family. Jim and Patricia were the parents of two young daughters. It was a shock when thirty-six-year-old Patricia fell ill and eventually succumbed to breast cancer. The family had not thought it necessary to insure Patricia, who worked as an executive secretary. In an interview Jim said, "I didn't see a need for covering my spouse. It just didn't occur to me that there would be such a financial burden if anything ever happened to her."

Patricia's income had been used to pay for things like movies, shopping, and restaurants. But without her income, it was difficult for Jim to meet expenses. The family was forced to relocate from expensive New York to rural Vermont for a lower cost of living. The pressure of financial obligations made grieving all the more difficult. An often overlooked benefit of life insurance is that it can buy beneficiaries the luxury of time off from work—time to be together as a family and come to terms with the loss. Years later daughter Gina regretted the circumstances. "If my mom would have had insurance, I would have been able to spend more time with my dad, and do the things I wanted to do when I was younger . . . more activities, more quality time with the family."

Child care is one of the many services a family would need to purchase in the event of the loss of a homemaker. In the book *What Is a Wife Worth?* Michael Harry Minton applied national-average wages to daily spousal tasks including nurse, dietician, housekeeper, child psychologist, food purchaser, and public relations/hostess. The total cost of services provided: $108,048.73 per year.

Of course, many people do not have such significant obligations. If you are a swinging single with no debt or dependents, you can forgo life insurance entirely and spend the money elsewhere. But beware, all that extra cash is likely to make you seem extremely attractive to the opposite sex. You'll meet someone, fall in love, get married, and BANG . . . you need life insurance!

And let us look with a jaundiced eye on the sales practices of the life insurance biz.

Term vs. Cash-Value Pitch

Although not technically a rip-off, this sales pitch merits criticism because it rewards disregard for the consumer's best interest. Life insurance products break down into two main groups: term insurance and cash-value policies (called whole, universal, or variable). Cash-value policies combine insurance with a savings element while term insurance gives you only a death benefit.

A term policy offers you coverage for a period of time. The term is normally one, five, seven, ten, fifteen, or twenty years. You pay a premium and the policy provides a death benefit. Say you buy a $1 million, twenty-year term policy. If you should die during the twenty-year term, your beneficiaries receive $1 million. If you do not die, your premium is gone.

With a cash-value policy you get both a death benefit and some equity in your policy. If you live (as you hope you will), you get some money back for all those premiums. Cash value seems like a great way to save you from throwing all your premium money out the window.

Temptation

It does sound tempting, but it's a rotten investment. With a few rare exceptions, financial planners recommend you always buy term insurance. You'll pay lower premiums (especially when you are young and need a lot of insurance to raise a family in the event of your death), and you'll get bigger and broader coverage for your buck. You will spend five to eight times more with a cash-value policy than with a term policy for an equal amount of coverage.

Perhaps the most awful thing about cash value is that young breadwinners (the main group for life insurance sales) rarely can afford as much coverage as they'll actually need. A thirty-year-old with two young children may need $500,000 worth of coverage. Term insurance may cost him or her (depending on health history) between $400 and $1,000 a year. But for the same cov-

erage, cash value would cost conservatively $2,000 to $6,000 a
year!*

---

*Rates are based on a quotes from a random company.

The Cash-Value Sales Script
But agents are motivated to sell cash-value policies because they
are compensated handsomely and quickly. Commissions are
built into the front end—which means part or all of your first
year premium goes into the agent's pocket. Here's how they convince you.

- "A cash-value policy is all paid up after a certain number of
  years. A day will come when you have coverage but no
  premium!"
- "You won't be able to afford term insurance as you get older
  . . . because it gets more expensive as you age."
- "Cash-value policies give you something back for your insurance premium dollar."
- "It's forced savings!"

The Reality
But don't believe it. First of all, an agent cannot guarantee when
or even if your policy will be paid up. The insurance company
takes your premium money and invests it internally and exter-
nally. So if it performs badly or if interest rates go down, you
will receive a lesser dividend and may be paying premiums indefinitely.

Agents argue that term insurance gets more expensive as you
age. True. If you take out a twenty-year term policy and you decide to renew it after it expires, your premium will go up because you are now older and a little closer to death. Sorry, but
it's true. But during the twenty-year term your dependent children will have grown and your mortgage will have been heavily

paid down. For twenty years you will have been able to invest the money you didn't waste on cash-value insurance. The aim is to need little or no coverage by the time you are of an age when term insurance gets really expensive.

The most convincing sell is that you get money back for your premium dollars. You get very little back. It takes years for these policies to accumulate enough for you to break even. And most policyholders drop out before that day comes.

And the contention that it's forced savings is weak and wimpy. It's forced savings with a horrible return on your money. Get your bank or employer to make savings deductions if you have trouble disciplining your spending.

Scams by Name

As we said before, cash-value life insurance sales is completely legal although widely maligned as a crummy deal. But this kind of policy is sold every day. And holders of such policies have to be extra cautious because some of the biggest rip-offs involve cash-value policies. *Wall Street Journal* reporter Leslie Scism wrote in a January 1998 article, "After years of scrutiny of the life-insurance industry, and well-publicized efforts by major insurers to clean up their shops, you'd think it was finally safe to listen when an agent makes a pitch." But Scism goes on to report that the industry continues to be accused of the same old scams. Among them, these:

•*Churning:* The industry is notorious for churning scandals. Churning involves replacing existing policies with new policies. The new sale generates a fat commission for the agent, who often has advised clients they'll be getting the new (and better) policy virtually for free! There are a lot of consumers out there holding onto cash-value policies—and they should be warned it rarely makes sense to switch and replace policies. What often happens is that the equity in the old policy is drained to pay new premiums and eventually the policyholder is left with no equity and new premium bills. Prudential, John Hancock, and Metropolitan Life, just to name a few, have all faced allegations and civil suits regarding churning.

After much public outrage, the big insurance companies claim they've implemented systems that will catch agents who are attempting to churn. But the truth is, the commission system rewards agents with big commissions for new sales and small commissions for renewals. Until the commission system changes, the temptation to churn will remain.

•*Vanishing premiums:* "Vanishing premium" life policies are a figment of the imagination. Agents promise that the dividends (earnings) on the cash-value policy will accumulate at a certain rate. They use fancy laptop computers to illustrate *overly optimistic* growth projections. Eventually these fabulous earnings can be used to pay the premiums. Supposedly your premium bills will vanish. But if interest rates or dividends go down (as happened in the early 1990s), guess what? Policyholders are outraged when the promise falls flat and premium bills fill their mailbox!

•*Insurance as investments:* This is a ploy used by agents who may be posing as financial planners. A product is sold as a retirement investment when it's actually an insurance policy. Agents toss around terms like "private pension plan" or "supplemental retirement plan" and tout the fact that your money grows tax deferred. It sounds like a retirement plan but it's really a cash-value life insurance policy. Putting retirement money into a growth fund is a much better way to go.

•*Forgery:* Insurance companies and their agents have been accused of forging signatures for any reason that suited them. Any change made to a policy requires policyholder authorization. Sometimes the agents are forging signatures in order to churn, other times they are simply too lazy to contact policyholders for issues they view as minutia. Many, if not most times consumers don't find out about it. After all, the majority of policyholders don't end up making a claim. But other times agents get caught.

Sign Here and Here and Here

CNBC's *Steals & Deals* reported on a heart-wrenching forgery/churning scandal. Randy Clark held a $94,000 life insurance policy with Prudential Insurance Company of America. After Mr. Clark was diagnosed with an inoperable brain tumor, the insurer rescinded the policy. Prudential claimed Mr. Clark knew about his brain tumor before filling out his application. Mr. Clark told us, "I'd never had any kind of neurological problem at all when I applied for this policy."

Clark also claimed he had been urged to replace a former policy with a new one. He wasn't told that his new policy could drain the equity from his original policy . . . which would be churning.

When Clark received a copy of his application, he noticed something amiss with the dates and signatures. Clark believed that Prudential altered the application to make it appear it was filed *after* his diagnosis.

Clark was subject to a lot of suspicion, even from his own attorney. It seemed plausible that a person diagnosed with a terminal illness might attempt to conceal his problem when applying for life insurance. But two handwriting analysts, including one hired by Prudential, concluded that the signatures were "not genuine."

Former Prudential district manager Howard Siegel spoke to us about the practice of forgery. "There were many forgeries. I know of one agent who had a box with a light under it, a little screen, and he would write the signature and trace it from another signature he had." Siegel said when he refused to participate in forgery, among other questionable practices, he was fired.

In a telephone interview Prudential responded that Siegel was a disgruntled employee and the reasons for his separation are other than he is alleging. Nonetheless, Siegel sued for wrongful termination and after the case was remanded to private arbitration, Siegel was awarded $338,014 plus an additional $1 million in punitive damages. Prudential labeled the arbitrators' $1.3 million award "grossly excessive and unwarranted" and filed an appeal.

Randy Clark, who lost his successful paving business and a five-bedroom home, was reduced to bankruptcy. Prudential offered to reinstate his policy and also offered him a settlement of $150,000. But Clark refused to settle and proceeded with his lawsuit alleging fraud and breach of contract. "I don't want to be shut up. My parting effort in life is going to be making sure this never happens to anyone again."

In a written statement Prudential said, "We have tried to resolve this matter with Mr. Clark by reinstating his life insurance and by offering him a settlement. Although we continue to have a serious disagreement with Mr. Clark over whether he told us the truth, we are anxious to address his concerns."

But eventually, in May of 1996, Clark settled with Prudential, after the life insurance company was forced to admit that documents in his file had been forged. Neither side would disclose the terms of the settlement. Clark was quoted as saying, "I'm very happy. I hope that this means that they will guard against these kinds of activities by their employees. That's what's important."

It Goes Both Ways
It would be unfair not to discuss the wrongs being perpetrated *upon* the insurance industry. Career criminals as well as so-called ordinary citizens have been known to participate in outrageous insurance fraud. Plenty of people are looking to live on easy street with a big insurance pay-off. And it doesn't stop with phony neck and back injuries either; insurance-related crimes include arson, kidnapping, and even murder.

But the insurance industry is very candid about the fact that it doesn't pay for the crime—consumers pay for the crime via higher premiums. And since you, the consumer, are picking up the tab, this chapter is written for you.

AGENTS AND THE COMMISSION QUESTION

One way to get the best for your insurance buck is to understand agents. Agents generally come in two types: the independent agent (also called a broker) and the exclusive agent.

Independent agents represent the products of many different companies and receive commissions based on a percentage of the price you pay in premiums. Exclusive agents sell insurance for one company only and also work on commission. You should choose between the independent and the exclusive agent after you understand the pros and cons of each.

The upside to working with exclusive agents is that they will have greater product knowledge because they sell only one line of insurance stuff, so to speak. The downside is that they may be subject to company quotas, which could result in high-pressure sales tactics aimed at you.

The upside to working with independent agents is that they can offer you more choice and get you a policy and price most suited to your needs. These agents will not have bosses pressuring them to meet quotas, but they may be swayed to recommend the product of the company that pays the highest commission. The downside is that these agents' product knowledge will not be as sharp because they deal with so many companies.

And what are those commissions anyway? This is where reading your policy very carefully will do you absolutely no good, because agent commissions are never itemized in your policy. Believe it or not, commission charges will not appear on any document you receive from your insurance company.

Ask Away

So the commission question is one you must ask. Ask your agent/broker to recommend at least three products in your area of need, in order of preference. After he or she has done so, ask what the commission on each product is. If the highest commissions correlate with the agent's top picks, it is probably not a co-incidence. If you don't get a straight answer or the agent is uncomfortable disclosing this information, then you certainly don't want to do business with him or her.

There is nothing evil about being made to pay a (reasonable) commission. Insurance agents will argue that it takes a huge amount of time and energy to convince people to let them into their kitchen to discuss things like death and destitution. And we agree. But it is evil to give bad or irresponsible financial advice in order to earn an extra buck.

Two Tips for Getting Unbiased Insurance Advice
It's scary to trust an advisor who may have a conflict of interest, but don't despair. You can get unbiased advice before, during or after (preferably before) you purchase your insurance. Try these approaches.

One way is to join a consumer advocacy organization. For a small fee, these groups will advise you on planning issues and act as an advocate for you if necessary.

You can join the National Insurance Consumer Organization (NICO), a nonprofit organization whose sole purpose is to provide assistance to insurance consumers. You can contact NICO at (703) 549-8050. Or check out www.theplan.com on the World Wide Web for a free look at what an online advocacy group offers.

Another method is to hire a fee-only financial advisor. Contrary to perception, you do not have to be wealthy to work with a financial planner. "Fee-only" planners charge you for the time they spend advising you and never get commissions from products they sell you. Look for these credentials:

CFP: Certified Financial Planner
ChFC: Chartered Financial Consultant
CLU: Chartered Life Underwriter

TIPS TO CUT YOUR INSURANCE PREMIUMS

> The only thing standing between your wallet and
> your insurance company's hands is your knowledge.
> —J. Robert Hunter, President, NICO

The following is a summary of simple tips that can save you hundreds or thousands of dollars on annual *premiums* (industry lingo for *your cash*).

Health Insurance Cost Cutters
Group Coverage
If you are offered HMO (health maintenance organization) or PPO (preferred provider organization) coverage through your employer, *sign up!* You'll get a much better rate as part of a group than you could buying it privately. If you have a choice of both, choosing the HMO will save you money. PPOs provide you with more choices and flexibility, but HMO coverage is less expensive. Opting for the highest deductible and copay also will cut your premiums.

Private Coverage
If you are not employed by a company with group coverage, keep trying! Alumni groups and professional business associations may offer group coverage to members. So get out there and start joining up. Paying for private coverage can be a bummer. If you must buy health insurance privately, you can lower your premium by purchasing only catastrophic coverage. This means, among other things, you'll have no dental or optical coverage but you can pay for those things out of pocket. Again, opt for the high deductibles and copays to lower premiums.

Disability Insurance Cost Cutters
Disability insurance pays you an income if you are unable to work. Rates are based on two things. The first is the risk level

and the second is the elimination period. Those actuarial wizards will have figured out a risk-level rating for your profession. Cops are deemed to be at greater risk than greeting card writers! (Surprisingly, administrative assistants are highly rated because of the prevalence of that modern malady: carpal tunnel syndrome.) There is not much you can do about your rating. But you can save by opting for a longer elimination period—the amount of time you agree to wait until your payments kick in. You'll normally have a choice anywhere between one and four months. Opting for four months rather than one month can save you between 60 to 70 percent on your premiums.

Life Insurance Cost Cutters
Saving money on life insurance is easy. Buy term insurance. It provides the coverage you need, when you need it, at the lowest cost.

Bonus Tip: If contemplating your exit from this world immobilizes you to the point of procrastination over the purchase of life insurance, try this. The general rule on life insurance is: You will know how much you need by taking your after-tax income and multiplying it by the number of years you expect to work. If you are still young, the number you come up with probably will impress you. This is the one part of the life insurance process that tends to cheer people up. It's nice to feel like a mogul for a minute!

INSURANCE ON POSSESSIONS
And then there are all the possessions that we work to acquire. Two types are available, homeowner/tenant and automobile.

Do You Need Homeowner/Tenant Insurance?
Renters and owners alike need insurance to protect them in case of damage, destruction, or theft. Homeowner/tenant policies also provide liability coverage, which, in the age of the 1-800-UCANSUE law firms, may be needed if someone has an accident while visiting your home.

Renters sometimes assume that the landlord's insurance will cover them in the event of a disaster. Not so. Because landlords have no "insurable interest" in your belongings, their policy will not pay to replace your things. Another benefit of home-owner/tenant insurance is that it will replace possessions stolen from you when you are not at home, such as a laptop computer or camera equipment.

Homeowner/Tenant Insurance Cost Cutters

When it comes to saving money in the areas of homeowner/tenant and automobile insurance, the key is to ask about discounts. Insurance companies almost always give discounts for having your home and auto policies with the same insurer. You may be eligible for additional discounts if you are a nonsmoker and if you have a smoke alarm and security system. You also will save on your homeowner policy by insuring the value of the house, not the value of the land the house is built upon—rarely is land stolen or damaged! Senior citizens can get a rate cut because they tend to be home more often than others—there is no better security system than being home! Discounts are rarely offered to you unless you ask, so ask!

Do You Need Automobile Insurance?

If you drive, you need it. Uncle Sam has decided this one for you. Most states mandate liability coverage at the very least.

Automobile Insurance Cost Cutters

Again, you'll get the best deal if you qualify for discounts. Auto insurance will be cheaper if you have your homeowner/tenant policy with the same company. And of course, if you appear to be low risk, the insurance company may give you a break. Discounts are available for clean driving records, security systems, automatic seat belts and air bags, and for drivers with special driver training. Senior citizens get lower rates, as do students with good grades. Residency in a low crime area is also in your favor. You also can cut your premium by skipping costly auto insurance "extras" like coverage for glass breakage, towing, rental reimbursement, and medical (called PIP—personal injury insurance). A comprehensive health insurance policy should cover you on the medical front. Again, high deductibles mean lower rates.

THE LOYALTY DISCOUNT

State Farm Insurance agent Kimberly Nuelle of Philadelphia told us that consumers often respond to a rate increase by switching insurers. But what policyholders don't realize is that most insurers also give discounts for the amount of time you hold policies. And if you stay with one company over a number of years, the discounts you receive most certainly will outweigh the cost of what is likely to be a temporary rate increase. This also may apply to automobile and homeowner/tenant policies.

Rate-Hike Revenge

You've heard the infuriating story: A driver with a clean record gets one traffic ticket or makes one claim and her insurer responds with an immediate rate increase! Those boneheads! So the angry consumer exacts revenge by canceling the policy and taking her business to the competitor.

The Coverage Crisis

There is one catastrophe for which no insurance policies are sold. That crisis is being unable to obtain insurance. Besides learning to be a savvy insurance consumer, you also must be prepared to possibly be declined, canceled, or denied!

Are insurers able to pick and choose whom they do business with? Yes and no. If it were entirely up to the insurance companies, only the genetically perfect and extremely lucky people of the world would hold policies.

Each insurance firm has a set of underwriting guidelines that are filed with their respective state. These guidelines are basically the rules by which the firm decides who gets insurance,

at what rate . . . and who does not. Each firm is legally obligated to abide by its own underwriting guidelines, and it cannot
employ underwriting guidelines that are in violation of state
laws.

Unspoken Underwriting Guidelines

One area where state laws have collided with underwriting
guidelines is in the area of discrimination. Property insurers
cannot refuse to insure anyone based solely on age, sex, marital status, job status, or zip code. They can charge higher rates
to someone who lives in a high-crime neighborhood, perhaps,
but in most cases they cannot refuse coverage based on residency.

But property insurers have been accused of "redlining" certain neighborhoods and individuals, therefore denying them the
right to purchase coverage.

Although the practice is illegal, minorities, single people, and
the unemployed have all been victims. Denial or cancellation of
coverage for these reasons would not be in accordance with
company underwriting guidelines, but it has been found to be an
unspoken rule with certain companies.

Red in the Face over Redlining

Nationwide Insurance Company, the fourth largest homeowners
and auto insurer in Florida, was fined $100,000 in 1997 by the
state insurance commissioner when it was found to have prac-
ticed redlining. Agents were encouraged not to sell insurance in
certain low-income neighborhoods that were still recovering
from Hurricane Andrew damage. If agents did sell policies in
certain zip codes, management retaliated against them by giving
them low ratings on their performance evaluations. And auto
applicants were redlined due to anything from temporary unemployment to marital status. The discrimination was discovered when more than thirty Nationwide agents came forward of
their own volition and testified to the state insurance depart-

ment. The agents were shielded from repercussions by federal whistleblower protection regulations.

GIVE ME COVER

What would you do if you were told you weren't eligible for needed coverage? Certainly there are situations in which insurers are within their rights to deny you coverage or cancel existing coverage. The following will explain a bit about how this might happen—and give you strategies to fight back if you are arbitrarily or unfairly discriminated against.

Declined or Canceled—Personal Insurance

Cancellation of life, health, and disability policies happens most often when premiums are unpaid or overdue and the policy lapses. You must pay all premiums on time and keep good records in case of a dispute. With personal insurance, it is legal for insurance companies to decline to cover you or to charge you the highest rates if you are found to have a preexisting medical condition.* When applying for personal insurance, you normally submit to a medical examination, and/or blood tests and/or review of your medical history. Denial based on medical health seems cruel, but without this rule no one would buy coverage until after he or she already was ill.

---

*Certain states recently have enacted regulations nullifying the preexisting conditions exclusion on health insurance. Contact your state department of insurance for information. Their number appears in the front of the white pages telephone book.

Strategies

If you are denied personal insurance coverage, your first strategy is to act like an insurance salesperson. Don't take no for an answer! Just because one company declined to cover you does not mean you are uninsurable. Apply to other companies. It is a little-known fact that certain insurers specialize in covering clients with specific medical conditions. Prudential Insurance Company, for example, has made a commitment to researching cardiac health. Because the company is well versed on heart-related disorders, it is more willing to consider underwriting individuals who have problems in this area.

Your second strategy is to find out the exact reason for the denial. Ask for a full explanation with verification. Another little-known fact is that anything negative in your medical history may be a matter of record. The insurance industry uses a national database of medical information to determine insurability. It's called the Medical Information Bureau (MIB) and is the insurance industry's answer to a credit bureau. If you have ever been declined coverage based on a medical problem, the insurers report you to the MIB. Almost any insurance company can access this information so it's crucial you check your records for accuracy. You are entitled to a copy of your record by calling 617-426-3660.

Declined or Canceled Coverage—Homeowner/Tenant

Fortunately, denial of coverage for homeowner/tenant insurance doesn't happen all that often. If you own or rent and are willing to pay the premiums, you usually can get coverage. The main exclusion on these policies is for expanded riders covering floods, earthquakes, mudslides, and the like. Residents of areas particularly susceptible to natural disasters may be denied coverage. If you find yourself in this boat, so to speak, the only strategy we can suggest is to shop it around until you find an insurer willing to sell you a policy. If no company will sell you a policy, then you can deduce that the actuarial wizards figure there's a darn good chance you'll be quaked, flooded, or covered in mud.

Strategies

Consider moving elsewhere.

Declined or Canceled Coverage—Automobile

Automobile insurance is required by law. The good news for motorists is that in most states you can't be canceled or denied auto insurance if you hold a valid driver's license. One automobile insurance agent described the feeling of being forced to insure high-risk drivers: "Uncle Sam divides up all the crappy drivers and requires each agency to underwrite their fair share." It's called being in the *assigned risk* program. Need we point out that if you are insured under the assigned risk program you will be assigned the highest rates?

Strategies

If you are in the assigned risk program, believe us, the insurance company would cancel you if it could. Pay your premiums on time and you shouldn't be canceled or declined.

If you have been placed in the assigned risk program, talk to your agent about steps you can take to be rated more desirably. Traffic violations eventually are erased from your record and enrolling in driver training courses can be helpful. Ask your agent about which vehicles are considered to be lower risk. For example, the Department of Highway Safety reports that Camaros are involved in more fatal accidents than any other vehicle on the road. So you might want to consider selling the sports car.

The Fully Paid Claim

As if faithfully paying your premium wasn't enough, having a claim denied is an upsetting experience. You've just suffered a loss and now insult is added to injury. Often claims are deemed valid, but a dispute arises between the insurer and the insured about the amount the claim is worth. And still other times, it seems as if your insurance company is trying to frustrate you to death with the red-tape run-around.

But experts advise that a proactive stance is the best approach. While many companies pay claims in an expeditious and fair manner, there are also those that won't fork over your claim money unless you kick and scream. Remember, the squeaky wheel gets the grease, so don't be afraid to squeak loudly. The following ten tips summarize the steps and tricks you need to know to get your claim paid in full.

▶ Top Ten Tips

1. *Stay calm.* Depending on the scope of your loss, you may be in an agitated state of mind. Take a little time to get your wits about you. You're going to need them.

2. *Read your policy.* Yes, dig the thing out and read it. It is crucial to determine whether your claim rightfully falls under the terms of the policy.

3. *Don't call your agent!* If you are at all unsure about the validity of your claim, don't call your agent or claims office until you've been advised by an objective professional. Any information you share with your insurance company could be used against you in a claim dispute.

4. *Document your loss.* If property was destroyed, damaged, or stolen, document the event with photographs, video, witness accounts, and police reports. The same process applies if you are injured. If the injury renders you unable to perform these tasks, enlist a friend or relative.

5. *Use your own experts.* Depending on the type of loss you have suffered, you may need to call on any number of professionals including doctors, lawyers, contractors, mechanics, inspectors, and adjusters. Your insurance company may want you to use the professionals it recommends, but this isn't advisable. Get an objective assessment. Unless it is a condition of your policy (and it usually isn't), you should not trust someone who has the interest of the insurer at heart.

6. *Follow the rules.* When filing your claim, be meticulous. Provide all supporting documentation within the time limit specified in the policy. If claims are only valid for thirty days, the insurance company can and will refuse to consider a claim received on the thirty-first day. Fill in the en-

tire claim form without error. Provide original receipts. Don't let the company get out of paying you your due due to a technicality.

7. *Document some more.* Keep copies of all forms and paperwork. Send correspondence via certified mail. Log calls made and received. Take notes during conversations with your agent or claims department. You may need corroborating evidence in the future.

8. *Use your clout.* Dealing with a large claims department can make you feel like the little guy. But you may have clout you aren't even aware of. Complain directly to your agent. Let him or her know you may take your business elsewhere and will encourage others to do the same. If coverage is arranged through your employer, ask the director of benefits to intercede on your behalf.

9. *Speak to Mr. Big.* Claims departments have been known to drive policyholders bonkers with their tortoiselike pace and penchant for losing important information. If inefficiency is the issue, insist on dealing only with the director of the department. If he or she won't return your calls, call his or her boss. Go to the top to get attention if necessary. No one wants a complaint letter with their name on it sitting on the president's desk.

10. *Get fighting mad.* Don't roll over. If you've exhausted all possible methods of getting satisfaction, file a complaint with the state office of insurance. Although they may investigate your claim, it is probable that you also will need to hire a private insurance attorney to pursue the matter through legal channels. If you are a member of a consumer group like NICO, you may have access to legal advice and counsel through the organization.

Our hope is that you never ever need your insurance.

Suggested Reading

Ron Alford, *How to Win the Insurance Claim Game,* Queens, NY: The Plan Publishing Company, 1992.

Ralph Nader and Wesley J. Smith, *Winning the Insurance Game,* New York: Doubleday, 1993.

Dave Ramsey, *The Financial Peace Planner,* New York: Penguin Books, 1998.

CHAPTER 7

JEWELRY

If you don't have an uncle in the jewelry business, this chapter is for you. Don't be a victim of "fools gold"!

Buying jewelry should be a wonderful, emotionally charged experience. You should walk away with a piece of art, a remembrance of a wonderful occasion or something you just can't live without. The most heartbreaking scenario is finding out too late that your cherished gem is not worth the price you paid. More often than not, the bargain you were promised is not really a bargain. Remember, jewelers are not in the business of handing out money and gems, they are in the business to make money. With the help of some of our "inside" tips, we hope to make you a smarter shopper. Although there are many, and maybe mostly, honest, reputable jewelers out there, getting ripped off is not uncommon enough.

Newsmagazine shows and consumer reporters love to do stories on gems. It's almost a newsmagazine formula. We gear up with our hidden camera tucked away in a baseball cap, a purse, or even a bra, and head out shopping for jewels. We make our purchase at a less-than-honorable establishment, and then go to a reputable dealer and find out we have been taken. We go back with our visible camera rolling and confront the jeweler who lied to us. We are in business! We get great ratings, and our viewers are more informed and leery the next time they set out to shop. We scare a few shady jewelers temporarily, but time goes by and the scams resurface. So try to use our experience, learn the tricks of the trade, and educate yourself about what could be a pricey investment not only for your wallet but for your heart.

DIAMONDS

Let's start with diamonds. Many young lovers will head out on that exciting search for the "perfect" diamond to express their love and commitment and because, as they say, "a diamond is forever." Most will live with that very same diamond for at least as long as the "knot" stays tied. With all that pressure and all the emotions running hot, a diamond dealer can use just a little psychology and sales pressure to win over any romantic.

Our first tip is to think with your head and then with your heart. So try to pick a jeweler you can trust. As you soon will see, buying a diamond from the wrong dealer can cost you thousands.

ABC's *Primetime Live* ran an exposé about buying diamonds. Diane Sawyer's producers hit New York City's diamond district with $25,000 to spend and went to purchase diamonds at bargain prices. They bought one "top-of-the-line" diamond at a negotiated rate of $3,700. Right down the block they bought another "near-colorless" diamond for $3300. Both jewelers raved about the quality and superior color of those bargain diamonds. Sawyer's team then took the diamonds to two different reputable gemologists who told ABC News that the color of the diamonds was definitely *not* "top of the line" or "near colorless." Instead they said the stones were brown. To make sure it wasn't just an honest mistake, the crew sent a different producer back to one store to try to sell that supposedly "colorless" diamond back to the retailer. Imagine her surprise when the very same dealer told her the diamond was anything but colorless— it was brown. The producer then informed the salesman that she had been told this was a good-quality stone. The salesman told her she was naive and that salespeople tend to "lie a little bit." When she went back to the second store, that jeweler offered to buy back the ring just purchased from his store not for the original $3,300 but for $800! Clearly, ABC News was taken.

Diane Sawyer later went back, this time with cameras rolling. One vendor refused to talk and the other denied he was the man who had sold the ring to her producer.

So what's going on here? Aside from downright sleazy sales tactics, insiders call it "overgrading." Honest jewelers tell us it happens a lot. It's an easy way to make money on a lower-grade stone, a deceptive trick that probably goes undetected by most unsuspecting buyers. Disreputable jewelers sell you on a stone that they have told you is a better cut, color, clarity, or carat than it really is. Of course you find out too late, if you find out at all.

Are you terrified to buy a diamond now? You don't have to be. There are ways to protect your purchase. The most important protection you have is to get the jeweler to put the specifics in writing. Make sure you get the color, cut and "map"—that's the actual configuration of your diamond—on your receipt. If you find out later the jeweler misrepresented the gem and the color and cut are not what you were told, you may have a case. Educating yourself on finding the perfect diamond and outsmarting the jeweler is your best line of defense. Learn as much as you can about diamonds from books, associations, and educated jewelers before you make that everlasting purchase. Here are several ways you can start to level the playing field with your jeweler.

Romancing the Stone: Choosing a Good-Quality Stone

Know your four Cs before you head out. That's color, cut, clarity, and carat weight. And remember, there's a fifth, and that may be the most important: *cost.*

We'll start with the cut because that may have the most influence on how your diamond will look. A well-cut diamond enhances the light that is reflected out of your diamond. Jewelers refer to a beautiful diamond's "fire," or the rainbow colors that flash from within, and the "brilliance," or the liveliness that emanates from the rock. These two qualities are directly influenced by the cut. Many people think cut refers to the shape of a diamond. Is it round, triangle, oval, marquise, emerald, heart, square, or pear? Not so! The cut determines the depth, width, and angle of the facets. Expect to pay for that fire and brilliance. A good cut takes the expertise of a skilled diamond cutter. A poorly cut stone may even compromise the durability of the stone. Some cutting faults may weaken the diamond, causing it to split or break. The price of a diamond can change by up to 30 percent depending on the cut. Unskilled diamond cutters usually sell their smaller diamonds for mass-market jewelry. Seasoned cutters, with years of experience, command much more for their stones. Those diamonds will find their way into the better retail shops.

•*Color:* The best color for a diamond is no color. A "colorless" or "white" diamond is extremely rare and very expensive. When jewelers speak of color, they are referring to the body color and not the rainbow-reflected light. The best way to judge color on your own is to look at the diamond on its side next to a white background. If the jeweler displays the diamond on dark velvet, ask to have it shown against white. Almost any diamond will sparkle against a dark background. Even "white" or near color-less diamonds will have a tinge of color.

Diamonds are graded on an alphabetical scale, with D being the best and Z the worst. Each letter after D represents more yellow or brown in the stone. Although determining color may be slightly different from jeweler to jeweler, a shady dealer will grossly overgrade on color and in some cases may even be as bold as to put it in writing. That's why it's up to you to verify the facts with an honest outside appraiser.

•*Clarity:* There is no such thing as a "flawless" diamond. That's because nature has a way of issuing birthmarks to its stones. As diamonds form and crystallize over millions of years, small inclusions or imperfections will be inherent in the gem. Since marks, bubbles, and lines are formed over centuries, no two diamonds will be alike. When inclusions do not interfere with light passing through it, the beauty will not be compromised. Rare and very valuable stones may just have small specks, visible only with a jeweler's loupe. The fewer the inclusions, the better the quality and the higher the cost. The Federal Trade Commission mandates a diamond may be called flawless only when no imperfections are visible to a trained eye under a ten-power magnification and in good light.

•*Carat:* Carat is the unit used to measure the diamond. The term comes from carob seeds used to balance scales in ancient times. A carat is comprised of 100 parts, each called a "point." It is much easier to find good-quality smaller diamonds. The larger, more valuable stones are quite rare and therefore have a greater value per carat.

•*Cost:* Set your price before you shop. Study up on the terms and language used in the industry. Give the jeweler a lowball figure because he or she will try to sell you "up." Say you are looking for the nicest stone in terms of cut and overall look. A great cut can make a so-so diamond seem to sparkle brighter.

Cracks in the Ice: Clarity-Enhanced Diamonds

A new twist to make your shopping even tougher is the introduction of clarity-enhanced or fracture-filled diamonds. These are usually low-grade diamonds with inclusions or cracks that have been either zapped by a laser or filled with a substance that covers the flaws. It's estimated that 10 percent of the diamonds out on the market have been enhanced. These enhanced or treated diamonds look fabulous. They offer a nice option to those who could not otherwise afford a good-quality diamond.

But it's a nice option only if you are told exactly what you are buying and you pay a lower price than you would for an "untreated" stone. CNBC's *Steals & Deals* visited one of the top clarity enhancers in this country. The company is Yehuda Diamonds and it is quite reputable. President Ron Yehuda was very candid with us and told us his method works to greatly improve the appearance of lower-grade diamonds, offering a better-looking stone for a lower price. His diamonds did indeed look good. A person who could not otherwise afford a top-quality stone could do very well with a treated diamond. But disclosure is key.

The law requires that buyers be told if a diamond or any other gem has been enhanced.

Ron Yehuda tells us he insists his retailers inform their customers in a written statement that their diamond has been treated. Yehuda Diamonds also come with a lifetime guarantee and specific care instructions. Consumers need this information not only so that they pay a fair price—a price that should be much lower than the cost of a nonenhanced diamond—but also so that they know how to care for the diamond.

Yehuda Diamonds and a few other companies are vigilant about telling customers the truth about their stones. Gemologists worry that treated diamonds coming from other countries, such as India, may not be labeled. When those untagged stones hit the United States and get into the retail mix, it's easy to see why retailers, and certainly customers, may never know what they are buying. Not only does the value of the stone come into question; caring for certain treated stones can be tricky.

Here's a scary example. Let's say a woman takes a diamond to be remounted. She doesn't know it's a treated stone. The jeweler working on it also doesn't know it's been treated. The use of excessive heat could destroy the benefits of the treatment. The natural cracks in the stone once again become visible. Not only is the customer upset, but the jeweler who is doing the repair work probably is going to be blamed. No doubt the customer will claim her diamond was switched, believing her diamond never had those cracks. Proving who is at fault is not a pretty situation. You first have to wonder if the original salesperson ever told the customer that the diamond was enhanced. Then you have to wonder if the young man buying the stone ever told his fiancée the truth. You answer that one! So it's easy to assume these clarity-enhanced diamonds are floating around the marketplace, first as original sales and then as resales, without many potential customers or even uneducated jewelers ever knowing that's what they have purchased.

Investigative producer Norma Morato and reporter Roseanne Colletti took to the streets for a report done at WCBS-TV and decided to test the market. They brought along gemologist and author of *Jewelry & Gems, The Buying Guide,* Antoniette Matlins, to check the diamonds. Dressed in disguise and carrying a hidden camera, the three women set out to shop. They purchased an engagement ring for $1,000. They were never told the diamond had been treated.

After examining the diamond with a special jeweler's loupe, Matlins confirmed the diamond was treated. Morato and Colletti then took the diamond to an appraiser; the appraiser told them it was worth $2,300, and again, there was no mention of the treatment. When they sent a different troubleshooter back with the same diamond for a second appraisal, the appraisal was valued at $800 less; still, there was no mention of the clarity enhancement. Talk about depreciation! To find out just how common this variation in appraisals was, the team took two clarity-enhanced diamonds to several New Jersey mall stores for appraisals. *No one* picked up on the treatment. So if all these "professional" jewelers could not identify the treatment, how are you ever to find out?

Fracture filling is not limited to diamonds. Emeralds, rubies, and other stones of color also come into this country filled. A Washington, D.C., woman purchased an emerald for $24,000. When she brought the ring to a jeweler to be resized, she was handed back an emerald that was full of cracks. Then she confronted the jeweler at the store where she made her original purchase. He denied the stone was filled. She took her case to court, and for the first time ever, a jury awarded a purchaser of an enhanced gem three times the purchase price because she was never told about the true nature of her emerald. Her insurance company was off the hook, because it believed the original appraisal. The appraiser, however, was fined $9,000. As you might imagine, this court case has jewelers running scared.

Getting a handle on how to detect these filled stones is a challenge for the industry to tackle. We are sure to hear more about this in the future. In the meantime, what can you do so you know exactly what you are buying? Here's a tip: The GIA,

Gemological Institute of America, will not grade clarity-enhanced gems. They will, however, confirm if the gem has been enhanced with a filler material. So if your gem does not come with a GIA grading, and if your jeweler tells you he or she will not send it to them to be graded, it's time to be suspicious.

There is another way to check it out for yourself. A reputable jeweler who invests in a $150 dark field loupe can show you whether a gem has been treated. Looking through this special loupe (which differs from the common loupe found at jewelers) at Yehuda's diamonds, we could clearly see a purple flash of light. The purple flash appears only if a diamond has been treated. Unfortunately, many jewelers don't know about the tool or have decided it's not necessary to have on hand for their customers.

If you do decide to buy an enhanced stone, take special care. The material used in the treatment may expand or contract in extreme temperatures. Experts advise you not to use ultrasonic or steam cleaning or you may see those cracks reappear. Our best advice is to ask the jeweler the following questions: Has the stone been treated? How has it been treated? How do you care for it? Can you have it cleaned with an ultrasonic machine? How can it be reset? Is it sensitive to heat? Some of the poorer treatments can even disintegrate from exposure to the sun. And if your stone has not been treated, get it in writing.

Getting the Best Deal
Everyone wants a deal. Radio ads blast the airwaves promoting "direct diamond wholesalers." These wholesalers claim to sell you the same price they sell to the retail industry. Think about it; who is paying for all those ads? And who pays for those pricey rents? Unless you have an uncle who is a diamond wholesaler, you are not getting a stone wholesale. True wholesalers don't need to take the chance of being robbed by someone posing as a retail customer.

The world supply of diamonds is shaped by an international cartel, overseen by the South African–based De Beers Consolidated Mines. De Beers controls 80 percent of the world's production and determines how many diamonds will flow onto the market. The company does this to keep the supply tight and diamond values stable. So the prices are pretty much set by the time jewelers get their supply, leaving little room for negotiation.

Unlike gold, the price of diamonds does not fluctuate that much. Therefore, jewelers do not have a lot of room to discount the stones. So when you hear about rock-bottom prices, going-out-of-business sales, and direct-from-the-wholesaler prices, be wary about how a jeweler can afford to charge so much less than the competition. Can you get a good deal at a jewelry exchange? Sure, you can get a good deal at lots of places.

Do your homework, ask the jeweler to show you the stone through a loupe or microscope, and most important, as we've said a hundred times (well, almost), *get it in writing*. If the diamond does not come with a certificate, have the jeweler write it on the sales slip. Lab reports and pregrading by a reputable grading firm can help you comparison shop. If one dealer offers you a price much lower than other jewelers for a comparable stone, be wary!

Should you buy a loose stone while on travels to Africa or the Caribbean? You answer that one. Do you plan on going back to see the retailer if there is a problem? In general, when buying a loose stone, examine the stone unmounted. You always can choose the setting you like later. In fact, the jeweler can recommend a setting that shows off your diamond and may make it look bigger or brighter than it really is. A setting can hide a stone's defects. The mounting and any side stones may obstruct the flaws. Make sure you view a clean diamond. Ask the jeweler to steam it for you; if that's not available, experts suggest using your breath and a handkerchief to wipe off whatever grease or film may be on the stone. One former mall salesman tells us he constantly polished his diamonds. Customers often came back to buy his diamond, saying "Yours was much shinier than the one we saw at a different shop." Don't be fooled by the flash, though; it may not be worth all your cash.

Sizing It Up

Make sure your jeweler tells you the weight of the main stone, not the *total* weight of all the stones. The Federal Trade Commission is clear about requiring jewelers to tag the piece with the weight of the individual stones as well as the total weight. And make sure you ask the jeweler the right question when inquiring about the weight. Don't ask how "large" the stone is. Ask what the stone "weighs." You should be told the carat size. Be careful of jewelers who use the word "spread" when referring to weight. A disreputable jeweler may say the diamond "spreads one carat"; all that really means is that the stone looks like a one-carat stone in its width.

Creative Lighting

One of the tricks of the trade to sell inferior diamonds is using tricky lighting. Many jewelry stores are filled with incandescent spotlights, usually recessed in dropped ceilings. There's nothing illegal about using strong lights, but there's also nothing wrong with the consumer asking to see the diamond in natural light, outside the store. A diamond will take whatever light you give it and throw it back at you. To compare diamonds at two different stores, check the stones under similar lighting. This advice is hard to follow when buying a diamond from a TV screen (more about that later). To compare diamonds in different stores accurately, look at the diamond through a gem scope, not a jeweler's loupe. Gem scopes have their own light source, and jewelers say they are much easier for untrained eyes to use. Inexperienced shoppers may see nothing through a loupe, especially if the light in the shop is poor. Don't be intimidated, ask the jeweler to show you how to look through the scope or loupe.

"Frozen spit" and "rock salt" are inside terms for poor diamonds. These junk stones look great only because of bright hot lights in a shop. These stones may be acceptable in tennis bracelets and earrings, but they are not engagement-ring quality. These are the stones you'll see in those advertised specials: "One-carat tennis bracelet for $199!" The jeweler is still making money because the diamonds are basically unsellable in any other form. The price you are paying usually just covers the price of the gold, the diamonds themselves are almost worthless. These tennis bracelet diamonds are set in white-gold illusion plates. If the stone happens to catch the light, it's probably coming from the white trim around the rim.

Is It for Real?

Here's another insider's trick. If your diamond is round or a cut that allows you to put it facedown over a newspaper, try to read the fine print on the paper. If you can read the words, it's a fake. A real diamond should not refract the light in a way in which you could read the lettering. Also, make sure your diamond is set in its setting, not glued. Rhinestones are usually glued, but diamonds rarely are. Look for imperfections: Fakes don't have them. Either you have a flawed diamond or it ain't for real!

The Old Switcheroo

Okay, you are finally comfortable with your purchase. You are confident you got the diamond you really wanted. You live with your diamond for a few years and decide you want to change the setting or you want your ring repaired. Go to a jeweler you can really trust. Believe it or not, it is not unheard of to have your diamond "switched" by jewelers when you leave the piece with them.

An ABC News diamond investigation revealed a horror story from one New York woman, who brought her diamond of thirty-seven years in to be reset. She later found out her diamond, which was worth about $7,000, was switched with a cubic zirconia worth about eight bucks! ABC's *Primetime Live* wanted to see if this really is a common trick, so they bought a diamond worth about $6,000. They then had the diamond "plotted," which maps out the individual stone with all its inclusions. The news team went a step further and had a serial number lasered into the stone. They then had the stone mounted. A producer went into several shops requesting the band be stretched. No problem; the same stone was there when they picked it up.

They then sent an older woman in for the same repair job. After she picked the ring up from the store, *Primetime Live* brought the diamond ring back to their expert, who told the news team the diamond was not the same. It had been switched! The diamond given the woman did not have the serial number and had major flaws. The diamond expert estimated the difference between the two diamonds at about $5,000.

So what's your best line of defense to make sure the diamond you walk in with is the same one you walk out with? If you can, stay and watch the jeweler do the cleaning or repair work. If that's not possible, make sure the jeweler fully describes the diamond you have brought in and puts it on your receipt. Ask the jeweler to write all the jewel's dimensions: diameter or length and width, depth and weight. This information also protects the jeweler from having a shady customer claim the diamond was switched. This is a win-win solution for both the reputable jeweler and the customer.

Appraisal Collusion
So now you have found that perfect piece of ice. You still aren't sure the jeweler is being honest with you. You say you want the stone appraised before you buy it. He says: "Sure, I encourage you to get it checked out." Many people will figure if he says that he must be honest, and they don't need an outside appraisal. Others will say "Great, let's go." Of course the diamond seller won't let you take the stone out of the shop without his armed guard. You might ask the guard for a recommendation. The guard tells you he can't because you might think it was a setup. So now you really trust him. He then points to different appraisal offices, saying this one is good or the one upstairs is good. "Oh, I have heard people were very happy with that man across the street." You don't realize you've been led to the appraiser he wants you to see. You ring the bell, the appraiser sees the guard, recognizes whom he works for, tells you to wait, he

will be right with you. He then calls the diamond vendor you just left, jots down all the information the jeweler told you, and tells it to you the exact same way. You walk out and the collusion has been a success.

Gemologist Antoinette Matlins tells of her experience with WCBS's Roseanne Colletti and Norma Morato as the jeweler they chose directed them to the GIA. That sounded legit. When they arrived at the office it was indeed the GIA . . . not the Gemological Institute of America, but another, much less reputable appraiser with the same initials.

Choosing an Honest Appraiser
You'll need an appraisal to insure not only your diamond but any valuable gem or gold piece you own. You'll need to update that appraisal every few years as the price of jewelry fluctuates. You should send the new appraisals to your insurance company for updated coverage and replacement value costs. You also may want the appraisal to determine part of your net worth. So with all the horror stories we've just told you about, how do you pick a reputable appraiser?

First of all, almost anyone can hang a shingle and call him- or herself an "appraiser." There are no standard guidelines or licenses needed. Your best bet is to call around and ask several appraisers for their credentials. Are they gemologists? Do they belong to a gemological association? Make sure the association really exists and isn't a clever take-off of a professional organization.

Appraisers should charge you an hourly rate. It is unacceptable to have the appraiser base a fee on a percentage of the appraised value. That's a scam. Ask appraisers ahead of time what they think the job will run you. Be wary of appraisers advertising low, low rates and those who use "percentage" in their fee structure. An appraisal doesn't usually take much time, so stay with your gem.

Insuring Your Gem

Once you have your gem appraised, get that appraisal to the insurance company. Homeowner and tenant insurance usually has limits on how much you will be paid for your lost, stolen or damaged gems. Some policies don't cover them at all. Check with your company. If your piece is worth more than $2,000 you should consider getting a "floater," a policy just on that piece. A floater will run you about $10 per $1,000 of coverage. Floaters generally protect you in a variety of situations not covered by standard homeowner's insurance, such as having your ring fall down the sink drain.

Compare companies for coverage. Some cover loss, some just theft. Ask about damage coverage as well. Gems can crack. The coverage usually is called "all-risk" and may be a few more dollars, but it is definitely worth it. You also should know that sales tax and deductible are not included.

Try to get your jewelry appraised every two years. The jewelry may appreciate, and you will be out of luck if you need to collect and your appraisal reveals a lower value. Make sure the insurance company allows you to replace your gems at the jeweler of your choice. Keep your appraisal in a safe place with your other insurance documents.

Diamonds Are Forever: If You Take Care of Them

The Jewelers of America Association recommends the following for keeping your diamond sparkling and safe.

- Don't wear it when you are doing rough work. Even though a diamond is durable, it can be chipped by a hard blow.
- Don't let your diamond come in contact with chlorine bleach when you are doing household chores. Bleach can damage and discolor the mounting.
- See your jeweler at least once a year for a check of the prongs and mounting.
- When you are not wearing your diamond, store it in a fabric-lined jewel case, or wrap it in tissue paper.

• Don't mix your diamond pieces in a drawer, because diamonds can scratch other jewelry and can even scratch each other.

Cleaning Your Diamond

Diamonds get smudged and dusty. Lotions, powders, soaps, and even your own skin oils put a film on diamonds and cut down their brilliance. A clean diamond "glows" because the maximum amount of light can enter and return a fiery brilliance.

Here are two ways you can keep your gem sparkling:

Use a detergent bath: Prepare a small bowl of warm suds with any mild liquid detergent you have at home. Brush the pieces with an eyebrow brush while they are in the suds. Then transfer them to a wire tea strainer and rinse them under running water. Pat them dry with a soft lintless cloth.

A cold-water soak also works: Make a half-and-half solution of cold water and ammonia in a cup. Soak the pieces for thirty minutes. Lift them out and tap gently around the back and front of the mounting with an old soft toothbrush. Swish the pieces in the solution once more and drain on tissue paper.

Your other alternatives involve buying a jewelry cleaner or taking your gem to your jeweler for a thorough cleaning.

ALL THAT GLITTERS MAY NOT BE REAL GOLD

Be careful where you buy your gold and how your piece is marked. The Federal Trade Commission is very clear about karat markings. A piece of jewelry cannot be labeled as real gold unless it is at least 10K. There is a big difference between fourteen-karat and gold-plated jewelry. Fourteen-karat gold contains fourteen parts of gold, mixed throughout with ten parts of base metal. Gold-plated is much cheaper; all it has to be made of is at least ten-karat gold bonded to a base metal. That's why you have probably had problems with gold plating wearing off on an inexpensive watch band or necklace.

Underkarating

You probably figured there's a scam in karat markings, and you were right! When you buy real gold, you expect it to be at least fourteen karat. But how do you really know? To check the karat of your piece you need to check the karat marking usually found on the clasp. The problem is you don't really know if the marking is legit.

Street vendors have been caught putting bogus karat stamps on inferior pieces. Several years ago the *Washington Post* hit the streets of Georgetown in search of gold. The *Post* purchased twelve pieces of gold jewelry and had them tested for content. Seven of those items turned out to contain less than 10K, which under the law is not considered gold.

The Jeweler's Vigilance Committee (JVC), a self-policing industry organization, also has conducted sweeps of street vendors to expose those who sell underkarated goods as the real thing. The JVC claims kiosks at malls and fairs are notorious for selling these goods. Their investigators found these kiosks also selling counterfeit Nike, Warner Bros., and Disney charms and chains. Most of these bogus goods come from Southeast Asia.

One way you can check to see if the gold is real and not underkarated is to look for a manufacturer's trademark. Under the Gold Standards Stamping Act, jewelry manufacturers must stamp their trademark on their pieces. The trademark stamp can be on a clasp, a brooch, or a pendant, and varies from manufacturer to manufacturer. This act was set up to hold the manufacturer accountable for the karating. It helps the retail jeweler as well as the customer have recourse in court if the gold isn't what it was sold to be. Unfortunately, some clever con artists have come up with ways to counterfeit the trademarks. Be careful of sidewalk sellers who claim to have manufacturers trademarks on their wares—they could be bogus.

Our best advice is to buy from a reputable jeweler who will still be around if you have a problem. Who can you go to if the kiosk closes or the fair leaves town? When buying from an established jeweler, safeguard your investment by getting the gold content in writing. Once again you will have the documentation you need if you find out later that you were duped.

PEARLS OF WISDOM

You can pay hundreds and hundreds of thousands for a strand of pearls. Real pearls come from oysters or other mollusks. All others are man-made. Cultured pearls are a lot less expensive. They also come from mollusks, but they are assisted by humans. Natural pearls are very rare and very expensive.

The luster of the pearl is extremely important. The skin should shine and not be dull. The more brilliant the luster, the more expensive the pearl. Shape also determines the value of the pearl. Since pearls are formed by oysters, no two are the same, and finding like pearls can seriously impact the price. The two best colors of pearls are rose with a touch of white or white with a touch of rose. You can find colors ranging from cream, gold, blue/gray, and black. Genuine black pearls are very expensive. The shape of the pearl also affects the cost. They could be round or baroque. Baroque pearls are long and skinny and less pricey. Round pearls are more desirable. Whatever your price range, you should look for the best quality you can afford. Experts say it's better to get a less flashy strand that will last you forever than a cheaper one that will deteriorate over time.

Is It for Real

The only way a pearl can be called natural or cultured is if it comes from the sea. Imitation or man-made pearls are created in a factory without the aid of an oyster. Most artificial pearls shine on the surface like nail polish. Man-made pearls must be labeled as such.

Right around Valentine's Day in 1997, the Federal Trade Commission (FTC) forced Zales, the nation's largest jewelry retailer, to settle charges it deceptively advertised its "Ocean Treasures" line of imitation pearls as "cultured" pearls. The FTC came down on Zales for using false advertising copy. The ads included phrases like "Created by nature, enhanced by man."

Right next to the copy were pictures of the Ocean Treasures line. The FTC claimed the ad led you to believe the pearls were cultured, not imitation. So even when buying at an established retail store, get the facts in writing on your receipt.

Shopping for Your Grand Strand
The Jewelers of America offers these tips.

- Check the surface for a satiny smooth finish. Look for unsightly blemishes, spots or pits.
- Look for luster in the shadow area of the pearl, not in the area on which the light is shining.
- All pearls in a strand should blend well together in regard to luster and color.
- Roll a strand of pearls along a flat surface to determine if all pearls are strung through their exact centers. All pearls should roll evenly, without an eccentric wobble.
- Buy the best quality you can afford. A good strand of pearls will last you a lifetime. Shoddy pearls may peel and crack. They are the cultured pearls that are removed from the mollusk too early to form a nice thick coating. You may spend a lot of money on poor-quality pearls, only to have them deteriorate after a year. Some disreputable jewelers may even blame you for mishandling them and not refund your money.

Protect Your Pearls
Once you've splurged on the best pearls you can afford, it makes good sense to take care of them. More tips from the Jewelers of America:

- Don't toss them carelessly into a purse or jewel box where they can become scratched by hard metal edges or harder stones.
- Don't expose them to acid-based hair sprays, cosmetics, or perfumes. You can bathe with pearls, but it may stretch the

stringing. So you should dry pearls with a tea towel so the necklace doesn't stretch.

• Don't clean them with chemicals or abrasives.

• Do treat pearls gently. Place them in a chamois bag or wrap them in tissue paper when putting them away.

• Do put on pearls after applying cosmetics, hair sprays, and perfume.

• Do bring your pearls back to your jeweler for restringing once a year, because cosmetics and ordinary wear weaken and stretch the nylon threads on which the pearls are strung.

• Do have the pearls strung with a knot between each pearl. This will prevent loss of pearls if the string should break.

• Don't keep your pearls in a safe deposit box for a long period of time. The lack of humidity may evaporate the moisture content of the pearls and dull the luster.

• Wear your pearls. Pearls that are worn frequently retain their moisture by absorbing it from the air or from your body.

SHOPPING STRATEGIES

Where should you buy your gems? We've shown you ways to shop for gems and gold. We've offered tips and exposed some of the underhanded tricks. Now it's time to discuss where you should purchase your pieces. You have many options. You can go to an established jeweler, a jewelry exchange, a mall store, a foreign country, an auction, or even shop off your TV screen. We are not advocating any one place. We just want to offer you insight as to what to watch out for at any one of these venues.

Buying off the Box

Let's start with shopping from the tube. Many people swear the cable shopping networks offer the greatest deals and are very happy with their purchases. After all, some of our favorite celebrities hawk their goods and offer us a chance to dress like them. Great, if that's how you like to shop. Realize, however, that you are only seeing a picture of the piece; you can't try it on, feel it, or really see its size and sparkle. High-pressure sales make you feel like you should get in on the deal before the deal expires. If that gives you a charge, then by all means charge it.

Heed these words of warning before you place your purchase over the phone. Several years ago New York Attorney General Oliver Koppell forced the Home Shopping Network to change its advertising of gemstone jewelry after charges that it was inflating the suggested retail value to make shoppers think they were getting a bargain.

The attorney general said the agreement ensures that the Florida-based network will adhere to certain guidelines in appraising jewelry, its best-selling line. Koppell said, "Home Shopping Club's suggested retail prices were so inflated that they were no more than a fantasy. A ring they were selling for $400 was probably worth about that. The trouble is, they were saying it would cost $1,200 elsewhere."

The case against HSN also claimed that in addition to flashing an unrealistic retail price on the television screen, the network hyped the products by saying there were only a few items left when, in fact, they had access to many more.

A HSN spokesperson said the settlement was not an admission of guilt. The network did agree to set guidelines everyone could agree on because there have been instances where people did not agree with their appraisals.

We checked consumer agency files recently and found that people who were dissatisfied with their purchases from these TV shopping networks did get their money back in a timely fashion. The New York Attorney General's office also told us HSN is adhering to the guidelines.

Even if the values the programs tout are correct, you should realize that the savvy hosts who sell to you are selling you mostly on romance and their own personal experience with the jewelry rather than specific details about the piece. So during all those late nights you stay up watching the shopping channels be sure you know why you are buying what you are buying!

Going, Going . . . Gone!

Auctions can be great places to get deals on rare and magnificent gems and jewelry, but they're also a source of major rip-offs. If you plan to spend a good deal of money for a rare piece at auction, the first thing you should do is hire an expert by the hour or by the job. Only an experienced gemologist can determine if a gem is worth the selling price. The second thing you should do is make sure there is documentation, such as a laboratory report, that provides full disclosure about those gems.

If you've got the cash to invest, and the adventurous soul and stomach for an auction, there are great deals to be had. But you better be crystal clear on what you are buying. Antoinette Matlins, author of *Jewelry & Gems, The Buying Guide,* was a guest on CNBC's *Steals & Deals,* and brought with her examples of fabulous deals at auction and outright rip-offs.

She showed us a Sotheby's buy—a ruby and diamond set complete with earrings. The set was purchased for $240,000 a few years ago. Matlins suggested it could not be made for $350,000 today and probably would retail for somewhere between $500,000 and $750,000. Not a bad buy!

After showing us some other great gets, she showed us what can happen when you don't know what you are buying. She displayed a beautiful pink topaz antique necklace purchased at a different auction house. The stones looked pink to us. Matlins told us they are genuine topaz, but colorless! She removed a stone from the setting and showed us a completely clear stone. Where did the pink color come from? She revealed a piece of pink foil set underneath the colorless stone. The ad at the auction said in bold print it was "pink topaz." Very misleading. Our advice here is, if you are willing to spend that kind of money at an auction, spend a little more by hiring an expert to come with you. You will save a lot more in the end.

Malling It

Have you ever stopped at a mall jewelry shop for absolutely no reason? You had no intention of buying or even looking at jew-

ercent off because there isn't that kind of markup, unless the rice is grossly inflated.

Do your own snooping; keep going back to see if the price ever changes. We've had honest salespeople tell us not to buy it, it will be on sale the next day.

Comparison Shopping

This is a tough one. Rarely are two pieces exactly the same. Unless you are buying a watch where the model numbers can be shopped, you will have a hard time playing one jeweler against another. Your only shot at knowing if you are getting a good deal and having some bargaining power is to get as many details about the piece in writing as possible. When shopping for a gem, having a lab report in hand and a price will help you compare a comparable stone at a different retailer. You won't be able to examine a stone carefully if it is already set.

Comparison shopping really doesn't work all that well with jewelry. As we said in the beginning of this chapter, buying jewelry is emotional. It's also like buying a piece of artwork. If you love the piece, buy it and keep all the records.

We love jewelry and gems and think you should too. Jewelry is an expression of love, art, and craftsmanship. Don't let a crafty jeweler rob you of an incredible experience. Stay away from high-pressure salespeople. Find a jeweler you can trust, one who is willing to spend time with you and educate you. Buying gems should be fun and one of the more celebrated and sensuous shopping experiences you will have. Use our advice so that your jewelry sparkles and you beam with pride knowing you truly got "a gem of a deal."

▶ Top Ten Tips

1. *Get everything in writing.* And we mean everything: the gold content, the weight of the stone, the warranty, and the appraisal.
2. *Get the lab report on the gem.* This map of the stone should include inclusions.

elry that day. And if you even had jewelry on you
probably would have thought of going to your fam

Mall stores are set up to grab your attention. Yo
notice that many of them are located on a corner with
entrances. Walking through the store just to browse i
convenient! There's nothing wrong with that; it's just sm
keting, and the sparkle of the jewels is very tempting. O
you have been drawn in by the sonic cleaning machi
makes noises, a type of circus atmosphere that captures yo
tention without you really knowing why. A former mall je
salesman clued us into those clever attention grabbers.

You should realize, however, that those are premium sp
and even just paying the rent at upscale malls does add
Those costs have to be made up in high volume or they have
be passed on to you in higher prices.

Sale or Scam?

How many times have you seen major retailers offer 50 percent
off sales on jewelry? It seems those sales are always running just
when you need them. Valentine's Day, Christmas, or Mother's
Day are hot times for these terrific savings. Department stores
are notorious for advertising these types of sales, and they are
also famous for not really ever having the before-the-sale price
for more than maybe a day or two. We sent our researcher,
Lamar Goering, into a major New York City department store
to look for a necklace for his girlfriend. Every time he checked
on the price—and this was over several months—the sale price
was constant.

According to the law, a retailer must sell the piece at full price
for a reasonable number of days. The retailer can be fined if
caught running a phony sale. So be aware the next time you hit
a department store jewelry counter expecting a great deal. If you
love the piece and still think it's a fair price, buy it. But don't believe you are actually getting a half-price bargain. Industry insiders say no one can afford to sell jewelry legitimately at 50

3. *Shop at a store where there is a gem scope for you to use.*
4. *Find your own reputable appraiser.*
5. *Stay with your jewelry while it is being repaired, or get a detailed receipt of the piece you have left behind.*
6. *Find a retailer that will still be there if you have a problem.* Be careful of buying at fairs and kiosks.
7. *Don't buy on impulse.*
8. *Don't always trust advertised sales.*
9. *Be careful when shopping abroad.* Buy jewelry as a souvenir, not necessarily as a bargain.
10. *Be careful shopping at auctions.* Pay a professional to shop with you.

Glossary

Clarity enhanced: A process to artificially fill in cracks of lower-grade gems.

Diamond switch: Jeweler switches your diamond for an inferior one.

Flawless diamond: No such thing.

Floater: Extra insurance to cover your jewels.

Frozen spit, rock salt: Poor-quality diamonds.

Overgrading: Jeweler misrepresents grade of gem . . . in his or her favor!

Spreads one carat: Diamond looks like a one-carat diamond in width.

Underkarated: Karat stamp on jewelry is higher than the true gold content.

Suggested Reading

Antoinette L. Matlins, P.G., *The Pearl Book: The Definitive Buying Guide* Woodstock, VT: GemStone Press, 1996.

Antoinette L. Matlins, P.G. and A. C. Bonanno, FGA, PG, ASA, *Jewelry & Gems: The Buying Guide,* Woodstock, VT: GemStone Press, 1993.

CHAPTER 8
MATTRESSES

Everyone wants a good night's sleep, but the nightmare of mattress shopping can keep you up at night. Mattress sales is an industry practically set up to be consumer unfriendly. We first investigated this field for a piece on NBC's *Today* show. At the time some of our friends and coworkers thought it was a strange subject to tackle. "What can you say about mattresses?" we were asked. "How much interesting information can there be?" Well, after our story aired these skeptics had learned exactly what anyone who's ever shopped for a mattress knows: Finding the mattress you want at a good price can be a monumental task. At its best, the retail mattress industry is set up to create consumer confusion. At its worst, it uses unscrupulous salespeople and high-pressure sales techniques to make a buck.

IS IT TIME TO SPRING FOR A NEW BED?

Since we spend a third of our lives sleeping, it's not surprising that a mattress is probably one of our most-used purchases. Because it's such an intricate part of our lives, when buying a mattress it's important to not only consider the cost, but to search out good value. You want to find a comfortable, quality bed at a great price.

Mattresses aren't cheap. There are plenty of ads out there claiming mattress sets for as low as $100. But in reality, a decent queen-size mattress and box spring cost about $800. For that kind of money, the first question you need to ask yourself is whether you really need a new one. If your mattress is eight to ten years old, strip off the sheets, take a good look, and ask yourself the following questions.

- Does the mattress look like it's sagging or uneven?
- Is the cover soiled or torn?
- Do you or your partner tend to roll toward the middle?
- When you roll around, do the coils squeak, creak, or crunch?
- Are you always adjusting your sleeping position to get more comfortable?
- When you wake up each morning are your muscles sore? Do you still feel tired?

If you answered no to all the above questions, you can probably skip this chapter, at least for now. But if some of your answers were yes, it's time to tackle the perplexing world of the mattress trade.

UNDER THE COVERS: IT'S WHAT'S INSIDE THAT COUNTS

Put several mattresses next to one another and the average consumer usually can't tell them apart. That's why a mattress is called a blind item. You're just never certain of what you're buying. The only thing you really see is the mattress ticking (the fabric that covers the mattress or box spring), which comes in different colors and materials. But the ticking doesn't indicate a bed's quality. In fact, some mattress makers actually cover cheap mattresses with expensive ticking so consumers think they're getting a better product. Certainly ticking can add to the quality of a mattress, but it's what's inside that counts. The coil construction, wire gauge, and amount of inner padding all determine the feel and quality of a mattress. Unfortunately, consumers can't dissect a mattress to inspect what's inside, and even if they could, to an untrained eye it just looks like a bunch of wires and upholstery. To help you find a bed that will hold up night after night, here's the anatomy of a typical mattress set.

Innerspring: The innerspring system is what provides support; it's how a mattress responds to the pressure of your weight and contours to your body. Each manufacturer claims to use the latest "innovative coil technology" to construct their beds. Sealy has trademarked their "PostureTech Coil with Sensory Arm," which they claim senses and cushions movement, then responds with increasing support. Serta uses "a network of interconnected steel Posture Spirals" made from continuous steel wire, and connected by "helicals." And Simmons Beautyrest has patented their individual "Pocketed Coil" innerspring that "reacts independently to pressure." With all this high-tech talk, it's easy to forget that we're talking about a mattress.

Naturally, every manufacturer claims they have the best system. But regardless of new technology and marketing mumbo jumbo, the different coil systems feel pretty much the same once you lie down on them. Two things you do want to pay attention to are coil count and coil gauge. A full-size innerspring mattress should have at least 300 coils, a queen-size at least 375, and a king at least 450. Understand that a higher coil count doesn't necessarily mean a superior product. A queen-size bed with 600 coils might prove to be less durable and comfortable than one with only 500. You also should ask about the gauge of the coil wire. Typically, the thicker the wire, the firmer and more durable the mattress. With wire gauge, the smaller the number the wider the wire; so a 12-gauge coil is thicker than a 16 gauge. High-quality mattresses generally have a wire gauge between 12$\frac{3}{4}$ and 14.

Padding: Padding is what's sandwiched between the coils and the cover of a mattress and makes it feel soft and cushy. Insulation padding lies on the coils so they don't poke you and it prevents the mattress from forming pockets. The middle and top padding is made up of several different materials, including wool, polyurethane foam, polyester, cotton, and felt. More expensive beds usually have more padding, including a pillow top which is a puffy cushion sewed onto the outside of the mattress. Beds with a thick cotton or polyester batting or layer tend to lose their loft over time compared to most foam material. Also, premium beds with pillow tops—currently very popular—are nice and fluffy but will compress with age.

Ticking: Ticking is the material covering a mattress or box spring. Although it's mostly a matter of aesthetics, ticking can manipulate a consumer's perception of mattress quality. Some industry insiders maintain it's the ticking that sells the mattress. "Ticking has ten seconds of life on the retail floor," one marketing executive told a home-furnishing trade journal. "What we try to do in those ten seconds is attract the consumer's eye—bring her in." Generally, the more you pay for a bed, the softer and more distinctive the ticking. Most ticking is made with polyester or cotton, but premium beds often use silk. You'll hear salespeople tout damask ticking, which is high-quality ticking with a woven pattern. While fancy ticking is attractive, the only time you'll ever pay attention to it is when you're in a mattress store. You want a durable cover, but unless you plan on foregoing sheets, never judge a mattress by its ticking cover.

Box Spring: Also called the foundation, the box spring is the bottom piece of a mattress set and contributes to a bed's overall comfort and support. Box springs are usually made with a combination of wood and steel covered with fabric and are designed to work in tandem with the mattress. As they do with innersprings, manufacturers patent their foundation systems. We're not bedding engineers, but we can tell you that the foundation is important and will affect how firm your bed feels. The foundation is like a shock absorber, and your bed won't have the bounce without the box spring. That's why mattresses are usually sold in a set with the box springs. You should not put a new mattress on an old foundation. Without a box spring your mattress will wear out a lot faster, one reason why many manufacturers' warranties are only valid if you buy the mattress and foundation as a set.

There are a few other catch phrases you're bound to hear while mattress shopping. Edge support is one feature you'll find on some mattresses. Because the edge of a mattress gets a lot of use, some manufactures put more durable coils or firmer padding on the perimeter of their beds. Sealy claims that their Edgeguard system provides a firmer edge and 10 percent more sleep space. Contour support is another popular trend. Mattresses with this feature provide firmer padding or extra coils in the area of your shoulders and hips, where your weight is concentrated. Manufacturers say this helps prevent sagging and gives you support where you need it most. Don't worry too much about special features like these unless you feel they contribute to your overall comfort.

EXPOSING SLEAZY SALES PRACTICES
"It's a dirty business," one mattress retailer told us. "That's the way it's been done for a hundred years and like many industries they just don't change." Buyer certainly beware when it comes to purchasing a mattress. Shopping for a new car can be less frustrating. Our investigation revealed the bedding industry is actually set up to confuse consumers, so it's difficult to know whether you're getting a bargain or a bad deal. On top of that many retailers employ sleazy and sometimes illegal sales tactics meant to manipulate unknowing and unprepared consumers.

The Name Game

As you know by now, we're big fans of comparison shopping. Checking out merchandise at several different stores can save you money and protect you from being ripped-off. But it's almost impossible to comparison shop when buying a mattress because the industry is built on a system that flies in the face of the smart shopper. "It was very frustrating," says Todd of New York City. We met Todd at a department store while he was shopping for a mattress. He had just moved to New York to start a new job and was trading in his college futon for a real bed. "I felt like the more stores I went to, the more confusing it became. My clarity of knowledge of beds didn't increase as I shopped around, it just got worse and worse."

Todd's confusion is understandable. For example, let's say you go to a store, bounce around on a few beds, and pick out one you like. Naturally, before you buy you want to shop around to see if you can get a better deal. You write down the brand and model name of the mattress you like, the Sealy Posturepedic Paisley for instance, and head out for another store. But you can't find the Paisley anywhere else. Why? Well, all major mattress manufacturers provide different stores different names for essentially the same mattress. The Sealy Posturepedic Paisley in one store might be labeled the Genoa, Ashton, Mayfield, Optimum, or Escort in another, depending on where you shop. There might be cosmetic changes to each of these differently named mattresses, like the color of the ticking, but they're essentially all identical inside. The industry calls these mattresses "comparables" and the main reason comparables are produced is to make it more difficult for consumers to bargain hunt. We found for that similar Sealy Posturepedic mattress set we could have spent anywhere from $579 to $1,500. But most consumers just never realize that these are all basically identical mattresses sold at a wide range of prices.

Joe Vicens runs 1-800-Mattress, a company that sells mattresses over the phone. He says the industry devised the comparables system to confuse consumers. "The department store, retail store, whoever it is, they want to have exclusivity on a name," explains Vicens. "So if you go into a store and see the mattress you like in pink, then walk into a store across the street, that exact same mattress would be blue and have a different name. It becomes very confusing." Manufacturers make anywhere from six to twelve basic mattress models, called levels, then make several comparables for each level. Therefore, a level 2 Sealy could be called a Sonora, Camelot, Winfield, or St. Phillip depending on where you shop. To make matters even more confusing, companies change their mattress names every few years.

Comparables exist in other industries, but are most prevalent in the bedding business. Some say the system started back in the 1970s when new trade laws prohibited all manufacturers from setting minimum retail prices. As a result many discount mattress stores opened up and cut into department and furniture store profits. The department and furniture stores wanted consumers to think their store carried exclusive products and not just something that could be picked up at any store, so they used their power to force the manufacturers to produce different-named mattresses for their stores. Soon the mattress chains wanted their own models too. Now manufacturers can have more than ten names for essentially the same bed.

The retailers claim their models are different from those of their competitors and this may be true to a certain extent. Many retailers request the manufacturers to add things like extra padding, a certain type of ticking, or special lumbar supports for their comparable mattresses. However, most of these changes are relatively minor, and the average consumer won't be able to tell the difference.

We tried to ask the manufacturers about "comparables," for our *Today* show report but both Simmons and Serta turned down our request for an interview. Sealy, however, invited us to one of their factories and explained that changing the system is almost impossible. "What sounds easy isn't," said a Sealy spokesperson. "Even though we produce the product, it's sold by independent merchants who have the right to buy or not buy the products they want." Although he admitted that it would be much more cost effective to avoid making over fifty different types of beds, he also said it wasn't feasible "We would not be successful in marketing our product," he explained. "The [retailers] would not buy the same product that everyone else carries."

We found that the manufacturers blame the confusing system on the retailers, and the retailers pin it on the manufacturers, but in the end it's the consumer who loses. Some industry insiders criticize us for making too much of the name game. They say buying a mattress is like buying a pair of shoes or clothes. Most consumers usually don't comparison shop for these items; they simply try something on, and if it's comfortable and attractive they buy it. But we think buying a bed isn't a fashion choice. You don't have to look good in your mattress. You want to shop for comfort, but you should also be able to shop for price.

This bedding industry tactic occasionally draws the attention of the government. Both the Connecticut and New York state legislatures have considered laws that would put an end to the comparables system, and the Federal Trade Commission did a preliminary investigation into the trade practice, but nothing has changed. Let's face it, regulating the mattress industry isn't exactly the government's top priority; so you'll need to protect yourself. Comparison shopping for a mattress isn't totally impossible and later on we'll give you some shopping strategies to ensure you get a fair deal. (See Consumer Challenge: Dare to Compare)

Sales, Lies, and Videotape

Our hidden camera investigation for the *Today* show revealed that running bogus sales and using high-pressure sales tactics are rampant in the mattress industry. Although the practices have gotten many stores in trouble with the law, they're such effective techniques that they're still prevalent in the industry. Salespeople are taught that once a customer leaves their store, odds are they're not coming back. Since most mattress salespeople get paid by commission, if they can't close the deal, they don't get paid.

"Buying a car was easier," says Todd, who was surprised at the high-pressure sales techniques he encountered while shopping for his mattress. "The salespeople say they just want you to be comfortable, but at the same time they're sort of hovering over you." Todd found that just about every store he went to had a big sale going on. "At one store the salesman threw like twenty different sales at me," recalls Todd. "He said, 'Didn't you read the paper! Big Sale! Big Sale!' " Todd also says that almost everywhere he shopped the store's sales staff made him feel like it was the last possible day he'd be able to get the special deal. "They were like this is the last second you're going to get this price," he says. "There was a real immediacy about the whole thing."

Retailers know that the notion of a "sale" always creates a feeling of urgency and gives the customer an additional incentive to buy. Consumers assume a sale is a rare event, but in the mattress biz there's often a sale every week. When the Labor Day Weekend Sale is over, the Bonus Saving Sale starts, followed by the Big Anniversary Sale, the Blowout Sale, and the Coupon Sale. We shopped at ten stores, eight had sales going on. Our experience at a New Jersey mattress discount store was typical. When we asked for the price of the specific mattress we wanted, the saleswoman said, "Are you looking to purchase now? I got a one-day sale working." Imagine our good fortune when the special one-day sale could save us over $400. When we told the saleswoman we wanted to get a cup of coffee and think about it she said, "You're going to think about a price like that?" She told us the price was good for that night only and the next day the bed would be back up to its regular price of $919. As we walked out of the store she warned, "I'm not kidding you, they're running one-day sales." However, we had the feeling that she was kidding, so we sent a coworker back to the same store five days later. Sure enough, the bed was still on sale.

The department stores we shopped at had their own trick.

While there is less sales pressure, these stores often use a technique known in the retail world as "high-low pricing." That's when a store sets prices at an initially inflated price for a limited period of time and then discounts the merchandise for weeks, making an item sound like it's on sale. For instance, the regular price for one queen-size set at one major department store was $1,735. But, thanks to a week-long sale, the price was dropped to $779. It may sound great, but the fact is that most department stores sell few beds at the ridiculously high "regular" price. We couldn't find any other store that sold a comparable bed for over $800. High-low pricing practices are a gray area of federal and state laws. As long as a store occasionally sells their merchandise at the higher price, it's not illegal. But some stores don't even bother trying to sell beds at "regular" prices. Sales that never end are a deceptive and fraudulent business practice and occasionally a state attorney general slaps a store with a fine or penalty, but the effect is usually only temporary.

Another illegal maneuver to beware of is the old bait and switch. For example, a store will advertise a mattress at a great price, but when you go to buy the mattress the salesperson tells you it's either not available or they bad mouth it and attempt to switch you to a more expensive mattress. They might try to sell you a mattress made by a company you never heard of. An off-brand might be cheaper, but they're frequently of lower quality. Off-brand mattresses also often have a large markup, so the store can make a bigger profit if they can get the consumer to switch. Generally it's best to stick with mattresses made by manufacturers you recognize. However beware, even the major manufacturers make cheap beds that are known in the industry as the "promotional" or "sub-premium" line. These beds are also of inferior quality and probably not suitable for most people. Remember, quality costs money, but if you're being pressured to buy or you're uncomfortable with a salesperson's technique, simply walk out of the store.

Let's Make a Deal

You'll find more old-fashioned and intense haggling at a mattress store than a used-car lot. During our undercover shopping trips the salespeople tried some real doozies on us. High-pressure humdingers like: "Let me ask you this. If I can get my boss to do it for $795, would you take it? I mean, I can't do any better than that—that's the cost of the mattress." And, "Are you ready to make a decision today? Tell you what: It will run you $599 for the set—save you $200." At most every mattress store the price tag—even on sale items—was very negotiable.

If you're not good at haggling, don't worry. Once a salesperson sees you're a serious customer or if you try to walk out the door, prices will magically start dropping, sometimes by hundreds of dollars. Though once they do, you'll feel the sales pressure intensify. If you tell a salesperson you want to shop around, they'll probably demand you leave a refundable deposit to guarantee the special price. Don't give in to the pressure. A price that's good today should still be good tomorrow. We don't recommend leaving a deposit, but if you do, make sure it's completely refundable.

Personally we despise high-pressure haggling. If a salesperson is willing to drop a price by hundreds of dollars at the drop of a hat, it means the store's price tags have no credibility, and it makes us wonder what the mattress is really worth. But if you want to get a bed at a good price, you often have to play the game. Even buying a mattress over the phone can be a hassle. You'll find that those 800 numbers will often quote a different price for the same mattress each time you call. In addition, keep in mind you can haggle over price with telephone retailers as well. If the bargain-bazaar atmosphere isn't for you, try shopping at department stores. Prices are usually nonnegotiable and there's a lot less sales pressure. However, you'll probably end up paying a little more for the calm and convenience.

Don't Let the Bedbug Bite

In the mattress industry that old phrase has new meaning. Have you ever wondered what happens to an old mattress? Some are recycled, which sounds like a sensible ecological practice until you hear the details. There are companies that specialize in taking old mattresses and simply putting new covers on them. They're called rebuilt or reconditioned beds, and they're sold at cut-rate prices. Rebuilt bedding is a multi-million dollar industry and experts estimate that in urban areas it accounts for up to 10 percent of all mattresses sold. Stores that sell reconditioned beds are naturally supposed to tell their customers exactly what they're getting. However, in 1997, a New York City Department of Consumer Affairs undercover investigation revealed that 45 percent of the stores inspected failed to identify their mattresses as used. "These kinds of sleazy sales tactics are not oversights," says Consumer Affairs Commissioner José Maldonado. "They are clear-cut cases of misrepresentation."

On the outside, reconditioned mattresses look like new, so it's easy for the unsuspecting consumer to be fooled. But rip off the new cover and you might find old padding soiled with urine, feces, or blood. Our colleagues at *Dateline NBC* bought nine rebuilt beds in three states—Maryland, New York, and California—at used furniture and small bedding stores. In every case a new cover had been sewn on top of the old soiled padding and foam. A forensic scientist analyzed the beds and found all nine beds contaminated with bacteria. The analysis also found dangerous levels of fungi, and yes, bedbugs. Even rebuilt mattresses that were supposedly sterilized contained high levels of contamination.

Most states don't have laws requiring sterilization and/or tagging of rebuilt mattresses to alert consumers that they are used products. Even the nineteen states that do have such laws on the books don't have the staff needed to enforce them. Here's what you can do to protect yourself.

•*Check the Tag.* You know the one. It has the scary, "do not remove this tag under penalty of law" warning. If you don't see one of these tags on a mattress you're considering, don't buy it. In states that require used mattresses to be tagged, usually a yellow tag indicates a supposedly rebuilt but sterilized bed and a red tag connotes a mattress that's been exposed to infectious or contagious diseases. Remember, the system can vary from state to state, and most have no regulation at all.

•*Try it Out.* If the bed is lumpy or making suspicious creaking and squeaking sounds, don't buy it, regardless of the price.

•*Check the Warranty.* Most new beds come with a ten to twenty-five–year warranty from the manufacturer. Used beds come with nothing.

•*Ask Around.* Run the name of the mattress store you're considering buying from by your local consumer affairs agency or Better Business Bureau. Stick with reputable stores that carry well-known brands.

SHOPPING STRATEGY
At this point we've probably scared and disgusted you to the point where you're thinking that old bed of yours isn't so lumpy after all. Fear not. Here we arm you with some shopping tips to ease the trauma of mattress hunting and help you find a bed that's just right.

BEDDING BASICS
Before you actually start visiting different stores, decide what you can afford to spend. There are so many models and such a wide range of prices that you'll save time and frustration by determining your budget up front. To get a good quality bed expect to pay at least $450 for a twin set, $600 for a full, $800 for a queen set and $1,000 for a king. Of course, you can spend a lot more than that. There has been a real industry push to create super premium beds costing from $2,000 to, believe it or not, $7,000. Such extravagance really isn't necessary. Features like a cashmere cover and brass air vents are overkill. Also, consider how the bed will be used. Obviously, a mattress set for a

guest room doesn't need to be as durable as one that's used every night.

When you hit the bedding stores, make sure to wear comfortable clothes and shoes you can slip off. When testing out a mattress, don't just sit on the edge and bounce up and down. You need to assume the prone position. You might feel self-conscious, but don't be embarrassed. The sales staff is used to it and they know that lying down is the only way to judge if a mattress is comfortable for you. This is a purchase that should last you ten years and that you'll use almost every night, so don't rush your decision. Spend a good ten minutes testing out any bed you're seriously considering. If your salesperson is hovering over you, don't be afraid to ask him or her for a few minutes of privacy.

Lying Down on the Job: Some Things to Consider
A knowledgeable salesperson should be able to determine your needs and help you narrow down your bedding choices based on variables like your sleeping position, weight, and body type. However, only you can determine the bed that's right for you. It's purely personal preference, but it helps to consider some basic criteria.

> **Space:** The average person turns about fifty times in their sleep each night, so you want some room to maneuver. When it comes to mattresses, bigger is definitely better. You want to have enough room to move, especially if you're sleeping with a partner. Here are the standard mattress sizes and dimensions:

Twin: 39″ wide × 75″ long
Full: 53″ wide × 75″ long; also known as a double bed
Queen: 60″ wide × 80″ long
California Queen: 60″ wide × 84″ long
King: 76″ wide × 80″ long
California King: 72″ wide × 84″ long

Comfort: Some folks like their bed hard, some like them soft; like Goldilocks, only you can determine the bed that's just right. The amount of cushioning or upholstery determines the comfort level for most people. That's the padding between you and the innerspring coils. There're two to eight layers of cushioning on the average mattress, each layer being anywhere from 12¼ inch to 2 inches thick. Plush and cushy mattresses will lose some of their loft and settle over time. Some premium beds have thick pillow tops on the mattress, but beware that this extra padding often starts to sag over time leaving an indentation, and because the pillow tops are sewed right onto the mattress, they can't be replaced easily. If you like your bed cushy, consider buying a thick mattress pad.

Support: Gauging mattress support can be more difficult than determining its comfort. When you mattress shop you'll hear the word "support" mentioned dozens of time. Salespeople and manufacturers also use terms like firm, super firm, ultra firm, extra firm, premium firm, and cushion firm. It gets to the point where the word "firm" has no real meaning. To make things more confusing, each major manufacturer offers several firmness levels and their definitions can't be compared with other brands. One company's "firm" bed might be harder than another brand's "super firm" bed.

The support or firmness of a bedding set comes from two places: the coils in the mattress and the box spring under the mattress. The amount of support depends on a person's weight. One mattress might support a 140-pound person, but not a 240-pound person. If you share your bed, you and your partner need to shop together. If one of you is heavier than the other, you need to make sure the bed is compatible for both of you. If the lighter person keeps rolling into the heavier one, it's not the bed for you.

Orthopedic experts say you can make your spine smile by buying the firmest mattress that you find comfortable. You want a mattress that supports your spine with little lateral bending. The mattress should contour to your body so there aren't a lot of gaps or spaces between you and the mattress. If a mattress is too firm, it can actually cut off your circulation, too soft and you'll get lower back pain. Remember, a salesperson can guide you along, but you have to decide based on personal preference. "The salespeople give you their spiel and talk about the scientific reason for this and that," says our mattress shopper, Todd, "but basically the most important thing is to find a bed that's comfortable to you."

Depth: Mattresses used to be about 7 inches thick, but today they are more than a foot in depth. Often the more expensive the mattress, the thicker the padding. You should realize that depending on the depth, you might have to buy special high contour or deep-pocketed sheets or use special lengthening straps on the regular sheets you already own.

Rest Easy: Finding the Store That's Right for You

You can buy a mattress at a furniture store, specialty shop, department store, factory-direct retailer, or even by telephone. Each has its advantages and disadvantages. For instance, department stores usually don't use high-pressure sales techniques and the shopping environment is relaxed, but the prices tend to be higher. At specialty stores the salespeople can drive you bonkers, but you can usually bargain your way to a good deal. You can't beat the convenience of ordering by phone, but it's risky since you can't try out what you're buying until it arrives at your home. Even if the telephone sales representative tells you a mattress is comparable to the model you liked in a store, there's no guarantee. To get the best deal it pays to shop at a variety of stores and pick the shopping environment that's best for you. There are plenty of reputable stores with knowledgeable sales staffs, so if you think a salesperson isn't attentive to your needs simply walk out the door.

Consumer Challenge: Dare to Compare

The mattress industry's name game makes it difficult to comparison shop, but it's not impossible. Consider it a challenge because by daring to compare you can save hundreds of dollars. Not only will you be able to compare prices but you'll increase your knowledge and leverage when it's time to negotiate the price.

Your first instinct might be to call the manufacturer and just ask which models are comparable, but that won't do much good. Manufacturers guard that top secret information as if it's a matter of national security. Retailers will often point out mattresses that are similar to their competitors' models, but there is no guarantee they're telling the truth. Beware of vague claims from salesperson, like, "Yeah this model is every bit as good as the one you saw in the other store." All retailers have a "comp list" Each store compiles this list so they know the names of all comparable models and can ensure that they're pricing their own mattresses competitively. If a salesperson sees you're a serious customer, he or she might share this confidential information if you ask.

You can also find comparable models by doing a little detective work yourself. First find two or three beds you're interested in buying, then jot down the model name and some of the specs. Most manufacturers offer their dealers bed-end cards to display with each bed. Treat the information on these cards like an ingredients list. It's the key to detecting comparable models with different names. Make note of the manufacturer, the model line and the name, Simmons Beautyrest Royalty, for instance. Then check the display card or ask the salesperson for specifics like coil count, coil gauge, innerspring system, box spring construction, cover fabric, comfort level (firm or ultra firm), cushioning materials, and the length of the warranty. In addition write down any special features like extra edge support. Also make a note of the stitching pattern in the quilting. Although the color of the ticking will change from store to store, the stitching design often remains the same. (For instance, the rounded diamond stitching on the Sealy Eton is also used on the Essex and Hanover, a clue that these are essentially identical models.) You should be able to take your notes to the next store and find the comparable model. If you have access to the Internet, surf the mattress manufacturer's Web page to find more clues. You won't see individual model names, but you'll see the specs of each of the various mattress lines or levels they offer, which can help you recognize comparable models at each store.

If you find that the comparable model is not quite as comfortable in another store, it might not be your imagination. Remember that although the comparable models are usually very similar there might be differences, some significant. In a 1997 *Consumer Reports* investigation, the magazine found that different mattresses that were supposed to be comparable models were actually quite different. When their technical staff dissected three "comparable" Serta Perfect Sleeper sets, they found the coil system was identical, but the amount of padding and firmness level varied considerably. Although all the sets were well made, the variations resulted in different feels. Another word of warning: Occasionally manufacturers will change product specifications and materials, but keep the model name the same, so the mattress you saw in the showroom could be quite different from the one that is delivered to your home.

Once you have found comparable models and are sure that they're similar, it's time to negotiate the best price. Most bedding stores, mattress telephone services, and even some department and furniture stores will meet or beat a competitor's price. But don't buy at the first store you go to just because they say they'll match the price if you find it lower somewhere else. After all, what sane person continues to look for a mattress after they've bought one? Another trick the store might try is to refuse to match a competitor's price, claiming that since the names are different the products aren't the same. Regardless, armed with your new knowledge you can shop at a minimum of three stores, play one store against another, and ultimately find a bed that's comfortable for both you and your wallet.

Rude Awakening: Don't Sleep Through the Fine Print

While everyone wants to get a bargain, don't jump at a rock-bottom price without considering the store's reputation and service. Although comparing mattress model prices is difficult, it's easy to compare service among stores. Review the charges for delivery, set-up, removal of your old bedding, and a bed frame. Many stores might throw these extras in for free to close the deal. You also need to ask about refund and exchange policies. Most stores don't offer refunds, but many have some sort of "comfort exchange policy" that allows you to exchange your mattress within a certain time period, usually about a month, if you're not satisfied. Understand all the terms of the policy. Often when you exchange a mattress you won't be able to negotiate the price of the replacement bed so you'll end up having to pay more for the new mattress. You should also find out if the store will charge you additional service or delivery fees if you decide to make an exchange. If you're buying a mattress over the phone, sight unseen, make sure it comes with a generous refund policy.

Verify that your sales receipt has the model and name of the mattress you're buying and it doesn't allow the store to make substitutions, otherwise if the model you ordered is out of stock, the store could deliver an "equivalent" mattress. Also get the delivery date in writing, because the salesperson's promise of next day delivery could end up arriving two weeks late. With the date in writing, should your delivery get delayed for an extended period of time, you should be able to cancel your order and get a full refund.

Before you buy you should also take a look at the manufacturer's warranty, but recognize that a long warranty does not guarantee quality. Most mattress warranties are for ten to twenty-five years, which sounds a lot better than it is because they are quite limited. Frequently the warranty only covers manufacturing defects like a bad spring, and doesn't protect against problems caused by general wear and tear. If the manufacturer determines you abused the bed, say there's a stain on the cover or your kids were jumping on it, your warranty will be void. In addition many warranties are prorated, so for each year you own the bed, you'll get less money for the repair or replacement cost.

When your new bed is delivered, inspect it carefully. Make sure it's the model you ordered and is in good condition. If there are any problems, don't be intimidated, simply refuse delivery. Don't remove that "Do Not Remove Under Penalty of Law" tag. Although you won't be arrested if you cut it off, you'll need it and your receipt to take advantage of your warranty.

Finally it's time to put on the sheets and get some rest.

Sweet Dreams: Taking Care of Your New Bed

After going through the ordeal of buying a new bed, you don't want to have to do it again soon. If you give your new bed set a little tender loving care, you'll extend its life. First off, tell the kids it's not a trampoline. Even little feet jumping will break down the inner construction of the mattress. When you move the mattress don't bend or fold it or lift the bed by the handles. The handles are meant to help you position the bed once it's on the foundation and will not support the full weight of the mattress. Also protect your bed with a good mattress pad.

During the first six months you have your new bed you should turn the mattress over and end-to-end once a month. After that you should turn it twice a year. Rotating the bed will equalize the wear and tear and ensure the bed stays comfortable longer. If your bed is very plush or has a pillow-top, rotate it more often because it will tend to show body impressions more quickly. Don't forget to rotate your box spring at least once a year also.

▶ Top Ten Tips

1. *Shop at reputable stores.* Stick with stores that carry well-known brands, and beware of cheap reconditioned (used) mattresses. Ask friends and coworkers for store referrals. If you aren't confident with the salesperson, or he or she is pressuring you to buy, leave the store.

2. *Set your price.* A good mattress isn't cheap. Expect to spend about $800 for a quality queen-sized set, although you'll find mattresses for much less and much more. You can save a lot of shopping time by only looking at mattresses that are within your budget.

3. *Shop for comfort.* You and your spine are looking for a mattress that offers superior comfort as well as good support. You don't want to buy a rock-hard bed thinking you'll just get used to it. Don't just shop for a bargain; you're looking for value. A mattress on sale at a great price is no bargain if you wake up sore each morning. The same rules apply if you're buying a mattress for your child. A durable high quality bed will help ensure a good night's sleep for years to come.

4. *Use the salesperson's knowledge.* Finding a mattress that's comfortable is a personal decision, but a competent salesperson can guide you through the process. With dozens of mattresses in a typical showroom, they can help you find a bed that suits your needs and your budget. If you think a bed is too soft, they should be able to lead you to a model that offers more support. A qualified salesperson can also explain the various models and clarify why one bed feels different than another. If the salesperson can't answer your questions, find a store that has a sales staff who can.

5. *Lie down on the job.* You won't consider buying a car without a test drive. Well, you'll use your mattress more and possibly own it longer than your automobile. So, wear

some comfortable clothes and get horizontal. Lie down on the bed the way you normally sleep and close your eyes. Don't be embarrassed. Ask the salesperson to give you some time, and spend at least ten minutes on any bed you're considering. If you share the bed, make sure you and your partner go shopping together so you can find a mattress that is compatible for both of you.

6. *Shop around.* Comparing prices is such a challenge one consumer suggested mattress stores should put up signs that say, "No shoplifting or comparison shopping." It does take effort to compare prices, but it's worth it. Once you become familiar with how the name game works, you can shop for price. Investing the time to shop around can save you hundreds of dollars. Try to persuade the salesperson to show you their confidential comparison list.

7. *Negotiate.* It's a competitive market and mattresses have huge markups, so make the retailer work to get your business. A price can drop by $200 the moment you start to walk out the door. Bargaining for a bed is pretty easy if you've done your homework and shopped around. You'll get the best price if you play one store against another.

8. *Take your time.* Don't be intimidated. Most mattress salespeople work on commission and they are trained not to let you leave the store without closing the sale. You're bound to hear high-pressure sales tactics like, "If I cut $100 off the price will you buy it right now?" Don't give in to pressure. Stores also use "special" sales to create urgency that motivates you to buy, but these sales are often bogus. The moment one sale ends the next one begins. An offer that's good today should be good tomorrow. Some stores will let you put down a deposit to guarantee the sales price, but make sure your money is fully refundable.

9. *Read the fine print.* Verify the quoted price includes both the mattress and the box spring. Ask about the price for delivery, set up, and the removal of your old bed. Understand all the restrictions of the store's return and exchange

policy. Make sure the sales receipt doesn't allow the store to substitute an "equivalent mattress," if the one you want is out of stock. Finally, get the delivery date in writing.

10. *Take advantage of the comfort guarantee.* If after a week or two you find that your new bed just isn't comfortable, exchange it for another model. Sure, you might have to pay more for a replacement, but it's a small price to pay for a good night's sleep.

Glossary

Coil count: Number of coils in a mattress. Determines how well the mattress will contour to the body. A full-size mattress should have at least 300 coils, however, a high coil count is not necessarily better.

Comparables: Mattress industry practice in which similar models are given different names at different stores to make it harder for consumers to comparison shop.

Foundation (or box spring):   support system upon which the mattress rests. Meant to work with the mattress to provide cushioning and support.

Full (or double):   Mattress 53″ wide × 75″ long.

High-Low pricing: Promoting a sale price based on an inflated regular price so the customer thinks he or she is getting a huge discount.

Innerspring: Metal spring system composed of hundreds of wire coils that respond to the pressure of the body and give the mattress its support.

King: Mattress 76″ wide × 80″ long.

Plush: Mattress that offers more cushioning for a softer and fluffier level of comfort.

Prorated warranty: The amount of coverage depreciates over a set number of years that the customer owns the product. Offers less protection than a regular warranty.

Queen: Mattress 60″ wide × 80″ long.
Twin: Mattress 39″ wide × 75″ long.
Wire gauge: Thickness of innerspring's wire coils.
The lower the gauge, the thicker the wire. Generally,
thicker wires are less flexible and more durable.

CHAPTER 9

MOVING

Humorist Dave Barry has some helpful advice if you're planning to pack up your entire life and move it: "Don't do it. Set fire to your household goods right now and just walk away from them without so much as a backward glance!" While Mr. Barry may be exaggerating a bit, studies have shown that moving is the third most traumatic event in a person's life (following death of a loved one and divorce). Considering that almost 42 million Americans move each year, there are plenty of stressed-out folks.

The mere idea of pulling up roots is traumatic enough. It gets worse when you add the physical and emotional exhaustion of boxing up all your worldly possessions and seeing them loaded onto a truck and driven away by strangers. In this frazzled state, you're primed for a rip-off, and with hundreds of dishonest moving companies out there waiting to take advantage of you, it's easy to see why Mr. Barry's bonfire idea doesn't sound so bad.

AMERICA ON THE MOVE
Moving is big business—a $7 billion-a-year industry. While thousands of moves go off without a hitch every week, plenty of disreputable companies are giving consumers nightmares and the industry a bad name. Even honest companies have dishonest people working for them. Each year the moving industry ranks near the top of the Better Business Bureau's list of total number of complaints against businesses. If your move is being paid for by your employer, there's probably less to worry about. If something goes wrong, at least you have your corporation to back you up. For consumers who are paying their own way, there's less protection. And professional moving is expensive. The aver-

age cost of an interstate move is estimated at $3,700. Plus, the process is complicated; there's a great deal of paperwork and fine print. By the time a consumer realizes the mistakes he or she made during a move, it's usually too late.

In this chapter we'll explain how the moving process works, the different options you have, and how to arm yourself with the knowledge you'll need to ensure a safe trip for yourself and your possessions.

TYPES OF MOVES: LOCAL, INTRASTATE, AND INTERSTATE

When hiring a moving company, your move is generally classified as one of three basic types—local, intrastate, or interstate. The main differences between the three are the distance you're moving, whether you cross state lines, the way you're charged, and who regulates your move. Here's how the American Moving and Storage Association, the national trade association of the moving industry, generally defines each move.

Local: A move is considered local if the distance traveled is no more than sixty miles within one state. It's estimated that 85 percent of all moves in the United States are local ones. Local move charges usually are based on the number of hours it takes to complete the job. .

Intrastate: An intrastate move is one over sixty miles within the same state. Generally, this type of move should be billed by the weight of your shipment and the actual distance traveled. (Keep in the mind that this sixty-mile figure isn't written in stone. Different organizations or state regulations might use a figure slightly higher or lower.)

Interstate: This involves a move across state lines. Charges for interstate moves usually are based on the weight of your shipment and the distance traveled. These rates are regulated by the federal government.

LOCAL AND INTRASTATE MOVES

Just because you're moving down the street doesn't mean you can't be scammed. Following are the things you need to know if you're planning a local or intrastate move. If you're moving a long distance within the same state and it can't be completed in one day, you might want to take a look at the interstate moving section later in this chapter for some additional advice.

Who's Protecting Your Possessions?

One of the biggest misconceptions about any type of move is that the government will protect the consumer if something goes wrong. Unfortunately, this misleading idea can cost you a lot of money. It's important to understand that when you hire a mover, you're buying a service, similar to buying a sofa or a microwave. If you're not satisfied or have problems, it's usually up to you, not the government, to resolve the matter, sometimes in court.

Both local and intrastate moves are regulated by the state where the move takes place. With fifty states, each one regulating movers in a different way, things can get confusing. Some states license moving companies and have laws on the books to protect consumers. However, several states are totally deregulated and don't even require movers to have a license to operate. As a spokesperson for Central Florida's Better Business Bureau told us, "Pretty much all you need is a driver's license and a pickup truck, and you can call yourself a mover." Besides Florida, other states that have little or no regulation and don't require movers to have a license are Alaska, Arizona, Delaware, Idaho, Maine, Maryland, South Dakota, Tennessee, Utah, Vermont, Wisconsin, and Wyoming.

The agencies that regulate movers and handle consumer complaints in each state vary widely. For example, in California, moving companies fall under the jurisdiction of the Public Utilities Commission, while in New York movers are regulated by the state Department of Transportation (DOT). States with strict moving laws might require companies to provide estimates that guarantee the price of your move, offer a variety of insurance coverage for your shipment, or address your complaints within a certain period of time after your move. But even states with such rules in place find they frequently don't have the power or resources to enforce them and put law-breaking companies out of business. For instance, New York's DOT has levied fines of hundreds of thousands of dollars on companies skirting the law, but 55 percent of those fines go unpaid each year. When New York actually revokes an operator's license, the company often simply changes its name and applies for a new license. Many companies defy the DOT completely and operate without a license. What does this all mean to you? Buyer Beware.

Households Held Hostage

The major consumer complaint about in-state moves is low-ball estimates. When your shipment arrives at your new home, you're expected to pay the full balance of the bill before the moving van is unloaded. This final bill can be hundreds of dollars more than the original estimate. Unfortunately, at this point you have little recourse; if you don't pay the bill, the driver may threaten to take off with your stuff until you pay up. It's a typical story we've heard many times.

Milton and his family were moving about five miles within the state of New Jersey. He got several price estimates to move his two-bedroom apartment and signed with the company that offered the lowest estimate of $300. At the time, Milton knew the estimate was too low, but he figured that even if he ended up paying more, it would still be cheaper than any other company. When the movers arrived at his apartment, they immediately jacked up the price to $800. "What was I going to do?" asks Milton. "It was the last day of the month, my lease was up, and I didn't have a choice." Milton had packed most of the apartment himself, but the movers had to wrap some furniture and fragile items. When they got to his new home, they demanded $1,900, which included $350 for bubble wrap, $150 for boxes, and $75 for tape. The movers refused to unload his belongings until he paid up. "It was complete extortion," recalls Milton, still angry about the incident today. "It's like they put a gun to my head. They had all my stuff in their truck. They had my kids' beds. I didn't know what to do, so I jumped in the truck and just sat there and told them I was staying there until they started unloading." The police soon showed up, but when Milton realized the officers weren't going to do anything to help him, he settled with the movers for $1,500. Says Milton, "When they finally got everything into my apartment, I couldn't believe it when they then asked for a tip!"

Milton got what some in the industry call a "spanking." He went for a low-ball estimate, only to be taken in the end. Since local movers usually charge by the hour, unscrupulous companies purposely underestimate the time it will take to do a job, just to get your business. The actual move ends up taking several hours longer than estimated, and exorbitant extra charges for things like packing materials are tacked onto the bill. When customers balk at paying the much-higher cost, the mover threatens to drive off with their belongings.

One former mover told a reporter at Fort Lauderdale's *Sun-Sentinel* how he "spanked" the elderly in Florida: "We would go to the house we were going to move, and if they were old we would get them to sign a contract, pretty much without reading it. Then we would go grab two or three of the most expensive items and put them in the truck. That was called 'leverage.'" Once movers have your stuff, there is little you can do. If you can't pay the bill, they'll put your possessions in storage until you come up with the cash. And every day your things sit in storage adds more to your bill because you're responsible for all warehouse charges.

Some states do have laws to protect consumers from low-ball estimates. In New York, for example, you're only required to pay 25 percent over the original estimated price to get the movers to unload your belongings. You'll then have fifteen days to pay the remainder of the bill. In California, the law is even stronger. Movers are required to give you a written estimate that the final cost cannot exceed. But other states have no such laws.

Regardless of the state you live in, if you don't know your rights, it's easy for a deceitful mover to give you a major "spanking."

Bandit Movers and Highway Robbery

Even states with good regulation find it hard to put unlicensed movers out of business. These scofflaw companies are mostly responsible for giving the moving industry a bad name. "You rarely hear stories in the news about good movers," says Doug Hill, president of the California Moving and Storage Association. "The vast majority of stories you hear are about these 'bandit movers.' " These companies make huge profits by undercutting the prices of legitimate movers and then taking advantage of consumers. When they get a bad reputation, they simply change their name. "We have one guy who's notorious," says Delores Liberatore, of Orlando's Better Business Bureau. "He's had three companies. The first one got a bad reputation, so he started another. When that one got a bad reputation, he changed the name again. They'll do anything to confuse the consumer." And these companies are brazen. They advertise in the phone book and even use fake license numbers in their ads.

Beside getting ripped off, there are additional concerns if you hire an unlicensed mover. Legitimate companies have insurance and worker's compensation for their employees, unlicensed companies don't. If your belongings are destroyed because an uninsured moving truck has an accident, you might not be able to collect a cent. Likewise, if a worker gets injured during your move, since he has no insurance from the moving company, he can turn around and sue you.

Several states are trying something new to stop moving companies that have a high number of egregious complaints against them—criminal prosecution. After a two-year investigation by Fort Lauderdale detectives, the Broward County State Attorney's office charged a local mover with racketeering, extortion, and grand theft. Police claim Prudential Van Lines was making about $3 million a year by deliberately giving customers low-ball estimates, then charging up to four times the original price quote. (This company is not affiliated with the Prudential Insurance Company of America.) One of the prosecutor's witnesses could well be Daye, from North Palm Beach. Based on an estimate of $400, she hired Prudential Van Lines (which was then using another name) to move two chairs, a sofa bed, and some dishes and pots approximately 300 miles. But after her belongings were loaded onto the truck, she says the movers demanded $2,700 in cash. According to Daye, when she called the company's office to complain, she was told to pay up or the truck would leave with her belongings. As of this writing, the case is still pending, but in news reports Prudential's attorney has said that his client committed no crime and is the victim of overzealous prosecutors.

Paying by the Hour: What to Expect

As we've mentioned, local moves usually are charged by the hour. When you get an estimate from a moving company, they'll tell you how many men they think it will take to do the job properly. Depending on the size of your home, you can expect anywhere from two to four movers. The hourly price per man depends on where you live and the prevailing rates in that area. As a general guide, we've found that three men plus a moving van cost from $50 to $80 per hour. In addition, you also can expect to pay for what's called "travel time." Most consumers make the mistake of thinking travel time means the time it takes to get from your old home to your new one. In fact, travel time is the time it takes the movers to drive the truck from their office to your home to start the move. The industry standard for travel time is about an hour and is billed at the same hourly rate as your move. However, travel time is certainly negotiable, especially if the moving company is located close to your home.

Please remember that when you're paying by the hour for anything, it pays to be organized. If you tell your moving company that you'll be completely packed when they arrive, but half your apartment is still unboxed when they get there, it's naturally going to take more time to complete the job, and the extra cost will come out of your pocket.

The Tale of the Tape: Exposing Hidden Charges

In addition to hourly rate and travel time, a plethora of extra charges can make your final moving cost soar. These charges are the bane of many a moving consumer. Tacked on to your bill you might find charges for things such as flights of stairs, elevators, awkward pieces like pianos, and especially packing materials. While these charges are standard and legal, you should know exactly what extras you'll be billed for before you sign up with a company. In addition, it's not uncommon for unethical moving companies to overcharge for these extras. "It was a total nightmare," Marilyn of New York told CNBC's *Steals & Deals*. Marilyn had hired a company to move her after seeing a flyer advertising low rates. She received an estimate over the phone of $147. To save money, she packed almost everything herself. All the movers were supposed to pack were a TV, VCR, computer, and glass tabletop. But Marilyn says when the movers arrived they pressured her into signing a blank packing form. "When they handed me a bill for $900 I almost died. I couldn't believe it," she says. Where did some of these extra charges come from?: $168 for bubble wrap, $77 for tape, and $48 for six mattress covers, even though Marilyn only has one bed. Unfortunately, it was too late for Marilyn. Don't let this happen to you. Never sign any kind of blank packing form or any paperwork that isn't completely filled out. (See "The Paper Trail: Before You Sign on the Dotted Line.")

In any local move, even if you pack everything yourself, there will always be legitimate packing charges, including tape to wrap furniture or other bulky items in blankets and boxes to transport unwieldy plants and frames. These costs can escalate quickly to $100 or more. Guard against these surprise charges by asking your mover exactly what packing materials you'll be charged for so you can work the extra cost into your moving budget.

INTERSTATE MOVES—CROSSING THE LINE

When you pack up all your belongings and move them across state lines, you're faced with a whole different set of potential problems. So before you relocate your life, bone up on your rights and responsibilities.

Who Is Protecting Your Possessions?

Unlike in-state moves, interstate moves are regulated by the federal Department of Transportation. However, while there are plenty of laws in place, the federal government doesn't enforce them or intervene on behalf of consumer complaints.

It wasn't always this way. The 1980 Federal Household Goods and Information Act laid down the law for interstate moving. For fifteen years these basic laws were enforced—and the interstate moving industry regulated—by the Interstate Commerce Commission (ICC), which received 4,500 consumer complaints each year. Unfortunately, due to budget cuts, the ICC was downsized continually until Congress pulled the plug on the agency effective January 1, 1996.

Some of the ICC's responsibilities, including regulation of the moving industry, were transferred to the Department of Transportation's Federal Highway Administration (FHWA). Unfortunately, Congress never gave the DOT the authority or the money to enforce the moving laws for which they were made responsible. In what seems like a classic case of government bureaucracy, the FHWA can accept consumer moving complaints but is forbidden to act on them. "We can't do a damn thing," explains FHWA office director John Grimm. "Sure we can advise the citizen of his rights, but we cannot intervene. Congress has determined that is for the court system." In other words, if you have a complaint about a moving company, you'll probably have to sue to get results. Grimm says that people are often bewildered and upset to learn that there is no government agency to protect them when hiring a mover, but he reminds consumers, "There is no federal agency that's going to protect you from unscrupulous building contractors or used cars salesmen either. There are laws and there are regulations, but there is no federal agency that's going to go out there and argue with your mover about the fact that he quoted you $3,000 but won't unload your furniture without $9,000."

Grimm goes on to explain that while the FHWA does license interstate movers, it makes no evaluation of their honesty. If a company meets a few basic requirements and pays a $300 registration fee, the agency must give it a license. "We can do things like evaluate a company's safety record and insurance coverage, but we make no evaluation of a company's morality," says Grimm. "Just because they have a license doesn't mean they're not crooks."

One government source in the industry told us he thinks things have gotten worse since the ICC was abolished: "I just have the feeling that there are a few bad apples out there who are suddenly aware that they are not being regulated that tightly, and they are taking advantage of it more than they were before." So where does this leave the consumer? Well, if you have a problem with an interstate move, it's a catch-22. The regulating agency in your state can't help you because it's out of their jurisdiction, and while the federal government can tell you the laws, it can't enforce them.

Now, more than ever, it's vital to do your homework to ensure you've chosen a reputable mover. Your mover should provide you with a handbook titled "Your Rights and Responsibilities When You Move," which outlines many of the federal rules and regulations. You also can obtain a copy from your regional office of the FHWA. By learning about your rights and your mover's responsibilities, you can protect yourself and your possessions.

Van Lines: How the Big Guys Work
There are about 3 million interstate moves each year. The majority of these moves are done by the approximately twenty-five

national van lines that include Allied, Atlas, Bekins, Mayflower, North American, and United. While these names probably sound familiar, the way they operate can be confusing.

It's important to understand that a van line itself doesn't move anyone. The national companies don't even own any trucks or equipment. They rely on a system of approximately 4,500 affiliated local agents across the country who do the actual moves. Usually more than one affiliated agent will be involved in a single move, which can be a potential problem for consumers. Here's how it works: When you sign up with an affiliated agent of a national van line, that agent becomes the booking agent. The booking agent provides the price estimate, handles all the initial paperwork, and registers your move with the national van line. The van line's dispatching network will then assign your move to an actual truck heading in the direction of your new home. The agent who actually moves your shipment is the hauling agent. It's important to realize that the booking and hauling agents could be two different companies. Once your shipment arrives at your new home, a local destination agent will help unload it. The driver of the truck, also called the van foreman, works for the hauling agent. In most cases the driver who picks up your shipment is the person who drives it to its destination and supervises the unloading. The driver is ultimately responsible for getting your belongings to your new home safely and on time.

Unfortunately, you have little control over which agents are involved in your move after you've booked with a van line. This can be a problem since one agent might be more reliable than another. For example, Sue recently moved from New York City to Los Angeles. When she opened the yellow pages to find a national van line, she discovered there were several local agents in the New York area affiliated with each line. After investigating several agents, she chose one and booked her move. On the day of her move, she learned that the hauling agent, who would be moving her belongings cross country, was not the original booking agent she had signed up with. While her shipment was in transit, Sue had some concerns about the delivery date and charges on her bill. She says she quickly discovered that even though the booking agent had come to her home and sold her on the van line, he no longer felt any responsibility to provide customer service or assistance. The booking agent and hauling agent simply blamed each other for the move's problems. Sue says it was a frustrating to deal with two different agents, neither of whom would take responsibility. While the national van lines do try to set a standard of service, there are always unreputable agents, and it takes time to weed them out.

You might be curious, with all these different agents involved, who actually gets your money. An industry insider told us that the national van lines take about 10 percent of the revenue of every move. Twenty percent goes to the booking agent who sold you on the company, and 20 percent goes to the local hauling agent. The remaining 50 percent is for the driver, who does most of the hard work.

There are also some independent moving companies that serve the public without being affiliated with a van line. These companies can offer reasonable rates on interstate moves because they're smaller and have less overhead than the national van lines. But hire independent movers with caution. Make sure they have an interstate license to operate in all the states between your old and new homes. If they have a limited license, they'll have to relay your shipment to a licensed mover, or illegally haul it themselves.

Cost Considerations: Is the Price Right?
As we mentioned before, the cost of an interstate move is largely determined by two things: the weight of your shipment and the total distance of your move. These two factors combine to determine what the industry calls the "linehaul charge," which is regulated by the federal government. Never deal with a mover who wants to charge you an hourly rate for an interstate move.

Weight is determined by actually putting the moving truck on a scale. Before the movers arrive at your home, the truck is weighed at a state-certified weigh station. This determines what's called the tare weight. The truck is weighed again after your shipment is loaded. This weight subtracted from the tare weight determines how much your shipment weighs. Occasionally the mover will do a "destination weighing," which means that they'll get the tare weight after they drop off your possessions. This will not affect the accuracy of the measurement, but the mover won't be able to determine your exact bill until after he unloads your shipment.

Be aware that if you have an unusually small shipment, many van lines have a minimum weight of 1,000 pounds, and you'll be charged based on that weight. Movers must advise you of a minimum weight requirement. If they fail to do so, your move should be based on the actual weight.

By law, consumers must be given a copy of the weight tickets for their move. These tickets should include your name and shipment number as well as the truck's I.D. number. In addition, you have the right to observe each weighing. According to federal regulations, "The mover is required to inform you of the specific location of each scale that will be used and to allow you a reasonable opportunity to be present."

Even if you're not present at the weighing, but believe the weight is incorrect, federal law permits you to request a reweigh before your belongings are unloaded at your new home. The mover isn't allowed to charge for this reweighing. Be aware that if the reweight amount is different from the original weight, you'll be charged for the amount of the reweigh whether it's more or less. Before you request a reweighing, you might want to do your own rough estimate. Add up the number of boxes and items of furniture you've moved, then divide the shipment weight by this item total. If the resulting number is between 35 and 45, chances are the weight measurement is accurate. If the total is over 45, you should consider asking for a reweigh.

Although linehaul charges are regulated by the government, most movers will offer you a discount off this price. For example, the tariff-book rate of a move weighing 4,000 pounds and traveling 3,000 miles is about $6,000. But moving companies competing for your business might offer up to 60 percent off this figure. This discount is determined by the marketplace—where you live and where you're moving—and the time of year you're moving. For example, a survey of five of the major van lines found discounts ranging from 46 to 55 percent for a move from New York City to Los Angeles during the fall. Also remember that the summer is always the busiest time for moving and thus the most expensive.

Additional Charges—It's All in the Details

Besides the basic linehaul charge, additional charges will inevitably be added to your bill. In general, most of these charges are not as arbitrary as in local moves. For example, most interstate movers don't charge for the rolls of tape they use. But they will charge for boxes they supply and for any packing or unpacking services that you need. In addition, you'll be charged extra for unwieldy or heavy items like a piano or an automobile. Also, certain appliances like washing machines need to be unhooked and their parts secured before they're moved, so you'll either have to do this yourself or pay your movers to do it for you. If you're moving to or from a large city, most movers will add what's called an "Additional Transportation Charge" (ATC), which compensates them for high labor rates in the area and for such hassles as dealing with traffic. The ATC for New York City is about $200. It's approximately $100 if you're moving to or from Los Angeles.

Customers also are charged for obstacles that might make the movers' work go more slowly. If you're moving to or from an apartment building, you'll be charged extra for each flight of stairs the movers have to go up or down. Fewer than eight steps is not considered a flight, and this charge applies only to apartment-type buildings. You shouldn't be charged for any stairs in a traditional two-story (single-family) house. There's also an extra charge for elevator use since it takes extra time and effort to load and unload it. Another charge is for what the moving industry calls a "long carry." This long-carry charge is based on the distance between the truck and your home's front door. The first 75 feet are free, but for each additional 50 feet (or fraction thereof), you'll be charged extra. In the case of an apartment-type building, remember that the long-carry distance is calculated from the van to the door of your unit, not the entrance of the building itself. To avoid any surprises on moving day, you might want to pull out a tape measure and do a rough estimate yourself. Movers have been known to embellish long-carry distances. The rates movers charge for stairs, elevators, and long carries are set by law; however, movers can discount these rates as they see fit.

There's really not much you can do to avoid these extra charges, since they are determined by factors beyond your control. However, to ensure that you get an accurate price estimate, you should make the booking agent aware of any of these situations before your move.

At the time of your move, you'll be asked to sign a form that lists the additional services performed. Understand exactly what these charges are and if they are correct. Jason (one of your coauthors) learned this from painful and embarrassing personal experience. In his recent cross-country move with a national van line, Jason's driver tried to overcharge him for additional services. He was billed for five flights of stairs even though he lived in a second-floor apartment. Not only did the driver charge double for each flight, but he also considered the two steps that led from the sidewalk to the apartment building as an additional flight. He also estimated the long-carry distance at 290 feet, even though it was less than 75 feet. Not knowing the long-carry rules at the time, Jason initialed the paperwork after the driver assured him he wouldn't be charged extra since the distance was "under 300 feet." He told Jason, "You just need to sign it so I can show my dispatcher that we worked hard." Later, looking at the back of the form where the charges were explained, Jason realized he'd been deceived and had to go through the hassle of getting these charges removed from the final bill. Even those of us who work in the consumer business can be cheated! Learn from Jason's mistake. We'll say it again—read the front and back of any moving form carefully and understand the charges before you sign. (See "The Paper Trail: Before You Sign on the Dotted Line.")

Pickup and Delivery Dates: Covering the Spread

Your idea of pickup and delivery dates is probably to have the movers pick up your shipment on a scheduled day and deliver it on another. By and large, this isn't how the industry works. Most moving companies will offer you a general time period or spread of dates for your shipment to be loaded and delivered. For example, if you need to be out of your home by February 15, your company might offer to pick up your belongings between the twelfth and fifteenth and deliver them anywhere from seven to fourteen days later. We realize this isn't exactly pinpoint accuracy and is inconvenient for the consumer. However, it works this way because your shipment is probably not the only one on the moving van.

Since a household shipment averages about 7,000 pounds and a moving van holds about 30,000 pounds, most likely your possessions will be traveling with other households moving in the same direction. It only makes sense that the first household loaded onto the van will be the last unloaded. Depending where your shipment falls in the loading process, three or four other households could be unloaded before yours. Often the loading schedule isn't set until the last minute. That's why your agent will try to get as much leeway as possible when he or she books your move. However, since the driver who loads your shipment is usually the person who drives it to its destination and unloads it, he usually can narrow down the delivery date, but only on the day he picks up your belongings.

Never agree to have your shipment picked up or delivered "as soon as possible." This is just asking for trouble. The federal government advises that the range of dates you and the mover agree on should be specific. The agreed-upon dates should be entered onto what's called an Order of Service. This document is the initial paperwork you will sign with the mover to schedule your move. These dates must also be entered on the Bill of Lading, which will become your official contract with your moving company. The only defense for not honoring these dates is called "defense of force majeure." This legal mumbo jumbo means circumstances that are unforeseen or beyond the mover's control, such as hurricanes, tornadoes, and other acts of God.

If a moving company is unable to make the contracted pickup or delivery dates, federal law mandates that you be notified by telephone, telegraph, or in person about the delay. At the same time, the company must tell you when the shipment will be picked up and delivered. If you're unable or unwilling to accept these new dates, you should attempt to reach an agreement with the mover for alternate dates.

If your shipment is late and you have to pay for hotels and restaurant meals because of the delay, you can try to recover these expenses from the mover. Reputable companies will reimburse you for these expenses if you file a delay or inconvenience claim. If the company refuses to pay, your only option is to take it to court.

Be aware that federal law also protects the moving companies. If you need to change the contracted delivery dates after your shipment has been picked up, you'll have to try to reach an agreement with your mover. However, the mover isn't required to change the dates and has the right to put your possessions in storage at your expense if you're unable to accept delivery on the dates stated in your contract.

If you need to ensure specific moving dates, most van lines offer a guaranteed service option. For an additional fee, they'll guarantee your pickup and delivery dates. If they fail to meet these dates, they must pay a certain amount of money each day pickup or delivery is delayed. This per diem usually ranges from $75 to $125. Make sure the guaranteed dates and the late charge amount are written into your Bill of Lading. Also, know what the guaranteed service option will cost and what conditions or limitations apply. Since moving companies are all vying for your business, you have some room to negotiate. Companies have been known to throw in their guaranteed service option for free.

SHOPPING STRATEGY FOR IN-STATE AND INTERSTATE MOVES

You've read a few consumer horror stories and learned about some dirty industry tricks. Now we're going to take you through the moving process—from hiring a mover to filing damage claims after the job is done. We don't want to make you paranoid, but we encourage you to go into any move armed with as much information about the process and the specific mover you've hired as possible. This knowledge is definitely your best protection against problems later on. The following advice covers both in-state and interstate moves and should make your move less stressful.

WHEN AND WHERE TO START
Start your moving-company search at least six to eight weeks before your move. Take into consideration the time you're moving. According to the American Moving and Storage Association, the summer—June through August—is when over 35 percent of all Americans move. The end of the month, when most apartment leases expire, is also busier than other times of the month. If you have to move during these peak periods, be sure to book your move well in advance. By starting to plan at least eight weeks ahead, you'll have a better chance of hiring movers who can meet your schedule. However, if you can be flexible and move during an off-peak period, you have a much better chance of getting the pickup and delivery dates you want as well as knocking money off your bill.

There are probably a lot of moving companies in your area, so it's important to narrow down the field. The best place to start is by getting recommendations from family and friends. There's no better way to get the lowdown on a moving company than by talking to people who have experienced it firsthand. If you're computer savvy, you can surf consumer newsgroups on the Internet for moving recommendations and warnings. If possible, try to get at least two opinions of the same company. Anyone can have one great or miserable experience. The yellow pages is a good place to turn to find all the moving companies in your area, but realize that just because a company has a big, full-page ad doesn't mean it's a superior company. Big ads don't necessarily equal reliability or honesty. And remember, even companies that don't have a license to operate still advertise in the phone book.

To Pack or Not to Pack
Let's face it, packing and unpacking are two of the worst things about moving. Searching for boxes behind your local liquor store and diving in supermarket Dumpsters is not a fun way to spend your weekend. Neither is trying to fit all you own neatly and safely in cardboard boxes. It's estimated that moving a four-bedroom home takes 120 to 200 boxes. That's a lot of work, so now is the time to decide if you're going to pack yourself or get professional help.

If you're relocating because of a job, and your move is being paid for by your company, there's no question: Have the movers pack for you. However, if you're paying for the move out of your own pocket, you can save hundreds, in some cases thousands, of dollars by packing yourself. Keep in mind that if you do your own packing, you're taking on more responsibility if things get broken. When you pack a box yourself, a mover isn't liable if anything breaks inside unless there is obvious damage to the outside of the box. On the other hand, there's evidence that moving professionals aren't always expert packers. A *Consumer Reports* magazine survey found that 55 percent of customers who paid movers to pack for them experienced damage, compared to 32 percent who did it themselves.

While liquor, grocery, and drugstores are good places to find boxes, particularly for a local move, you should consider using at least some professional moving boxes too. This is especially true for interstate moves, where a shipment generally travels longer and farther and is shipped with other households. Moving cartons are thicker than regular boxes, which helps protect your possessions, and are uniform in size for easier loading. There are also boxes made especially for things like dishes, clothing, and picture frames, which better protect these items and make packing easier. Movers charge premium prices for boxes. To save money, check your local yellow pages for moving-supply stores in your area. No matter what kind of box you use, it generally should weigh no more than 50 pounds when fully packed and should close completely. Most interstate (and some local) movers have helpful pamphlets that show the do-it-yourself packer how to get professional results. Make sure you ask for one.

When packing yourself, it's important to start far enough in advance of your move. You should start gathering moving materials and packing up things you don't need like books and glassware at least a week before your move date. Packing can be an overwhelming experience, and getting a jump on it will help make things easier. Never pack hazardous materials like paint, gasoline, aerosol cans, nail polish and remover. Check with your moving company for a complete list of forbidden items before you start packing. Your movers will inspect all packed cartons prior to loading them on the van. If they feel they're not properly packed, they can refuse to load the boxes until they're repacked.

For both in-state and interstate moves, everything you're transporting must be boxed, except for large or extremely unwieldy items like sofas, floor lamps, and dining tables. What goes in a box is basically at the discretion of the mover, and if they have to box it themselves it will cost you. During a local move, one New York City couple was charged extra when their movers insisted their floor plants had to be boxed. Even though the plants were simply set inside large, unsealed cartons, and the boxes were taken back by the movers to be used again, the couple was still charged $5 a box.

Packing doesn't have to be an all-or-nothing proposition. It might be worth the extra cost to have your mover pack your most fragile items for you. Such things as glass tabletops, chandeliers, fine crystal and china, and computers and other electronics might be better left to the professionals. But be prepared; it gets expensive. One major van line wanted over $300 to pack a desktop computer for a cross-country move.

A new trend on the moving market is packing services. These services generally are not affiliated with any moving company. They simply come to your home to pack or unpack your possessions. Typically charging $30 per person per hour, not only will they unpack you, they'll set up your kitchen, prepare your bedroom, and even hang up your pictures. Keep in mind that in the eyes of the moving company, when using these independent packing services you are as responsible for damage to your goods as if you packed them yourself.

Never pack anything you feel is irreplaceable. Boxes get damaged, items get lost, even stolen—it's a fact of life in the moving business. In a complaint to Southern California's Better Business Bureau, a San Francisco man claims that, among other things, the company that moved him from Los Angeles lost a box containing the ashes of his deceased friend. Although the moving company denied responsibility, it did pay a small monetary compensation. However, as the consumer told the BBB, "No small amount of money would help considering the sentimental loss this caused." While this example may be a bit extreme, it should make you think twice before handing anything over to a mover. Things you should consider taking with you include photographs and family albums, jewelry, cash, financial and legal documents, and medical records.

Never label the outside of a moving box with its contents. A box labeled "CDs" or "baseball-card collection" might mysteriously disappear before it gets to your new home. Better to label the boxes only with the room where they should be unloaded and a number. Then, in a separate notebook, list the contents of each box by its corresponding number. Not only is this safer, but it helps you dig out your coffeemaker without pillaging ten other boxes first.

Estimate: Making It More Than a Guess
An estimate is what a moving company predicts your move will cost. To secure an estimate, a representative from a moving company will come to your home to see what the job involves. This probably will be your first face-to-face contact with a potential mover. The representative will survey your possessions to determine the total weight of your shipment or how many hours it will take to move it. It's very important to communicate with the agent exactly what you'll be moving. Don't leave anything out. As you walk through your home, point out any items that you won't be taking. Make sure the person notes any items you plan to take that aren't evident, such as things stored in an attic or garage. Open up all your cupboards and closets too. An estimate is useless if you don't give the agent a precise idea of what you need moved.

This is also the time to discuss any items that need special care: a mirror or antique chair you'd like the movers to crate, for example, or a treadmill they'll need to disassemble. You also should show the movers what you want them to pack to see how much extra it will cost.

For local moves, many companies will try to do an estimate over the phone. They'll ask you how many rooms of stuff must be moved and give you an oral estimate. We discourage getting an estimate that isn't in writing. If there's a dispute later, a phone estimate is useless.

There are three types of estimates, nonbinding, binding, and guaranteed not to exceed. It's very important to understand the differences between the three. A nonbinding estimate means there's no guarantee that the final cost will not exceed the estimate. It's merely a guess—an educated one, it is hoped. Just because the estimate is in writing doesn't mean it's accurate. "This baffles most people," says Jerry DeSanto of New York's Better Business Bureau. "When a company comes into your house, looks at your belongings, and gives you a piece of paper that says it's going to cost $1,000 to move, most people assume it's going to cost $1,000 to move, but often the cost is more. Then consumers come to me and say, 'But it's on a piece of paper!' and I have to explain that it's just an estimate." Most moves are based on nonbinding estimates. A mover should never charge to give you a nonbinding estimate.

A binding estimate, on the other hand, is a guaranteed price. When you receive a binding estimate, you aren't required to pay any more than the binding-estimate amount. It doesn't matter how much your shipment weighs or how many hours it takes to move, you still pay only the price agreed upon in the binding estimate. Not every mover offers binding estimates, and some movers will charge to prepare one for you. In a binding estimate, the mover will make detailed notes of your shipment and all the services you need or request. Once you have a binding estimate, come move day, you can't add items you didn't show the agent who originally prepared your estimate. If a large piece of furniture is added, for example, the mover can either revise the estimate or void it completely. Once your shipment is on the van for an interstate move, federal law states that the driver cannot increase the binding estimate or withdraw it because of things like rate increases or miscalculation of the estimated weight of the shipment. However, if unexpected services are needed at your new home, such as a long carry or an elevator you didn't tell your mover about, or if your stuff has to be stored, then the mover can charge extra. A binding estimate also can be voided by the mover if you do not move within a specific period of time, usually sixty to ninety days from the date the estimate is given.

Finally, there's the guaranteed-not-to-exceed estimate, which is a hybrid of the first two. As with the binding agreement, for a guaranteed-not-to-exceed estimate you must show the mover everything you plan to move. Then you'll be given a price. For a move based on weight, if the linehaul charges of your shipment are less than the not-to-exceed estimate, you pay the lesser amount. If they are more, you only have to pay up to the guaranteed-not-to-exceed price.

Getting the Estimate That's Right for You

We strongly recommend trying to get either a binding or guaranteed-not-to-exceed estimate. Be aware that a binding estimate might cost a little more money. After all, movers are in the business to make a profit, and they'll have to pad out a binding estimate to make sure they can cover any unforeseen expenses. But a binding estimate gives you some piece of mind when budgeting your move and helps to avoid ugly surprises at the end. We also like the guaranteed-not-to-exceed estimate since it also gives you some price assurance. When Jason moved from New York to Los Angeles, he picked the only major van line that offered a guaranteed-not-to-exceed estimate. It worked out well. The company originally estimated the weight of his shipment at 5,200 pounds, but the actual weight turned out to be 840 pounds less. He had to pay the price calculated on the lower weight.

Be mindful that just because a company offers you a binding or not-to-exceed estimate doesn't automatically mean it is a legitimate company. You still need to check out the mover before you sign on. We've heard of customers who had binding contracts but still were forced to pay more before the movers would unload their belongings. Also, when you get a binding or not-to-exceed estimate, make sure it's dated and signed by the mover and includes any extra charges or services you know you'll need, like packing, storage, or stair and elevator charges. In addition, make sure any paperwork you are given or asked to sign includes the phrase "binding estimate" or "guaranteed-not-to-exceed estimate."

Unfortunately, for many local and intrastate moves, companies don't offer binding estimates. However, some local moving companies only do moves based on a flat rate. This flat rate is, in essence, a binding estimate and can protect you from surprise charges. If there are flat-rate movers in your area, it definitely makes sense to check them out and at least get an estimate from them.

To be fair, an estimator's job isn't always easy. You'd think they would have figured out how to do it by now, but estimating the price of a move is still far from an exact science. We had five national van lines estimate the weight of a small two-bedroom apartment. All five sent out a salesman to look at the apartment. After their careful calculations, the estimates ranged from 4,200 to 6,125 pounds. That's quite a spread. When the shipment was finally weighed on moving day, the exact amount was 4,360 pounds.

While a nonbinding estimate doesn't guarantee a price, you should know your rights if the total charge ends up being much more than the estimate. For interstate moves, federal regulations are in place to protect you. According to the law, at the time of delivery the mover cannot require you to pay more than the amount on the original estimate plus 10 percent. You then have thirty days after the date of delivery to pay any remaining charges. For example, if you received an original estimate of $3,000 for your interstate move, but the movers are waving a bill that totals $4,000 when they arrive at your new home, you only have to pay $3,300 to have them unload the truck. You'll still owe the company the additional $700, but you'll have thirty days to settle the bill.

Unfortunately, as we mentioned before, with in-state moves the laws differ state to state. To avoid lowball estimates turning into sky-high bills, compare your estimates carefully and ask potential movers specific questions. Make sure you know how many workers the per-hour price includes and if the truck is big enough to haul your belongings in one trip. Find out what additional charges there will be for things like travel time, stairs, elevators, and packing materials.

Whether you're moving locally or long distance, whether you're getting binding or nonbinding estimates, we implore you to get estimates from at least three different companies. Don't automatically go with the lowest bid. Treat bids cautiously. Companies without licenses and companies that do not hire trained movers can afford to charge less. A low bid now could translate into a lot of extra charges down the line.

Making the Right Move: Investigating Your Mover

After you've gotten a few estimates and narrowed down your moving company choices, it's imperative to gather as much information as possible about each company. One of the best ways to ensure that your possessions arrive on time and intact is by taking the time and effort to hire a responsible mover now.

Check out any mover you're considering with your local Better Business Bureau. They can tell you how many customer complaints they've received about a company. For a local move call the government agency responsible for regulating moves in your state. (As we mentioned earlier, the agency responsible for intrastate moves varies greatly from state to state. Check the government listings in your local phone book.) They can tell you if your potential moving company has a license (if required by your state) and how many complaints it has from other customers. To find out if an interstate mover is licensed, call your regional office of the Federal Highway Administration's Office of Motor Carriers or search their database over the Internet (www.safersys.org). It will help to have the company's motor carrier (MC) number, which is the license number assigned by the federal government. In addition, if you're considering using a major van line, you also should call the company's main headquarters to make sure the local agent you're dealing with is actually an affiliate of the national company.

When reviewing the number of complaints against a company, take into consideration how many moves that company does a year. For example, a company that does 3,000 moves a year will most likely have more customer complaints than a company that only does 1,000 moves a year.

You also can do a little footwork. Doug Hill of the California

Moving and Storage Association suggests you pay a visit to the office of any mover you're considering. "Just go in and buy a box," he advises. "This way you can make sure they have a legitimate place of business. By going into their office you'll see the kind of people who work there and how professional they are." Hill says this can help determine if it's a dependable business you can trust with all your possessions.

Insurance: Making Sure You're Covered

While you hope your move goes smoothly, you have to be prepared if it doesn't. When moving an entire household of items—whether across the street or across the country—there's a good chance something is going to get damaged or lost. That's why it's very important to make sure that your possessions are properly insured.

The first step is to check your homeowner's insurance. Some policies will cover your household possessions in transit. If this is the case, find out exactly what is and is not covered and what your deductible would be. If you have valuables you're particularly worried about, you can buy a rider through your insurance company.

If you find you need additional coverage, the next step is to turn to the moving company. It's important to realize that moving companies are not licensed to sell insurance. What they do offer is called "liability protection." Different states have different laws regulating the types of protection movers can offer consumers. But in most states the plans are very similar to the protection options that are mandated by the federal government for interstate moves.

There are basically four types of protection. The industry calls the most basic "released value." The good news is this coverage is free. The bad news is that on an interstate move, it offers you only 60 cents per pound per item regardless of its actual value. This might be a good deal if the most valuable thing you're moving is a brick collection. Otherwise, this coverage usually isn't sufficient for most consumers. Here's an example:

Your new color television is damaged in the move. For a 40-pound TV at 60 cents per pound, the movers owe you $24. And that super-light camcorder you just bought—if it's broken under this coverage, you'll receive a check for less than a dollar. For in-states moves, each state has its own regulations for release-value coverage, but they usually fall between 30 cents and a whopping $1.25 per pound.

The next level of protection is usually called "depreciation coverage." Here, if something is broken or lost, you'll get the re-placement value of the item minus depreciation. In other words, if your five-year-old television set breaks during the move, the moving company won't replace it with a new one. You'll get a cash settlement for the price of the TV minus depreciation. Therefore, you'll get more money for a broken two-year-old TV than for a broken five-year-old one. With depreciation protec-tion, the cost is determined by weight and the declared value of what you think your total shipment is worth.

The premier level of protection is "full-value protection." Un-der this plan if an item is lost or damaged beyond repair, you'll receive the full-replacement cost regardless of depreciation. If it breaks your five-year-old TV, and it can't be repaired, the mov-ing company will pay for a brand-new set. The cost for full-value protection is also based on the weight and declared value of your total shipment. To make this plan more affordable, you might be given a choice of deductibles, up to $500. The higher the deductible, the cheaper the plan.

Finally, if your mover doesn't offer any protection, or if you are not asked to sign off on coverage, an interstate mover auto-matically assumes liability for the entire shipment at an amount equal to $1.25 per pound times the weight of your shipment. Claims will then be settled taking into account depreciation. This automatic protection will cost you $7 for each $1,000 of li-ability.

These protection plans can be confusing. Make sure your moving company thoroughly explains your options and costs as well as the limitations of each plan you're considering.

The Paper Trail: Before You Sign on the Dotted Line

There's a lot of paperwork involved in any move. And although we've said the following many times already, we think it bears repeating again: Before signing any paperwork always read it completely, front and back, and understand what it means. Also, never sign blank paperwork.

We're going to take you through all the documents that are crucial to your move. This paperwork is required by law for all interstate moves, and, depending on your state's regulations, you'll probably see much of the same paperwork for an in-state move too.

ESTIMATE

The estimate states your mover's educated guess at how much your move will cost. Whether it's a nonbinding, binding, or guaranteed-not-to-exceed estimate, your mover should provide you with a signed copy. It should clearly describe the shipment and all the services provided that are known at the time it is signed. (See "Estimate: Making It More Than a Guess.")

ORDER OF SERVICE

For interstate and many local moves, companies are required to provide an Order of Service. It also can be called an Agreement of Service. This form, which usually is given to you two to three days before your move, contains all the details of your move, including pickup and delivery dates, the amount of insurance protection you want, and any special circumstances, such as guaranteed delivery dates, long carries, and special packing needs. If you have a binding or guaranteed-not-to-exceed estimate, these words should be written on your Order of Service. Usually there is also a box you can check off if you want to be present for the weighing of your shipment.

The Order of Service should clearly record the charges for everything involved in your move. The total charges on your Order of Service generally should match your estimate total, unless details of your move have changed. However, the Order of Service is *not* a contract. It does not obligate you to use the mover. It merely helps prevent misunderstandings between you and the moving company. Prior to loading your shipment, it can be amended at any time, even if you've signed it. Make sure it contains your mover's name, address, telephone, and license number.

BILL OF LADING

The Bill of Lading is the contract between you and your mover. It's probably the most important piece of paper you will sign. On a local move the document may be called the Bill of Freight. A mover is required by law to prepare a Bill of Lading for all interstate and most in-state moves. You'll get the Bill of Lading on moving day, and you should sign and receive a copy of it before the movers start loading your possessions. Make sure the information on the Bill of Lading matches the information on your Order of Service, particularly delivery dates, delivery address, and estimated cost. On the Bill of Lading you must select the type of liability coverage you want. If you do not fill in this section, you'll be stuck with standard coverage, which might not cover your belongings if they are lost or damaged. In addition, look very carefully at the name of the company listed on the Bill of Lading; only this company can be held responsible for your shipment and your satisfaction with the moving service. It's your responsibility to read the Bill of Lading carefully. Do not sign it if you disagree with something or if it doesn't reflect the services you want. Once you sign the Bill of Lading, you are obligated by law to pay for the charges agreed upon in the contract. There's no changing your mind.

INVENTORY

Before your shipment is loaded, the driver will probably prepare an inventory sheet. (This is not required by law.) This sheet lists every box and item that is loaded onto the truck and its condition before being loaded. The driver will tag each item with a number and then write a description of that item and its condition on the inventory sheet. Many times this will be done very quickly, during the heat of a move. Don't let yourself be steamrolled. Walk with the driver as he does the inventory. He'll be making notations in code; for example, PBO (packed by owner) means you packed the box yourself, while SC 10 usually means a scratch on the top of an item. Insist that he explain all his notations about existing damage as he's writing it on the inventory list. "If he writes down scratch, you make him show you the scratch," says Ron Rogers, a claims adjuster who works for dozens of moving companies and has written a book about the industry. (See "Where to Turn for Help.") This is crucial since the moving company will scrutinize the inventory list later to determine if it will pay you for any damage you claim occurred during the move. Rogers goes on to say that even if your dining room table has a hairline scratch before the move, your driver will probably just note it as "scratched." If the move then causes a large, obvious scratch, you might have problems collecting on your claim when the move is over. Rogers notes that drivers sometimes have their own reasons for being vague on the inventory sheet. "If items are damaged in your move, it's often the driver who has to pay for the damage out of his own pocket." You'll be asked to sign each sheet of the inventory list, which in essence acknowledges your agreement with everything the driver has written down. You have the right to note any disagreements on the form before you sign.

At your new home, when the movers unload your shipment, you'll be asked to check off each item by number on the inventory as an acknowledgment of receipt. You also must note any damage that didn't exist when the items were loaded. It's important that you inspect each and every item as it's brought into your home. It happens very fast, with numbers being called out that you're responsible for checking off. Again, don't be steamrolled. While you obviously can't open every box in the movers' presence, make sure to examine all furniture and the outside of each box. Any missing or damaged items should be called to the attention of the driver immediately. After everything has been unloaded, the driver will ask you to sign his copy of the inventory list. Make sure that all missing or damaged items are clearly noted on his copy before you sign it. While you do have some leeway to submit a claim if you find damage later, this is the best time to point out damage in the hopes of being compensated.

If your company doesn't use an inventory list, which is common in local moves, you should create one yourself. After the move is finished, physically check the moving van and truck's cab to make sure nothing has been left behind.

When It's Over: The Claims Process

Chances are something will be damaged, destroyed, or lost during your move. Filing a claim is your way of receiving compensation. It's estimated that three out of every ten moves results in a claim. Bear in mind that the amount of compensation you're entitled to is based on the type of insurance protection you have chosen. (See "Insurance: Making Sure You're Covered.")

For interstate moves, federal law gives you nine months from the day of delivery to file a claim with your moving company. However, we suggest the sooner, the better. After inspecting all your things carefully, if you discover something is damaged or missing, call your moving company as soon as possible and request its forms. "One of the biggest problems, particularly with local movers, is that you ask for a claim form and you don't get one, you call again for a claim form, and you still don't get one," says Ron Rogers. "A lot of people get sick of asking and just give up." Never give up. If you're having problems, Rogers suggests sending your request return-receipt, or insist that the company fax you a form.

Remember, if you've packed yourself, movers will accept liability for broken items inside boxes only if the outside of the carton has obvious damage. Be sure to save all damaged boxes until your claim is settled. We also suggest keeping the inventory tags attached to any articles you're claiming. On a claim form you'll need to list each item by its inventory tag number. You'll also need to describe the item thoroughly and give a complete description of the problem—broken, scratched, missing. In addition, you'll have to list the amount you paid for the item and the date of purchase. Finally, you must provide both the repair and replacement costs of the item.

We realize it can be difficult to estimate repair costs. Many moving companies realize this as well. Never low-ball yourself. For example, if your dining room table was scratched in a move, you're probably not going to know how much it would cost to repair. Consider calling a local craftsman and getting at least a general idea of what the cost would be. If you're still having trouble determining the cost, Rogers suggests leaving the repair cost blank.

On the claim form you also should list any property damage you feel was caused by the movers. This includes scratched floors, dented walls, and stained carpets. (Always point out any property damage to the driver before he leaves your home.) Property damage should be covered regardless of the protection coverage you have chosen.

After you submit your claim, federal law governing interstate moves mandates that a moving company has 30 days to acknowledge in writing that it has received it. It has 120 days to pay, deny, make a settlement offer, or advise you of the status of your claim and the reason for the delay. (For a local move, you're often on your own. Very few states regulate the claims process. Check with your state regulator or attorney general.)

The moving company probably will send a claims adjuster to your home to inspect the damaged items. That person will take photographs as well as notes on the damage to pass on to the moving company. Claims adjusters usually are not employees of the company. They're independent contractors who sometimes are also professional craftsmen. Reputable companies employ adjusters who are capable of repairing different things: a scratched wood or glass table, a broken mirror, a ripped leather chair, or a broken toaster oven. While this is convenient, some adjusters might not be qualified to make the repairs you need. (Or they simply might not be very good.) You don't have to use the adjuster to repair your damaged items. You can get your own reasonable estimate from an outside repair service and submit it your moving company for payment. If an adjuster does make a repair you're not happy with, contact your moving company and demand they pay for an outside service to do the job right.

When a company evaluates your claim, your inventory list becomes crucial. If there's any damage that sounds similar to damage the driver noted on the inventory sheet, your claim could be denied. This is the point when many consumers start kicking themselves for not paying attention to the inventory sheet at the other end of their move. "People don't look at their inventory sheets when they're being filled in, they just arbitrarily sign it," says Rogers. "They don't check what the driver's written down as damaged at origin. People who are transferred by big companies make out okay because they have their company to back them up," he continues. "If the mover has a contract with a big company, they're more apt to take care of a claim. But people who pay for their own moves don't make out as well."

When a Company Denies Your Claim: Fight Back

There are many reasons a moving company might deny your claim. For example: Your new television set doesn't work after the move, but there is no visible damage. Your coffee table is scratched, but it was noted as scratched on the inventory sheet and the scratch doesn't look new. China you packed yourself is broken, but the outside of the box isn't damaged. Your laptop computer is missing, and the movers didn't list it on the inventory sheet. If your mover won't pay for damage or loss you're sure they caused, you do have limited recourse. You can sue your mover or, in certain cases, go to arbitration, which is usually quicker and cheaper than going to court.

Arbitration is a process whereby a neutral third party listens to both sides of a dispute and comes to what is hoped is a fair settlement. An arbitrator's decision is legally binding and can be enforced by the courts. Although you do have a limited right to appeal the decision, courts usually won't revise an arbitrator's findings. When reaching a decision in moving cases, an arbitrator takes into consideration the laws and regulations that govern the industry. In addition, the amount an arbitrator awards cannot exceed the moving company's liability under the Bill of Lading. In other words, if you selected released-value protection for your move, which pays only up to 60 cents per pound for a damaged item, that's all you'll be able to collect, even if an arbitrator rules in your favor. Before arbitration can begin, you must have already exhausted your moving company's regular claim process, and the company must have made its final settlement offer.

While there are several arbitration programs, most of the major movers use the dispute settlement program sponsored by the American Moving and Storage Association (AMSA). For interstate moves, companies must submit to binding arbitration for disputed claims under $1,000. If the claim is over $1,000, the mover is not obligated to go to arbitration, but most do since it's a lot cheaper than court. In fact, according to the AMSA, in all but nine of their cases movers have agreed to go to arbitration. The American Arbitrator's Association, an independent, nonprofit organization that administers the AMSA dispute program, charges $300 for initiating a standard arbitration case, for which you must initially pay half. Depending on the outcome of the arbitration, your fee might be refunded. Keep in mind that arbitration is mandated only for claims involving lost or damaged items. Complaints about egregious service—late delivery, miscalculated weights, overcharges on your bill—are not required to go to arbitration. If you have these types of complaints and you're not satisfied with your moving company's response, you'll have to sue.

The federal government can't mandate arbitration for disputes resulting from local or intrastate moves, although some states' laws might require it. Even in unregulated states, reputable companies will agree to arbitration. Contact your moving company, local Better Business Bureau, or state Moving and Storage Association (if available) about arbitration in your area.

STORAGE: FINDING A SAFE PLACE FOR YOUR STUFF

If you can't move into your new home immediately, you'll have to store your belongings temporarily. It's what the moving industry calls "storage-in-transit." If you know you'll need storage before you move, you should ask each agent who comes to your home for an estimate. The price and services each potential mover offers for warehouse storage should be taken into consideration when choosing a company. Make sure the extra charge for storage-in-transit is listed on both your Order of Service and Bill of Lading.

For interstate moves, storage-in-transit rates are regulated by the government, just like linehaul charges. However, as with linehaul charges, movers can discount their price for warehouse storage.

Each time your shipment is loaded or unloaded increases the chance that something will be lost or damaged. Nevertheless, if you're using the storage-in-transit service, your moving company is responsible for your shipment during this time. Make sure you have the exact address of the warehouse where your possessions will be stored along with a complete list of contact names and phone numbers for the storage facility.

Legally, your shipment can remain in a warehouse as storage-in-transit for up to ninety days. After that it's considered long-term storage, and you'll either have to arrange for it to be moved elsewhere or negotiate a new contract with the warehouse you're using.

DO-IT-YOURSELF: IT'S MORE THAN THE COST OF PIZZA AND BEER

After hearing about all the pitfalls and potential nightmares of hiring a moving company, you might be thinking "Forget about professionals, I'll just do it myself." While do-it-yourself moving can be more economical, it involves a lot more than throwing stuff in boxes and recruiting a few friends with promises of pizza and beer. There are many things to consider in a do-it-yourself move.

Nationally known companies such as U-Haul, Ryder, Budget, and Hertz-Penske as well as local independents will rent you anything from a carrier to attach to the roof of your car to a 26-foot truck. They also can provide you with dollies, ramps, moving blankets, and anything else needed to move from one place to another. Packing a moving truck correctly is an art form. An incorrectly packed truck can lead to items damaged in transit. Many rental companies offer helpful booklets or videotapes to show you the best way to load a truck. You should study these carefully before your move.

As with hiring a moving company, you should shop around and compare the prices of at least three different rental companies before making a commitment. Rates can vary greatly. For instance, in a survey of three major rental companies for a move from New York to Florida, the cost to rent a 24- to 26-foot truck ranged from $1,093 to $1,314. Often you can save money by avoiding truck rental during peak times like the summer, most weekends, and the end of the month. If you must move during these times, make a reservation well in advance.

When shopping around for the best deal on a rental truck, there is more to consider than just the price quoted for the vehicle. You need to watch out for various extra charges. For example, be wary of special "in-town" rental rates for a local move. We've all seen great advertised rates—$19.95 for a truck rental—but you shouldn't assume that this rate is the price per day. This can be the rate for as few as six hours. If you go over the six-hour period, you could be charged an additional $20. If you're moving a two-bedroom home, trust us, it's going to take longer than six hours. In addition, for a local rental you'll probably be charged extra for every mile you drive at a cost of around 60 cents per mile. When you add it all together, a 60-mile move that takes eight hours can quickly escalate from the $19.95 advertised price to $76. But wait. There are even more charges to consider.

Expect to pay about $10 a day for insurance. This insurance should cover both the truck and your cargo in case you get into an accident. It won't cover items that are lost or damaged in the normal moving process. While insurance is optional, be aware that your own auto insurance policy might not cover you when renting a moving truck. Don't decline the insurance option unless you're certain your personal auto policy covers you. In addition to insurance, you'll need to rent other things that will raise your final moving cost. Furniture pads cost about $12 a dozen, a hand truck another $15, and to move extra-heavy items like a refrigerator you'll need an appliance dolly, which runs another $10. See how quickly those extra costs can add up?

When you're moving long distance, there are even more costs to consider. For instance, what are you going to do with your car? A car trailer that attaches to a truck rents for about $200. You also might have to pay an additional $5 a day for separate insurance on the trailer. Also, figure the cost of gasoline into your moving budget. A fully loaded, 26-foot truck gets only about 10 miles to the gallon, so a 1,200-mile move would cost about $150 in fuel alone. You also might need to factor in hotel rooms and meals.

In a long-distance rental where you need to drop off the truck at your destination (a one-way rental), your quoted rental price should include the exact number of days you will have the truck and a certain amount of miles. If the move takes more time than anticipated, or if you put on extra miles, you'll have to pay more.

If you're contemplating a self-move, in particular a long-distance self-move, you really need to add up all these additional expenses to get a better idea of what your actual cost will be before you sign a rental agreement. Don't jump automatically at the lowest per-day rate. If you like to haggle, this is a good chance to dicker for the best deal. Most companies will throw in free miles or lower their overall price to match a competitor's offer. Still, if your estimated total is much higher than anticipated, it might be worth calling a few professional movers for estimates. If their prices are close, go with the professional. You can save your back and your friendships in the process.

Self-Movers Beware: A Consumer Warning

Driving a 20-foot truck isn't quite like driving the family car. Although most rental trucks have automatic transmissions, they still drive like trucks. Many accidents are the fault of inexperienced rental-truck drivers. Also keep in mind that rental trucks rack up a lot of miles, and breakdowns can happen. Most responsible companies have a toll-free number you can call if you experience difficulties. However, a breakdown on a long-distance move is a major inconvenience. We've even heard complaints from consumers who've experienced multiple breakdowns during a single move or had accidents caused by poorly maintained trucks. We spoke with one consumer who rented a truck from a leading company to move from Florida to Georgia. He had to deal with four breakdowns before the truck finally died. And the stories get worse.

A 1997 investigation by the ABC newsmagazine *20/20* raised some serious questions about the safety of U-Haul, the nation's largest renter of do-it-yourself moving equipment. In a three-month investigation, *20/20* rented twenty-one trucks in five states. They then took the trucks to certified safety inspectors in each state. Inspectors found significant safety and maintenance violations. More than half the trucks had worn tires, bad brakes, and loose steering. Eleven of the twenty-one trucks were given failing marks. In a letter to *20/20*, U-Haul apologized for the condition of seven of the trucks the newsmagazine had rented and acknowledged that four had such serious problems that they shouldn't have been on the road. However, the company disagreed with some of the inspectors' findings and said the trucks that *20/20* rented did not constitute a representative sampling of its equipment nationwide. We tried to contact U-Haul to see what's happened since ABC's report, but they didn't return our calls.

Before you sign a rental agreement, make sure the truck has passed recent inspection. Also, before you drive it off the lot, do your own check. Even if you don't know the first thing about truck maintenance, you can look at the tire treads and make sure the headlights, turn signals, and windshield wipers work. As you pull away from the lot, test out the brakes and steering. If you hear any strange noises or something doesn't feel right, take the truck back and demand a replacement.

Finally, as when hiring a mover, call your local Better Business Bureau or consumer protection agency to find out about complaints against any company you're considering.

Self-Moving Alternatives: New Trends

There are some alternatives to traditional moving that could save you time and money. If you plan to rent a truck and do the driving, but don't want to do the hard labor of actually loading and unloading, consider hiring professional movers to do it for you. Many moving companies will hire out their trained workers to help you load and unload for about $10 to $20 per man per hour. Make sure these workers are covered by their company's worker's compensation insurance, in case they get hurt on your premises.

Another new trend in the moving industry is you-pack/they-haul. These companies actually drive the moving truck for you, but you need to do the loading and unloading. You're usually charged by the amount of truck space that your shipment occupies. As with self-moves, you'll need to pack the truck well and provide moving blankets, dollies, ramps, and any other equipment to do the job. Since you're charged by the amount of space your shipment occupies in the truck, it obviously pays to pack as efficiently as possible. For those seeking a bargain, this service may be the best of both worlds: It's often cheaper than hiring professional movers to do the whole job, and you don't have to deal with the hassles of driving a big truck yourself. However, before you sign up, carefully evaluate any extra costs and make sure you thoroughly check out the company.

SAVING EVEN MORE MONEY: MOVING AND THE IRS

Certain moving expenses are deductible on your income tax return. Obviously, your move must meet certain criteria, but if you're moving because your company changed locations or you're starting a new job, you might be able to deduct the cost of moving your household and storing it in-transit as well as some travel costs. If you plan to deduct your move, it's vital to save all receipts relating to it and keep good records. Like anything involving the IRS, the rules are complicated, so you'll want to consult with a tax professional. For more information, call the IRS and request "Publication 521: Moving Expenses" (800-TAX-FORM), or download the information from the Internet (www.irs.gov).

WHERE TO TURN FOR HELP

Local Moves
To see if a company is licensed, investigate its reputation, or file a complaint about your local move:

•*State regulatory agency.* This agency varies from state to state. It could be your state's Department of Transportation or public utilities commission. If the moving industry in your state is deregulated, try your local consumer protection agency.

•*The Better Business Bureau.* Call the office in the area where the moving company has its headquarters.

•*Your state's Moving and Storage Association.* Half the states have one. Often they're located in the state's capital, or ask a reputable mover for the phone number.

Interstate Moves
To see if a company is licensed, investigate its reputation, or file a complaint about your interstate move:

•Your regional office of the Department of Transportation's Federal Highway Administration, or the main headquarters for their Office of Motor Carriers:

4000 Seventh Street, S.W.
Washington, DC 20590
(202) 266-0665
www.fhwa.dot.gov
It can tell you if a carrier is licensed, but remember that while it takes complaints, it doesn't act on them at this time.

•The Better Business Bureau office in the area where the moving company has its headquarters.

•If you're using a major van line, call the national headquarters to make sure the local agent you're dealing with is an affiliate of the van line.

•The American Moving and Storage Association.

This association offers consumer booklets, advice, and information on claims dispute arbitration. It also might be able to help with other complaints if a mover is a member:
1611 Duke Street
Alexandria, VA 22314
(703) 683-7410
www.amconf.org

•Ron Rogers, a claims adjuster for dozens of moving companies, has self-published a book on the industry. He also has some helpful tips on his Internet site:
10240 Atascadero Avenue
Atascadero, CA 93422
(805) 461-5292
http://home.calinet.com/rrcs/

▶ Top Ten Tips
    1. *Plan your move at least six to eight weeks in advance.* This will give you a much better chance of getting the move

dates you need and will give you time to evaluate the cost
and services of potential movers.

2. *Interview moving agents.* Don't merely listen to their sales
pitch. Ask specific questions and have them explain how
your move would work from start to finish.

3. *Get at least three written estimates.* Beware of estimates
that seem too good to be true. To avoid being lowballed,
we suggest obtaining binding or not-to-exceed estimates.
Make sure all possible extra charges, including special
packing needs, long carries, and flights of stairs, are included. Ask specific questions about what is and is not included in your move.

4. *Investigate potential movers.* Before choosing your mover,
make sure it has a license and a good reputation. Taking a
little time to do this before you hire a moving company can
prevent a lot of frustration later.

5. *Photograph or videotape your valuables.* Doing so will
come in handy if something is lost or damaged in transit
and the moving company disputes your claim.

6. *Consider your coverage.* The various options for protection coverage can be confusing, so make sure you understand exactly what is and what is not covered. If you're
worried about damage to your possessions, spend the
money for full-value protection.

7. *Read all paperwork carefully.* Be prepared to be rushed
through the paperwork when the movers get to your
home. Don't be intimidated. Take the time to read all
forms, front and back, and ask questions if you don't understand something. Make sure the delivery dates, coverage option, storage information, and any other services
you have requested are on the Order of Service and Bill of
Lading. Make sure these charges are the same as on your
estimate. Keep a copy of all paperwork.

8. *Oversee your inventory.* If your moving company prepares
an inventory, make sure all items being moved are tagged.

Stay with the driver to assure he makes legible notations and that you agree with him on any preexisting damage. After your belongings arrive at your new home, note any damage to your boxes or furniture that occurred from the move on the driver's inventory sheet before you sign off on it.

9. *Don't give your mover anything that is priceless or irreplaceable.* Move things like family heirlooms, photo albums, financial or legal documents, cameras, and credit cards yourself.

10. *Follow through.* If you have a loss or damage claim, file it promptly. If you have other complaints about your move, report them to the company immediately. If you're not satisfied with the response, contact the appropriate agency. (See "Where to Turn for Help.")

Glossary

Agent: Affiliate of the motor carrier who is authorized to act on its behalf.

Bill of lading: Receipt for your belongings and the contract for their transportation.

Booking agent: Agent who sells you the company's service, handles all initial paperwork, and registers your move with the van line. The booking agent may or may not be your hauling or destination agent.

Destination agent: Agent located near your new home who can provide necessary services and assistance to either you or the van driver.

Hauling agent: Agent assigned by the van line to transport your possessions.

Long carry: A charge assessed when a shipment must be moved more than 75 feet from the truck to the door of your residence.

MC number: Motor carrier number assigned by the federal Department of Transportation granting authority for interstate operations. Movers regulated by state authorities should have a separate license number that authorizes them for in-state moves.

Order of Service: Initial document that authorizes the van line to perform moving services. Not a contract, you can cancel an Order of Service before the move day without penalty.

PBO (Packed by Owner):   Items you packed yourself that the moving company will not be liable for unless there's damage to the shipping carton.

Spanking: Industry slang for taking advantage of a customer, usually by giving lowball estimates, then charging the customer much more.

Van foreman: The van driver who has overall responsibility for the loading, transport, and unloading of your belongings.

Weight bumping: The falsification of a shipment weight to make it appear to weigh more than it does.

CHAPTER 10

TRAVEL

Travel offers the opportunity to explore a new city, experience a different culture, or just kick back in a chaise longue with an exotic drink in hand. But a vacation also can mean a lot of pressure and frustration. Traveling is expensive, and it's difficult to determine when you've gotten a good deal. Whether you're traveling for business or pleasure, it's disturbing to discover that the man sitting next to you on a plane or the couple in the hotel room down the hall paid much less than you. On top of that, there are plenty of travel suppliers out there preying on the unsuspecting consumer.

In this chapter we let you in on some insider secrets. We show you how to hunt down the best bargains on airfare, hotels, rental cars, and travel packages and warn you about the latest travel scams. Armed with this information, you'll be able to have an even better time on your next journey.

AIRLINES

Let's face it, delayed flights, cramped seating, bad food, and lost luggage are just a few of the inconveniences that can befall you when you take to the not-so-friendly skies. Adding insult to injury, buying a plane ticket has become something of a crap shoot. There's a good chance that the guy hogging your armrest paid half as much as you did for the same lousy experience. The deregulation of the airlines by Congress in 1985 has dropped fares across the board. However, the industry's pricing structure is now so confusing and unpredictable that it's almost impossible for consumers to tell if they've gotten a good deal. In this section we'll tell you what goes on in the airline industry on the other side of the reservation desk and teach you a few strategies to ensure you get the best deal.

FINDING A FARE THAT'S FAIR: HOW THE SYSTEM WORKS

If you ask a dozen passengers on any given flight what they paid for their round-trip ticket, you'll probably get a dozen different answers. Let's say you paid $550 for a round-trip coach ticket from Los Angeles to Washington, D.C. Well, the woman sitting next to you may have paid $298, the man across the aisle could have spent $856, and the woman one row over might have been charged $1,320. How can this happen? The airlines constantly change their fares in an attempt to squeeze the biggest profit out of each flight, averaging over 200,000 price changes per day. It's known in the industry as "revenue management" or "yield management." Each airline uses a sophisticated computer pricing system that constantly monitors the demand on every flight, analyzes historical purchase patterns, and keeps tabs on what competitors are charging. When demand is high, prices go up, and when it's low, fares are discounted. These discounts can last a few hours or a few days. A travel agent we spoke to compared buying a plane ticket to playing roulette—you just never know what's going to happen. "I've seen a fare jump $200 in thirty minutes," he told us. "A fare will literally change on the computer system while I have a customer on the phone. And if we haven't booked the flight yet, that person has to take the higher fare."

By purchasing a ticket well in advance, you usually can grab an airline's best deal, called an "excursion" or "supersaver" fare. To get this fare, you have to buy a nonrefundable ticket at least twenty-one days in advance and stay over a Saturday night. As you book closer to the departure date, the prices go up accordingly with different rates kicking in fourteen, seven, and three days in advance. The idea is that vacationers can plan their trips ahead of time and also put up with various restrictions in order to get the lowest rates. Meanwhile, business travelers often travel at the last minute and need more flexibility to change or cancel their trips, so they pay full fare—often three or four times higher than the excursion rate. In essence, these full-fare passengers subsidize those who travel on discounted tickets.

The airline ticket prices you see advertised in your local newspaper are often supersaver rates, with plenty of fine print that reveals a plethora of restrictions: things like blackout periods, day-of-the-week travel restrictions, minimum and maximum stays, among many others. These restrictions can be ridiculous. We saw one unbelievably cheap round-trip fare from Los Angeles to New York offered by a major airline. However, the fine print revealed you only had twenty-four hours to complete the entire trip. In addition, for each flight only a certain number of seats are sold at the excursion rate, so even if you call in advance, you're not guaranteed to get a cheap fare. Buying in advance can definitely be a solid way to get a good deal. But with prices fluctuating constantly and airlines jockeying to the squeeze the most profit out of each flight, the great deal you bought today—a month before takeoff—could end up being more expensive than a ticket purchased just a week in advance.

Although you always should ask your travel agent, airline representative, or whoever books your trip for the "lowest fare possible," recent studies have shown that even this doesn't always guarantee you the lowest price. A 1997 study by the Public Interest Research Group (PIRG), a nonprofit research and advocacy organization, investigated what it calls the "mind-numbing bazaar of air fares." Over a two-day period, they called both travel agents and airlines in twenty-eight cities to obtain quotes for the lowest airfares for specific round-trip itineraries originating in each city. When requesting a quote on a twenty-one-day advance purchase ticket, PIRG received 504 unique price quotes from 891 calls. In Seattle, for example, fifteen calls resulted in fifteen different fares. And the prices varied widely. When requesting the lowest full-fare ticket from Dulles

Airport in Washington, D.C., to Salt Lake City, one travel agent quoted $315 while two airlines wanted $1,649 and $1,642—all for the same route on the same day. It certainly isn't hard to see that the average consumer never knows if he or she is being quoted a bargain or a bum deal.

The reservation system used to book airline tickets can affect price. Most travel agents, airlines, and even do-it-yourself Internet booking sites use computer reservation systems (CRS) to ticket flights. There are four main systems, each owned by a different airline. Sabre is owned by American Airlines, Apollo/Galileo is owned by United and US Airways, System One Amadeus is owned by Continental, and Worldspan is the joint operation of Delta, Northwest, and TWA. In theory, despite the different systems, you should be able to buy any ticket for any airline from any system at the same price. For instance, if your travel agent uses Apollo to pull flights from Dallas to Chicago, she should be able to see all the majors carriers' flights and prices. But with constant fare changes and fluctuations in seat availability, it's hard for the systems to stay in sync. Usually an airline's own system will be more up to date with information for that airline than the other CRSs. In addition, some charge that the reservation systems are biased toward the airlines that own them. "The government has cracked down and stopped the blatant favoritism," one industry insider told us, "but the systems still favor the airlines that own them." For instance, it's often easier for a travel agent who uses Sabre to book an American flight.

The route you fly also can determine how much you'll pay. A route with a lot of competition, particularly one also serviced by smaller, low-fare airlines, will have lower rates. For example, you generally can find good deals flying between New York City and Miami or Las Vegas and Los Angeles because so many carriers are battling each other to get your business on these routes. On the flip side, if you live near the hub airport of a major airline, competition is minimal and airfares can be unusually high. According to a 1996 government study, in Cincinnati, a Delta hub, ticket prices run about 84 percent higher than average. In Pittsburgh, where the airport is dominated by US Airways, fares run about 75 percent higher than average.

In 1997 the Consumers Union petitioned the Department of Transportation to clear up pricing confusion and make it easier for consumers to compare fares. Their "Truth in Airfare" proposal requires airlines to disclose the average and lowest fares the carrier is charging on each route. Under the proposal, this information would be listed in computer reservation systems so travelers could be informed of this data whenever an airline or travel agent quotes them a price. "By comparing the quoted fare with the average and lowest fares, consumers can quickly tell whether they're getting a true bargain, a fair price, or a raw deal," writes the Consumers Union. But the airlines aren't fans of the proposal, claiming such statistics would be useless and confuse the public. Whether the proposal is passed or not, if you want to find the lowest fares you'll need to shop around. Great deals always can be had, if you know where to look.

BOOKING YOUR FLIGHT: WHERE TO TURN FOR THE BEST DEALS

Booking a flight isn't like it used to be. Different market conditions and new technology have changed how the industry operates. Today a resourceful consumer has to check out several different options to snag the best deals.

Airlines: Buying Direct

While you certainly can buy your tickets directly from the airlines, in most cases we don't recommend it. When you call an airline's toll-free number, you'll be quoted prices for that airline, but the agent obviously won't tell you if other airlines are offering lower fares. Also, the airline's agents might not make you aware of different options that could drastically reduce the cost of your trip; for example, leaving on a weekday could be cheaper than leaving on a weekend.

As with buying anything else, we strongly suggest you com-

322   TRICKS OF THE TRADE

parison shop before making a purchase. Use airline quotes to get an idea of how much they would charge for your trip, but investigate other options, including travel agents and the Internet, before booking anything. If you do end up buying your ticket directly from an airline, be certain you've asked for the lowest fare available. Make note of name of the agent you spoke with as well as your flight numbers and the agreed-upon price. Also be sure to jot down the confirmation number or record locator.

The airlines do offer some great exclusive deals, but you need Internet access to find out about them. Each week many airlines advertise deeply discounted fares exclusively on their Web sites. Most of the bargains are for restricted, last-minute weekend trips—a sort of a fire sale—as the airlines attempt to fill up empty seats. These special deals usually are posted on the Internet on Wednesdays for trips leaving that Friday or Saturday and returning the following Sunday through Tuesday, so you should have your bags packed and ready to go. (Airlines will also e-mail these deals to you each week if you register your address with them.) Most airlines also post other special promotions, such as sweepstakes, two-for one deals, and even auctions where you can bid on tickets.

Travel Agents: Your Personal Deal Maker
Travel agents are part of a unique business. There aren't many professions that supply consumers with expertise and service without charging them a dime. However, the travel industry is changing, and agencies have had to adapt in order to survive.

For each airline ticket a travel agent sells, he or she is paid a commission by the airline. The commission on a domestic ticket used to be 10 percent, but recently most airlines have cut it down to 8 percent. In addition, some airlines have placed a cap on commissions, never paying more than $50 on any round-trip domestic ticket. Since up to 80 percent of an agency's business consists of booking airline tickets, this commission cutting has come as quite a blow. Unlike most businesses that simply raise prices to earn more revenue, travel agencies don't set the airfare rates. Some agencies, finding they could no longer make ends meet, have closed their doors, laid off workers, or found other ways to make money. Many are now charging customers service fees—between $5 and $50—for every domestic ticket sold. Consumers have had mixed feelings. Some are upset and refuse to use agents who charge fees while other don't mind paying for the service. We don't think there's anything wrong with paying proficient travel agents a small fee if it means they'll do their best to find us a bargain.

How to Find a Good Agent
A travel agent can be your ticket to booking the lowest airfares. However, some agents are more skilled and motivated than others. How do you know if you're dealing with an agent who can get you the best bang for your buck? Keep the following in mind when looking for a good agent.

•*Experience is a mark of any good travel agent.* You want someone who knows the industry ropes and can deal with the ins and outs of the business. One way to verify an agent's experience is through the Institute of Certified Travel Agents. It certifies agents who have five years of experience and training in travel management. (See "Where to Turn for Help.")

•*A good agent knows the intricacies of the airline's computer reservation system.* It's truly human versus machine. An agent who isn't thoroughly familiar with the system can look up only the most basic information. A good agent needs to use the CRS aggressively and creatively to find the real bargains.

•*The best airfare deals aren't always on the computer system.* A good travel agent needs to be aware of other options. Charter flights, consolidators, and smaller, low-fare airlines are all potential money savers an agent should check out. A knowledgeable agent also will be aware of current airline promotions such as free companion fares, weekend specials, and kids-fly-free programs.

If you're not satisfied that your agent is doing everything he or she can to get you the best deal, it's time to shop around for someone else. Consider calling two or three other agents to see if they can get you a better deal. May the best agent win your business!

Also be wary of an agent who seems to be pushing a certain airline with vague claims like "they're just better." This agent might not have your best interests in mind. Some airlines and travel agencies form alliances that offer agents perks, such as overrides—bonuses on top of the standard commission. The more tickets an agent sells on the airline, the bigger the potential bonus. "I've seen airlines come in and say, 'We'll pay you $50 to $100 for every passenger you move to my airline.' And it's perfectly legal," explains Tom Parsons, editor of *Best Fares* magazine and author of *Insider Travel Secrets You're Not Supposed to Know.* "Agents will then steer all the business to that airline and tell consumers that that's the best price they can get." But a travel agent we spoke with defended the practice saying her company would go out of business if it didn't get paid the commission override, but added that "an ethical agent will not push a client onto a flight that's not right for them." Soft money is another airline industry incentive that offers travel agents things like VIP club memberships if they meet certain sales targets. Unfortunately, as standard commissions continue to shrink, these types of incentives will bias the travel agent industry more and more.

The Internet: Doing It Yourself
"A computer is infinitely patient," says John Levine, author of *Internet for Dummies.* "You can spend as much time as you want trying different times, different routes, and different airlines to compare different fares and the computer will never roll

its eyes and wonder when you'll be taking your wallet out."
Levine says he saves hundreds of dollars a year using the Internet to arrange his trips. "You can do a lot better on the Internet than you would with the typical agent who quotes you whatever shows up on the first screen of his computer," he says. Like Levine, hundreds of thousands of people are now playing travel agent and booking their own airfare, hotel, and car rentals from the comfort of home.

Internet booking sites are easy to navigate. You simply enter your departure city, departure date, destination, return date, and preferred flight times. Within moments all the flights that match your criteria will appear on-screen. Once you book your flight, you can even pick out your seat and have your tickets mailed to you.

Consumers tell us they love the Internet because it gives them control over their travel destiny. After all, you have to be tenacious to find the lowest fares. On the Internet you can check prices and flight options as often as you like in search of the ultimate bargain. Such persistence could try a travel agent's patience, especially if you're not a regular customer.

Booking via the Internet does have its problems. Although most sites have a search feature to help you find the lowest fare, sometimes it's not accurate. You might find that one Web site will offer a "low fare" that's hundreds of dollars higher than a quote on another site. The main reason for the discrepancy is that different sites use different reservation system databases, and each site's low-price search engine works in a slightly different way. We've also heard complaints about tickets that never arrive and bad customer service.

Some people have a real knack for using the Internet to find good bargains, but the process can be time-consuming. Professional travel agents use a more sophisticated computer reservation system that provides a little more information than Web services, and, as we said above, good agents know the secrets to discovering great deals. The novice do-it-yourselfer might be smart to surf the Internet but then check with a professional to see if the Internet price can be met or beaten. Here are a few tips for navigating a great fare on the Internet.

- •Make sure you understand all the rules and restrictions placed on your ticket before you buy.
- •Get quotes from two or three Web sites for each trip you're trying to book since there can be drastic price differences between sites.
- •If you're booking a complicated itinerary or flying internationally, consider using a travel agent.
- •Some of the smaller, low-cost airlines aren't on any Internet booking systems. Be sure to check out these airlines' home pages or call them directly.

The largest booking sites include:

- •Expedia (www.expedia.msn.com): Owned by Microsoft, it's one of the most popular sites. Uses the Worldspan database.
- •Travelocity (www.travelocity.com): A subsidiary of American Airlines, Travelocity uses the database of American's Sabre system, so you can book flights on any major carrier.
- •Preview Travel (www.previewtravel.com): Currently the exclusive travel provider to America Online and the search engine Excite (www.excite.com). Uses Apollo's reservation system.

Airline Consolidators: Buying Wholesale

Consolidators serve as a kind of factory outlet for the airline industry. They receive tickets that airlines fear will go unsold and then offer them to the public at considerable savings. Every airline, including the big guys, has at least one consolidator working for it under contract—something all companies prefer to keep quiet about. The airlines want to fill every seat but don't want to offer open discounts because it could start a fare war. So they sell tickets discreetly though consolidators.

Consolidators are almost always a good bet if you're planning to travel abroad, particularly to Asia, Latin America, and

Africa as well as Europe during the summer. By buying through a consolidator, you often can save hundreds, sometimes thousands, of dollars. In a typical example, we found a major carrier's cheapest rate from Chicago to Tokyo was $1,350, but through a consolidator that same flight cost 30 percent less. Different consolidators contract with different airlines, and some of the best deals for international flights are on small, foreign carriers. A particularly cheap fare to London, for instance, might be on Pakistan International Airlines or Air Madagascar. If that's not your cup of tea, you also can find consolidator tickets for flights on Delta, Air France, American, and all the other major carriers.

For domestic flights, consolidator prices usually aren't lower than the supersaver fares most airlines offer. But as we've said, these fares aren't always easy to come by and are loaded with restrictions. A major advantage of consolidator tickets is that advance purchase and Saturday-night stay requirements usually are waived. This makes going through a consolidator a particularly good deal if you're purchasing tickets at the last minute. And contrary to popular belief, you can find consolidator deals for first class and business seats too.

So what's the bad news when it comes to consolidators? With consolidator tickets there are usually no advance seat assignments or special meal orders, and you probably won't be eligible to collect frequent flyer miles. You also might have to endure awkward flight schedules, long layovers, and indirect routes with extra stops. If your flight has an excessive delay or is canceled, the airline might not transfer you to another carrier. In addition, it can be very hard to get a refund, and even if you do, there probably will be a whopping penalty.

You can buy from a consolidator in two ways, either directly or through a travel agent. It's probably safest to buy your ticket through an agent. Many work with reputable consolidators on a regular basis and can comparison shop for you. Also, if something goes wrong, you'll have the agent in your corner to resolve problems. If you do decide to go it alone, which many consumers do, you'll find consolidators listed in those tiny ads in the back of your local newspaper's travel section. Take these precautions if booking by yourself.

•*Buy from a local consolidator.* It's always safer to do business with a local company. You can make sure it actually has an office—not just a post-office box—and you can pick up your tickets in person.

•*Shop around.* Different consolidators have different prices for the same destination. It pays to call around and compare to get the best deal.

•*Investigate its reputation.* Check any consolidator you're considering with the Better Business Bureau or consumer protection agency where it's located. Dishonest consolidators have been known to sell stolen tickets or tickets bought with frequent flyer miles. There are also fly-by-night operations that take your money and run, so find out how long your consolidator has been in business.

•*Buy with a credit card.* Some consolidators charge an extra fee for credit card purchases, but in our opinion it's well worth the extra money for the consumer protection that plastic provides. Should a problem arise, using a credit card makes it much easier to dispute purchases.

•*Check with the airline.* After you buy your ticket, call the airline directly and make sure it has your reservation. If the airline doesn't have a record of your ticket, call your consolidator immediately.

•*Beware of ticket brokers.* Unlike consolidators who have contracts with airlines to sell tickets at cheaper rates, brokers act as middlemen, buying tickets from consolidators and then selling them to the public. Most brokers won't send you tickets until after they have your cash. Be careful. It's probably safer to buy directly from consolidators that contract with the airlines.

SHOPPING STRATEGY: HOW TO AVOID SKY-WAY ROBBERY

Now that you have a better understanding of how the airline industry works, it's time to learn some tricks of your own. With these shopping tactics you'll be able to snag the lowest rates and be assured you're getting a fair deal.

Shop Early and Often: Uncovering the Lowest Fare

The earlier you start to shop, the more likely you are to find a bargain. While you'll probably get the best rate if you buy at least twenty-one days before you fly, be careful of purchasing a ticket too early. If you can, start your search several months before your trip so you can get an idea of the going rates, but don't buy right away. Sales can happen at any time. With airfares fluctuating like the stock market, it takes timing and persistence to ensure you're buying low. You need to follow the market closely and be ready to pounce when there's a fare war and ticket prices plummet. As we've discussed, you have a lot of resources at your fingertips: airline toll-free numbers, travel agents, consolidators, and the Internet. Use them all. By checking fares frequently—several times a week—you'll know when a bargain fare becomes available. When you find a great deal, snatch it up, because it might not be available for long.

While airfare wars and sales are unpredictable, Wendy Perrin, consumer news editor at *Condé Nast Traveler* magazine and author of *Wendy Perrin's Secrets Every Smart Traveler Should Know*, notes that airlines usually drop domestic fares during three key periods: late May or early June, late August, and the days between Thanksgiving and Christmas. Perrin explains that these are times when business travel is slow and the airlines are trying to pull in vacation travelers. Also, you generally can find the cheapest fares in spring, as airlines jockey to get the most out of the upcoming summer vacation season.

What should you do if you buy your ticket only to find that the airline has dropped its fares? Even if you have a supersaver ticket that's nonrefundable, it can still be exchanged in what's called a "rollover" or "downgrade." To qualify for an exchange, your trip has to meet all the restrictions of the new fare, such as advance purchase or Saturday-night stay requirements. There also have to be seats available at the lower fare. The airlines usually charge around $50 to roll over your ticket, although on certain airlines you can avoid this charge by accepting a voucher for the refund amount, which is good for future travel on that airline. You can roll over your ticket through your travel agent, an airline ticket office, or at the airport.

The best deals go to the most flexible travelers. According to Tom Parsons, a consumer travel advocate and editor of *Best Fares* magazine, the trick is to find the best fare and then figure out how you can take advantage of it. If a low fare is sold out for the day you plan to depart, it might be available for the following day. "Don't let your travel agent dictate flights and times for you, and don't be so inflexible you miss the opportunity to save a couple hundred dollars," says Parsons. Run all the variables: What if I leave in the morning? Take the redeye? Fly on a weekday instead of a weekend? What about a nonstop versus connecting flight? By remaining flexible, you can save hundreds of dollars.

Ticketing Tricks: What the Airlines Don't Want You to Know

Tom Parsons is the king of what he calls creative ticketing. A former business traveler, he became obsessed with finding the best travel bargains. He has spent the last fifteen years analyzing airline prices and investigating just how the industry works. Now an author, magazine publisher, and frequent guest on television and radio shows, he reveals the inside secrets he has learned. Keep in mind that these strategies aren't for everyone. But if you can't meet restrictions like advance purchase and Saturday-night stays, these ticketing alternatives could save you money off paying the full fare. Sitting at a computer reservation system terminal in his office, Parsons explained some creative tricks and gave us some real-life examples.

Split or End-to-End Ticketing

Sometimes buying two separate one-way tickets is cheaper than buying just one. Tom showed us how it works. He found a one-way, nonstop fare from Dallas to Los Angeles on a major airline for $830. But with some creative ticketing, he quickly discovered you can fly one-way from Dallas to Albuquerque for $88 and then switch to another airline and fly from Albuquerque to L.A. for $107. "People say that's so inconvenient," says Parsons, "but you know what I say? When you start making $600 an hour you can be as convenient as you want." You'll find your best chances of getting good split-ticket deals on routes served by low-fare airlines.

Alternate Cities

When we were looking for a cheap rate on a round trip ticket from Los Angeles to Boston, we were dismayed to find high fares across the board. Parsons suggested flying to an alternate city, in this case Providence, Rhode Island. The fare was $250 less than anything into Boston, and it would only mean a one-hour drive into the city. For a family of four, that adds up to a savings of $1,000. "For a grand, you have to say, 'Get me a stretch limo and a bottle of champagne, and we're on our way,' " says Parsons. Anyone can take advantage of this strategy, so get out your atlas when you're booking your flight and keep alternate cities in mind.

Back-to-Back or Nested Ticketing

This ticketing method is particularly good for business travelers or anyone else who wants a cheap deal without the restriction of a Saturday-night stay. For example, when Parsons looked into an American flight from Los Angeles to Dallas with no Saturday-night restriction, the fare was $1,660. But if we bought two round-trip tickets, one originating in Los Angeles and the other in Dallas, both with Saturday-night stays, the total cost for both tickets was only $800. With back-to-back ticketing, travelers only use the outbound part of each round-trip ticket. They can save the remaining portions for use at a later date or simply toss them. Airlines frown on back-to-back ticketing because they claim it violates the contract they have with travelers. To avoid problems, experts suggest booking each half of your back-to-back tickets with a different travel agent or even on two different airlines. Beware that airlines have threatened to take away the frequent flyer miles of anyone discovered using back-to-back tickets and some have even stopped passengers at the gate, demanding they pay full fare. Although this has rarely happened, airlines warn they're cracking down on the practice.

Hidden Cities
No, we're not talking about flying to the lost city of Atlantis. Parsons coined the term "hidden cities" when he discovered that sometimes you can get the cheapest fare between point A and point B by buying a ticket to point C. Let's say you're in Los Angeles and you need to get to Dallas. You learn a one-way ticket costs $548, but you can buy a ticket from L.A. to Austin, with a stop in Dallas, for only $187. Now, you don't want to go to Austin, but you can jump off the plane when it lands in Dallas, the "hidden city." This fare difference is mainly due to the fact that airlines no longer base their prices on how many miles are traveled but on how heavy competition is on certain routes.

A downside of hidden-city ticketing is that you obviously can't check luggage. In this example, it would end up in Austin. However, because your savings can be dramatic, Parsons suggests, "Pack light, carry light, and keep your wallet heavy with greenbacks." Like back-to-back ticketing, a bigger drawback to the hidden-city strategy is that the airlines claim it violates their rules. It's not illegal per se, but if you're caught, you could be billed for the extra fare you would have paid for the shorter trip. If you still want to risk it, make sure you use it only for one-way travel because it's easier for airlines to catch you if you try to use the return portion of your ticket. If they know what you're up to, many travel agents won't book hidden-city tickets since getting caught could upset their relationship with an airline.

Back-to-back and hidden-city ticketing are particularly controversial. The traveling public and many consumer travel advocates question whether airlines have the right to tell you how to use tickets once you buy them. Ed Perkins, editor of the *Consumer Reports Travel Letter,* uses an interesting analogy: "What would happen if McDonald's usually sells a hamburger for $2.98, and it runs a special for a hamburger plus fries for $2.69, and then goes around and tries to collect an extra 29 cents from everybody who didn't eat the fries?" However you cut it, using these creative ticketing practices is a risk because the airlines carry a lot of clout.

Low-fare Airlines: Little Companies, Big Savings

Low-fare airlines are a cost-conscious consumer's best friend. Not only do they offer great fares, but they've forced the major carriers to drop prices on certain routes to remain competitive. The Department of Transportation (DOT) has estimated that low-fare carriers save travelers more than $6 billion a year. Some, like Southwest and America West, offer service to many U.S. cities, while others, like Tower Air, have broken into the international market. A majority of low-fare airlines concentrate on providing regional service; Reno Air, Spirit Airlines, and Pro Air are a few examples. By flying older planes, hiring nonunion workers, and contracting out aircraft maintenance, these upstart airlines keep overhead low and pass the savings on to the public. In exchange for cheap fares, most low-cost carriers have limited frequent-flyer programs, cramped seating, and offer minimal in-flight services. But when you're talking about coach, Ed Perkins points out, "The service on the big airlines is certainly no better than it is on the low-fare lines. It's bad everywhere."

The DOT collects fare information from most airlines for each route they fly. If you examine the data for the average round-trip coach fares consumers paid in 1996, it's clear that low-cost airlines can save you money. For example, on the Chicago–Minneapolis route United charged an average of $409 per ticket while Frontier averaged only $105. And passengers flying from Dallas to Salt Lake City paid American $365 on average for flights but only $192 to Vanguard. Along with everyday lower prices, low-fare airlines offer other advantages. Many don't require advance purchase or Saturday-night stays in order to secure a good fare. And though some low-cost carriers now utilize yield management—selling certain seats for more than others based on demand—even the highest-priced seat on these upstarts usually will cost you less than on a major carrier.

If you want to patronize low-fare airlines, you'll probably have to do some of the work yourself. Some travel agents are reluctant to book passengers on no-frills flights. A problem is that many of these smaller carriers aren't listed on computer reservation systems. And even when they are, the agent might have to call the airline directly to ticket the flight instead of doing it all from the computer terminal. Make it a point to ask your agent which low-fare airlines have flights to your destination, or call the carriers directly; all have toll-free numbers.

Ever since the 1996 ValuJet crash in the Florida Everglades, the entire low-fare industry has been stigmatized by the public's perception that it sacrifices safety for low prices. Are these airlines safe? While travelers have to make this decision for themselves, consider this. While most low-cost carriers haven't been around long enough to compile reliable statistics, Southwest, the granddaddy of the low-fare biz, has one of the best safety records in the entire industry. Low-fare airlines have made travel more affordable for everyone and might well be worth a try.

Airline Promotions: Hidden Deals with Big Savings
Travel expert Tom Parsons calls airline special promotions "buried treasure" for consumers and likens them to "hundred-dollar bills you can pick up and use if you know where to find them." These promotions take many forms, including dollars-

off coupons, two-for-one certificates, free upgrades, and discounted weekend trips. You need to keep your eyes open because they can pop up anywhere. Here are some examples.

- •Buy $250 worth of groceries at certain supermarkets and you're eligible for discounted airline tickets for anywhere in the United States.
- •Purchase a video for $19.98 and receive a certificate that gives you up to $400 off a round-trip ticket to London.
- •Stay at certain hotels and get free upgrade certificates that can bump you from coach to first class on future flights.

Also, if you're a senior citizen or a student you're eligible for various discounts on most airlines, so be sure to ask. Many of the major carriers also have senior coupon programs where older travelers can buy vouchers at a discount and then use them to fly to any domestic destination. You can stay on top of promotions by subscribing to one of the many newsletters and magazines devoted to travel.

And don't forget the greatest promotional gimmick of all: frequent-flyer programs. Even if you don't fly often, you can earn miles for doing just about anything: making phone calls, eating at certain restaurants, even purchasing a car or home. However, use these plans cautiously. The airlines don't offer frequent flyer miles to be nice. The programs have been extremely successful at increasing brand loyalty, and one way or another you're paying something for these freebies in the end. Don't be a sucker. Parsons says that a frequent-flyer mile is literally worth 2 cents, so if you receive 1,000 miles for purchasing something, it's really only worth $20. Shop around and buy products at good prices, not just because they earn you miles.

HOTELS

"I think the biggest mistake travelers make is obsessing about airfares and not spending as much time as they should on hotel prices," says Ed Perkins, editor of the *Consumer Reports Travel Letter*. Think about it. While it's the goal of most people to fly for as little as possible, they shouldn't forget what they'll have to shell out for a hotel room. "In an awful lot of cases, hotel accommodations are going to amount to a bigger chunk of a traveler's budget than airfare," Perkins notes. Just like securing a good fare, with a little work and some insider info, there's no reason why you should ever have to pay full price for lodging again.

ON THE RACK: THE TRUTH ABOUT HOTEL RATES
Did you ever notice that when you check into a hotel, the front desk clerk never says your room rate out loud? He or she simply circles it on your invoice, pushes it across the counter, and asks you to initial. Why the cloak-and-dagger routine? Well, the guy waiting in line behind you may be paying a lot more or less for the same type of room as you. To avoid a tussle in the lobby, hotels find it easier to keep their guests in the dark. As with airfares, you'll find dozens of different rates at the same hotel for similar rooms. Let's start with the rack rate. This is the published list price for any given hotel room, but it's a price you rarely should have to pay. For example, when we inquired about rates at a luxury hotel in Los Angeles, we were first quoted the rack rate of $390 per night for a deluxe room. But after a bit of prodding, we knocked that down to $255 in less than a minute. Getting discounts on hotel rooms is easy if you know where to look and what to ask.

BOOKING A ROOM: WHAT ARE YOUR OPTIONS?
Just like buying plane tickets, there are different ways to go about booking a hotel room. Getting a great rate takes patience and perseverance since there isn't one method that will always secure you the cheapest price. The important thing is to shop around and use all the resources available to you.

Toll-free Numbers, Direct Dialing, and Travel Agents

A good starting point in booking a room with a major chain is to call its toll-free number. A hotel representative can access price information for all the hotels in the chain and give you a quote for the location and type of room you want. However, many times you can get a better deal if you call the hotel directly. It will have detailed information about the property, be more up to date on room availability and special discounts, and have more authority to negotiate rates. For example, one chain's national reservation number quoted a standard room rate of $230 per night, but when the hotel was called directly it had a weekend special that knocked the rate down to $150. However, it always pays to call both numbers. Sometimes the left hand doesn't know what the right hand is quoting, so you can never be sure where you'll get the best deal.

A mistake many people make when calling for a reservation is simply asking for the price of a room. We can almost guarantee that the first rate a reservation clerk will quote is for something more luxurious—and thus more expensive—than the standard room. You need to emphasize that you are looking for the lowest possible price. For example, a hotel in Los Angeles first quoted us a room rate of $420. Although the clerk never volunteered the fact that less expensive rooms were available, with a little nudging she revealed there was a standard room available for $165 less. Another big mistake travelers make is failing to inquire about any specials that are going on at a hotel as well as discounts for certain organizations or age groups. (See "Discounts: Don't Ask, Don't Tell.")

Travel agents also can reserve rooms through computer reservation systems. Hotels pay agents a 10 to 15 percent commission on rooms they book. As with airfares, it takes a good travel agent to locate the best deals. Sometimes a hotel's special promotional rates are listed on the computer, and sometimes they're not. Jason, your coauthor, learned this firsthand when he booked a room at the Ritz Carlton in southern California. Even with a corporate discount, his travel agent couldn't get a rate under $245, but when Jason called the hotel directly, he discovered there was a special promotional rate available for $150. An aggressive travel agent will find the cheapest rate on the system and then call the hotel directly to see if he can get an even better deal.

Expert Ed Perkins also suggests finding an agent who has access to preferred rates—special discounted prices that hotels give certain agencies due to volume booking. "Any good travel agency will have access to a preferred rate program of some kind, and they can run as much as 40 percent off the list price," Perkins says. A hotel chain also might select certain travel agencies to be their preferred suppliers. For the consumer, this is a double-edged sword. It can bias agents toward their preferred supplier hotel, but at the same time they can use their clout to secure things like bigger discounts and free room upgrades.

Hotel Consolidators: Booking in Bulk

Hotel consolidators, also called brokers, contract with hotels to book rooms the hotels fear may go unsold. Since consolidators deal in volume—booking large blocks of rooms—they're able to offer consumers some excellent deals. According to Bob Deiner of Hotel Reservations Network, one of the best-known consolidators in the country, booking a room through a broker can save up to 70 percent off the rack rate. Bear in mind that consolidators work almost exclusively with moderate to high-priced hotels in major cities, both in the United States and abroad, as well as resort areas. Some offer rooms in dozens of cities; others specialize in just one city or region.

While brokers can save you money, they also can get you out of a jam when rooms are scarce. During certain times of the year, a city's hotels might be booked solid due to conventions, holidays, or special events. This is when a consolidator can come to the rescue. "When a hotel tells you 'sold out,' it doesn't really mean they're sold out because a consolidator may be holding rooms," explains Deiner. Take Orlando in July, when Disney World is overflowing with vacationing families. "We have rooms at probably fifty hotels in Orlando, even when the city is sold out," he says.

Many travel agents work with hotel consolidators on a regular basis, but you can call a broker directly. Some brokers require you to prepay a room reservation through them, while others will simply make a discounted reservation for you at a hotel and have you pay as you normally would, when you check out. Before you book, make sure you know what the cancellation policy is in case your plans change. Policies can vary from broker to broker and hotel to hotel, so it's best to get them in writing. Usually you can find hotel consolidators by calling the local convention and visitors bureau or chamber of commerce in the city you plan to visit. Here are a few of the better-known consolidators to get you started.

- **Central Reservation Service:** (800) 548-3311 (www.reserva tion-services.com). Most major U.S. and international cities.
- **Hotel Reservations Network:** (800) 964-6835 (www.180096hotel.com). Most major U.S. cities plus London and Paris.
- **Quikbook:** (800) 789-9887 (www.quikbook.com). Seven major U.S. cities.
- **Room Exchange:** (800) 846-7000 (www.hotelrooms.com). Major U.S. and European cities.
- **Travel Interlink:** (800) 477-7172. Major cities in Europe, Asia, and the South Pacific.

As with all businesses, there are unscrupulous hotel consolidators. To protect yourself, check out the company with the Better Business Bureau or consumer protection agency where it's located. Finally, "Never send cash and never pay by check," warns Deiner. "Always pay on a credit card. If someone is demanding cash, something is wrong."

Half-Price Hotel Rooms: Join the Club

Why sleep in a $75-a-night hotel room when you can rest easy in a $150 room at half price? That's what half-price hotel companies are all about. Hotels work with them because they would rather book their rooms at a discount than have them go empty. To join a half-price program, you pay a fee, usually $50 to $100 a year, and receive an I.D. card and a directory, which lists hundreds of participating hotels all over the world as well as discounts on dining, attractions, car rentals, airline tickets, and other travel services.

To book a room, you simply pick out the hotel you'd like and call it directly. Unfortunately, a 50 percent discount isn't guaranteed. If a hotel projects it will be over 80 percent occupied during the dates you want, it probably won't give you a half-price rate. There's also the question of how a hotel calculates its discount. Unfortunately, in some cases, hotels quote half off an inflated rack rate. "Sometimes the rack rate hotels calculate the discount from is fake," says travel expert Ed Perkins. "Even if you walked up to the desk you wouldn't have to pay that much." Also, be aware that some hotels that belong to half-price programs never offer 50 percent off their room rates. Many large chains give a more modest 25 percent discount. Unquestionably, it can be frustrating if the hotel you want won't honor a discount. Nevertheless, if you're a frequent traveler, a half-price program usually can save you money.

To become a member of a half-price program, you can call the company directly or join though various travel clubs, alumni associations, church groups, and similar organizations. Here are a few of the better-known programs.

- •Encore: (800) 444-9800 (www.travelfare.com/encore.htm)
- •Entertainment Publications: (800) 445-4137 (www.entertainment-gold.com)
- •Great American Traveler: (800) 548-2812 (www.member-web.com)

- ITC-50: (800) 987-6216
- Quest: (800) 742-3543

SHOPPING STRATEGY: GETTING A ROOM AT THE INN (AT A GREAT RATE)

In this section we provide some tips the budget-minded traveler should keep in mind to get the best bargains on hotel rates. We hope they'll help you get the room you want at a price that's right.

Shop Smart: Five Tips to Follow

Know what you need. There are countless hotels to choose from that offer a variety of rates, amenities, and services, particularly if you're traveling to a large city or resort area. Remember that while a hotel with a gym, sauna, and Olympic-size pool sounds great, if you don't have the time or inclination to use them, you're wasting money.

Plan ahead. Just like buying an airline ticket, often you can get good deals on hotel rooms if you book early. Many hotels offer advance-purchase discounts of up to 50 percent when reservations are made a month or so prior to your stay. But be careful; some hotels require prepayment, and it can be difficult to get your money back if you cancel your trip.

Be persistent. Many hotels change their rates frequently in response to market demand. Discounts and specials can pop up at any time. Keep calling a hotel even after you've booked a room to see if a better deal becomes available.

Travel the off-season. Hotels generally offer lower rates during their off-season, when demand for rooms is low. Naturally, the off-season depends on where you're traveling. Few people head to Phoenix during August, when even the sidewalks sizzle. Likewise, Chicago in January is not only windy but much too cold for most vacationers. During these off-peak times, you can nab some great rates at even the finest hotels.

•*Preserve paperwork.* A little organization can save you a lot of time and frustration later. When you book a room, make note of the rate, any discounts, the confirmation number, and the name of your reservation agent. Same thing if you cancel. Record the cancellation number, the date you called, and the agent's name. If you cancel a room you reserved on a credit card, keep a close eye on your monthly statements until you're satisfied the hotel hasn't mistakenly charged you. We've learned from experience that having documentation always makes clearing up billing errors easier.

Discounts: Don't Ask, Don't Tell

As we've said, only fools pay full price. With so many hotel discounts available, almost anyone can qualify for at least one. Here's a breakdown of the most common:

•*Corporate rates:* Most hotels in metropolitan areas offer a discounted rate for business travelers, usually a modest 10 to 20 percent. However, large corporations often negotiate special rates with hotel chains that can mean discounts of up to 40 percent for their employees whether they're traveling for business or pleasure. Even if you're self-employed, don't be afraid to ask for a corporate discount. Sometimes all you need is a business card to qualify. A word of warning: Don't assume the corporate rate is always the best you can get. We recently paid a "preferred corporate rate" of $165 at a national hotel, only to learn that the walk-in rate was $125.

•*Membership discounts:* If you belong to certain groups or organizations, often you can take advantage of special rates. The most prevalent is the American Automobile Association (AAA), whose members often get at least 10 percent off at participating hotels. Civic-organization or union members, government employees, and those who've served in the military are other examples of those who may be eligible for some kind of discount.

•*Family discounts:* You never want to pay full price when traveling with kids. At many hotels there's no charge for children under 18 who stay in the same room with their parents. If you need additional space, usually you can get a second room for up to 50 percent off. Most national chains also offer free meals for kids if they eat with their parents. Make sure you know the age limit to qualify for such discounts. At some hotels children qualify if they're nineteen or younger; at others the cut-off age is twelve.

•*Senior discounts:* Most hotels offer senior citizen discounts of about 10 to 30 percent, so be sure to carry your American Association of Retired Persons (AARP) card when traveling. Some hotel chains also run their own senior programs, which you can join for little or no charge and receive discounts of up to 50 percent.

To take advantage of any discount program you qualify for, you've got to speak up. First, ask the hotel for the lowest rate available, then run through the litany of possible discounts for which you are eligible. Don't be shy. If you don't qualify for a discount, try to negotiate your own preferred rate. If you're booking more than one room or staying several nights, see if they'll knock a little off the price. Travel expert Tom Parsons emphasizes that haggling shouldn't be restricted to room rates and suggests asking for a free room upgrade or complimentary breakfast too. The worst the hotel can do is say no. If you're booking at the last minute, Parsons recommends doing it over the phone. You don't have as much leverage when you're standing at the front desk with nowhere to go for the night.

Promotions: Keep Your Eyes Peeled for Savings
Like the airlines, hotels run special promotions to drum up business, and there are some great deals to be had if you know where

to find them. You can take advantage of offers like free room upgrades, discounts for using certain credit cards, free car rental, double frequent flyer mile credit, and specials for staying more than two nights. Weekend getaway rates are also popular at many hotels. In addition to low room rates, these getaway bargains might include free room service or a complimentary champagne brunch.

A hotel's frequent traveler program also can be a key to savings. Just like the airlines, most hotel chains have membership programs that earn you points with every stay. You can redeem these points for free stays at any of the chain's properties or, with some programs, trade them in for merchandise or airline tickets. As a frequent traveler member you also may be eligible for certain exclusive benefits like special room rates, automatic room upgrades, express check-in and checkout, and free morning coffee and newspaper. Examples of some of the biggest frequent traveler programs include the Hilton HHonors program, Marriott Honored Guest rewards, and the Holiday Inn Priority Club.

Where do you find out about hotel promotions? Your travel agent is a good source. You'll also find them stuffed in with your monthly credit card bill and frequent flyer club statement. Expert Tom Parsons suggests checking the Sunday travel section of the newspaper for your destination city as well as nearby cities. For instance, if you're traveling to San Francisco, check out not only the *San Francisco Chronicle* but the *Los Angeles Times* as well. Hotels will often advertise great bargains in area papers to attract guests from the region, but if you can learn of any special promotions, you'll be able to take advantage of them even if you're traveling from across the country. You can get out-of-town newspapers at larger newsstands or at your local library.

Another way to secure a promotional rate is simply to ask when you make your reservation. Again, don't count on the hotel reservation agent to immediately offer you the best deal.

Hotel Alternatives: Other Options for the Budget Traveler

If you're traveling on a shoestring budget or just tired of staying in drab hotel rooms with no character, there are options that can save you money and offer a unique experience.

•*Bed and Breakfasts:* For some charming ambience, consider a stay at a bed and breakfast. Accommodations vary, ranging from a historic inn to a spare room in someone's house. Often there are few amenities—no room service or swimming pool, perhaps— and you might even have to share a bathroom with other guests. However, usually you'll find a relaxed setting, comfortable room, and a homemade breakfast. B&Bs don't offer the anonymity of a big hotel, so they're not for the shy or introverted, but they always offer a unique experience at a bargain price. Most B&Bs require payment in advance, and many don't take credit cards. They also usually have strict cancellation policies. While people usually associate B&Bs with small towns and rural areas, you can find them in every big city in the country (and abroad). B&B listings can be found in guidebooks, newspaper ads, or through local tourist boards and chambers of commerce. There are also regional and national B&B booking services.

•*Apartment or house rentals:* Whether it's a condo in Maui, a flat in London, or a villa in the Caribbean, rentals allow you to live among the natives and save money too. Often they're large enough to accommodate an entire family and usually provide a kitchen for cooking meals yourself. Most rentals require at least a week's stay and provide no maid service. You can find rentals in your newspaper's travel section or book them through a broker or rental agent. But beware; Wendy Perrin, *Condé Nast Traveler*'s consumer news editor, has heard from many folks who thought they were booking luxury rentals only to discover the place was a dump. To protect yourself, do a little homework. Check out any broker or agent with the local tourist board and request photos or a video of the property and the surrounding area.

• *Youth Hostels:* Hostels offer the ultimate in no-frills accommodations. While they're most prevalent in Europe, where people of all ages take advantage of their low cost, there are plenty of hostels in the United States too. Remember that you get what you pay for. Hostels provide little privacy, men and women usually stay in separate dorms, there are strict curfews, and you need to vacate the hostel during the day. However, if you simply want a cheap night's stay, a hostel offers a good alternative.

Buyer Beware: Hidden Charges

Hidden charges are our pet peeve. You book a nice hotel room at a rate that suits your budget, only to find a slew of extra charges on your bill at checkout time. There's the parking fee, which can cost you up to $20 a day, even if you don't use the valet service. There's the $15 resort fee, even though you didn't stick a toe in the pool or run one step on a treadmill. And what about the excessive room service charges? Not only are the menu prices extravagant, but many hotels are now adding a 15 percent service charge on top of a separate delivery fee, while still expecting you to add a gratuity. Don't even get us started on those $8 bags of honey-roasted peanuts from the courtesy bar!

Another cash cow for hotels is phone calls. Forget the dime-a-minute rates you get at home. Hotels usually charge more than a dollar a minute on long distance calls and demand 75 cents for each local or toll-free number. Hotels in the United States are required to list their calling rates and the long distance carrier they use. They also must give you the option of using your own calling card. Understand what a call is going to cost *before* you pick up the phone.

Taxes also cause instant bill inflation. When hotels quote you their rates, they rarely include various hotel taxes, which can add 10 to 20 percent to your bill. In New York City, for example, we were quoted a room rate of $179 for the night. But add 8.25 percent state tax, 5 percent city tax, and a $2 occupancy tax, and our room rate skyrocketed to $205. And it's not just the Big Apple that's tax happy. Washington, D.C., Chicago, Dallas,

Houston, Los Angeles, and Miami are just a few of the many cities where hotel taxes run over 12 percent. Travel abroad and you'll be socked with even higher taxes—up to 25 percent. Protect yourself and your budget from a rude shock by asking what the room rate is, including taxes, when you book your room.

Finally, be sure to check out your bill when you check out. Hotels make mistakes on their bills—some studies suggest up to 40 percent of the time. Unless you want to pay for another guest's dry cleaning, scrutinize your bill and point out any errors to the front desk clerk immediately. Usually he or she will be happy to correct any errors on the spot.

CAR RENTALS

You have your plane ticket and hotel accommodations, now it's time to rent some wheels.

HOW TO DRIVE A HARD BARGAIN: BOOKING THE BEST RATE

The car-rental industry is dominated by the big guys—Hertz, Avis, Enterprise, National, and Budget—with increasing competition from smaller companies including Alamo, Value, and Thrifty. There are also regional and local companies out there vying for your business. With so much competition, there are plenty of good deals to be had.

To book a car, you can call individual companies directly (most have toll-free numbers), visit travel reservation sites on the Internet, or go through your travel agent. Car-rental companies typically pay agents a 10 percent commission for each booking. Here are some shopping strategies to consider.

•*Shop early.* It pays to shop early and often because car-rental prices change constantly, depending on demand. Although you might get lucky and secure a last-minute deal, we suggest booking in advance. By reserving ahead of time, you'll almost always get a good price. More important, you'll be assured of *getting* a car. At peak travel times—especially at resort destinations like Orlando—it's not uncommon for a company to run out of automobiles completely. True bargain hunters book in advance but continue to check rates as their trip draws near.

•*Shop around.* We've seen rental prices vary tremendously from company to company, so it's important to call at least three and compare. When reviewing quotes, there's a lot more to consider than just the basic rental rate; the cheapest rental-car quote could end up costing you the most. Pay particular attention to the amount of free miles included in the price of a rental, especially if you plan to drive a lot. One company might offer unlimited mileage, while another might allow only 100 free miles a day, charging for each additional mile driven. At 20 or 30 cents per mile, this can quickly add to your final cost. Also, if you plan to rent a car from one location and drop it off at another, ask each rental agency you're considering about the drop-off fee. These fees can vary by hundreds of dollars, so it's important to take them into consideration.

•*Find discounts and promotions.* Rental-car discounts are plentiful and can cut as much as 40 percent off your final bill. For example, as a member of the American Automobile Association (AAA), usually you can get $20 knocked off a weekly rental at most Hertz locations. Senior citizens, military personnel, and members of frequent-flyer clubs and other organizations can find similar discounts. Also, some companies negotiate special rates with rental-car agencies that their employees can take advantage of for either business or pleasure trips.

Rental agencies are always running promotions. You can find ads for free car upgrades, advance-purchase rates, weekend specials, and other bargains in the Sunday travel section of your newspaper. In addition, car-rental coupons can be found enclosed with frequent flyer statements and credit card bills. As with hotels, car-rental agencies rarely volunteer special promotional rates. Instead, you'll need to have the promotion code—a series of numbers or letters found on the coupon or ad; usually you can't get the special rate without it.

•*Consider your options.* Renting a car from an agency's airport site is almost always more expensive than renting from other office locations because operating expenses are higher out of an airport. In addition, many cities levy extra taxes and surcharges on cars rented at an airport. Denver, for instance, levies a $2.98-per-day surcharge on all cars rented from airport branches. You can avoid these surcharges by taking a cab or shuttle to your hotel and renting a car in town. This makes particular sense if you need a car for only part of your trip. Most national agencies have several branches in large cities; there might even be one right in your hotel. Another option is calling a company like Enterprise, which offers a unique service: It will either deliver a car right to your door or pick you up and take you to the nearest office. Enterprise's rates can be 30 to 40 percent cheaper than the competitors'. You also can check the yellow pages at your destination and find budget operators like Rent-A-Wreck as well as dozens of local companies and car dealers that rent automobiles at much lower rates than the major chains. Be careful of dealing with a company you've never heard of. While their rates may be cheaper, you want to ensure that the firm is reputable and rents well-maintained vehicles.

•*Rentals abroad.* Driving in a foreign country can be intimidating: signs in an unfamiliar language, freeways with no speed limits, and cars driving on the "wrong" side of the road. Unfortunately, getting a good deal on a rental car can be just as challenging. All the tips given above apply. In addition, keep in mind that foreign cars are generally much smaller than those in the United States. Make sure you, any traveling companions, and all your luggage can fit comfortably. If you can't handle a stick shift, you'll have to pay a premium for a car with an automatic transmission. Also, don't have a coronary at the pumps when you realize that gasoline can cost up to $5 U.S. per gallon.

Make your reservations before you go; you'll save money and frustration. Stick with major companies that have offices in the United States. Hertz, Avis, Dollar, and Budget are just a few of the U.S. chains that operate abroad. You also can use a rental wholesaler, such as Europe by Car (800-223-1516), Kemwel Holiday Autos (800-678-0678), and Auto Europe (800-223-5555). Many companies will let you prepay for a foreign car rental in U.S. currency, which is the best way to ensure exact cost. But before you prepay, make sure you're aware of any additional charges that might be added to your bill later. (See "Don't Let Extra Charges Drive You Over the Edge.")

HIGH-PRESSURE TACTICS: DON'T BE TAKEN FOR A RIDE

You're on vacation, you've had a long flight, and you just want to grab your rental car and be on your way. The last thing you need is some high-pressure sales pitch from a rental-car clerk. Well, brace yourself, because that's probably just what you're going to get. Most agents will try to convince you to upgrade to a more luxurious, and more expensive, vehicle. A convertible sounds fun, but is it worth the extra cash for a sunburned head? An agent also will try to push you to purchase the company's form of insurance coverage.

This coverage, called collision damage waiver (CDW) or loss damage waiver (LDW), produces huge revenues for rental-car agencies. The pitch sounds good: If your rental car is damaged or stolen and you've purchased the CDW—which can cost up to $16 a day—you won't be held financially responsible. While rental coverage itself isn't a bad thing, most people don't need it. If you own a car, your auto insurance policy probably covers you for rentals, although there might be a deductible. Similarly, if you're traveling on business, most companies have policies that protect their employees. Many credit-card companies also offer some form of built-in collision protection when you charge a rental to their card. (A word of warning: Some credit cards won't cover you if you rent certain types of vehicles, including vans, jeeps, and luxury cars.) Before you buy any coverage from a rental agency, do some research. Call both your private insurer and credit-card company to determine if the protection you have is sufficient.

Since many rental-car companies pay their agents a commission when they sell insurance coverage, you're bound to experience some high-pressure sales tactics. Some agents get customers to sign off on coverage without even explaining that it's optional. Others use intimidating scare tactics to get you to buy. If you decline collision coverage, you might hear, "Do you realize you'll be financially responsible for the full price of the car if you have an accident?" Or they'll try to plant a seed of doubt: "Are you sure your credit card covers you completely?" These tactics have gotten so bad that some states have placed caps on how much a company can charge for CDW coverage, and both New York and Illinois have outlawed it completely.

Car-rental companies push other types of insurance coverage:

- *Liability coverage* covers you if you're in an accident that involves bodily injury or property damage and you're sued.
- *Personal accident insurance* provides a one-time payment if you or your passengers are maimed or killed in an accident.
- *Personal effects coverage* reimburses you if personal property is damaged or stolen from your car.

Again, your auto or homeowner insurance might already provide this kind of coverage. If you rent cars often, a call to your insurance agent can save you hundreds of dollars a year on protection you don't need.

DON'T LET EXTRA CHARGES DRIVE YOU OVER THE EDGE

There's nothing worse than extra charges that make your final rental-car bill soar. A close look at your receipt will reveal that you're paying for a lot more than just a basic rental rate. The most common extra charges include drop-off fees, additional driver fees, and the following.

•*Taxes and surcharges:* Your final bill will most likely include a myriad of charges, including a vehicle license fee, airport access fee, and the usual state and city taxes. These extra surcharges can add as much as 25 percent to your final cost. And if you think the fees are bad in the United States, they're nothing compared to those in Europe.

•*Fuel fees:* Here's another way agencies pump up profits. Your best bet when refueling your rental car is to simply fill the tank before you return the vehicle. If you don't, the company will charge you a premium—about $3 to $4 a gallon—to do it. When you rent a car, the agent also might push the fuel-purchase option, claiming it will save you money. Trust us, it won't. The idea is to prepay for a full tank of gas at a fairly reasonable per-gallon rate. Your mission, should you choose to accept it, is to return the car with an empty tank. Any fuel that remains is essentially your gift to the rental agency. Unless you know you can return the car at the point where it's running on vapors, decline this option.

•*Cancellation penalties:* If you make a reservation but fail to cancel it, some companies will still charge you a day's rental fee as a penalty. When you book your car, make a note of the cancellation policy. If you do cancel your reservation, jot down the date you called, whom you talked to, and the cancellation number.

TOUR PACKAGES

Tour packages offer one-stop shopping convenience. If you're overwhelmed by all the details of planning a trip, these tours present an easy and sometimes economical option. But pick the wrong tour and your vacation can turn into a nightmare.

Dozens of tour operators go out of business every year, leaving hundreds of prepaid customers without trips or refunds. Even worse, travelers actually have been stranded during their vacations with no way to get home. In this section we look at the perks and pitfalls of tour package deals.

PICK A TOUR, ANY TOUR

When people think of travel tours, many picture themselves squeezed into a packed bus, visiting different countries at breakneck speed, and stopping only for quick photo ops and overpriced tourist traps. While package tours like that still exist, today there's a lot more variety. Tours can offer the traveler total structure or complete freedom. Some have experienced guides, others let you explore on your own. What can you expect from a tour package? Well, that definitely depends on the type of trip you choose. In addition to the traditional "Discover Europe in ten days" tour, many other types of packages are available.

Specialty Tours

Specialty trips can offer once-in-a-lifetime opportunities. On an adventure tour, you might hike in Nepal, bike in Napa Valley, or bungee jump in New Zealand, all under the watchful eyes of trained guides who are there to ensure you have fun and make it home in one piece. An art lover's tour might have you visiting the finest museums in Europe, guided by an art connoisseur, while on an ecotour you could be tagging along as a scientist and his crew study sea turtles in the Galapagos.

Fly/Drive and Air/Land Packages

These convenient package deals bundle your airfare with your hotels, car rental, or both. Most airlines have their own tour divisions that sell these packages, often to popular vacation destinations. For example, Delta offers Delta Dream Vacations, while American has Fly Away Vacations. They can be big money savers. In some cases, an entire package can cost less than a plane ticket alone. Keep in mind that these are package deals, not tours. You won't travel with a group or guide.

Charter Tours
Charter tours are usually air and hotel packages to resort destinations. Instead of flying on a major carrier, you take a charter plane. At your destination, the tour usually provides a free transfer to your hotel as well as an orientation program where you can purchase tickets for group sightseeing tours and activities.

All-Inclusive Packages
These are the ultimate in one-stop shopping. One price covers everything, from meals, to lodging, to activities of all kinds. There's no need to leave the property unless you really want to. Club Med is probably the most famous example of an all-inclusive vacation destination.

WHERE TO LOOK, WHERE TO BOOK
Although you can buy packages directly from tour operators, most are sold through travel agents. In fact, ever since the airlines put a cap on commissions, many agents have started selling more packages because they can earn up to 15 percent for every trip they book. Today more and more agents are specializing in certain types of travel, such as ecotourism, spa vacations, and family trips. So, if you're planning something unique, look for an agent who concentrates on the kind of trip you want.

If you can travel at a moment's notice, keep an eye out for any last-minute deals in the newspaper. Occasionally tour operators hold fire sales when they need to fill vacancies. There are great bargains to be had, but you also need to ask yourself why the tour isn't already booked.

PICKING THE PERFECT PACKAGE: HOW TO
DECIPHER THE BEST DEAL

Before you sink your savings into the trip of a lifetime, know what you're getting into. Package tours can be great, but when they're bad, they're awful. And because you pay for packages up front, you'll probably feel obligated to stick with your trip till the bitter end. You can prevent potential vacations from hell by doing your homework before you leave home.

Never take glossy brochures at face value. *Today* show travel editor Peter Greenberg suggests reading travel literature carefully and scrutinizing every claim. When a hotel touts a "beach nearby," it could mean you and your inflatable inner tube need to take a $15 cab ride even to see water. Likewise, "minutes from attractions" could indicate a five-minute stroll or a thirty-minute bus ride. "They play games like this all the time," warns Greenberg. "If your hotel claims to have 'old world charm,' translation: There's no private bathroom." Ask questions and don't assume anything. If the hotel says they're "steps from the shore," call up and ask exactly how many steps they're talking about.

Greenberg also suggests pulling out a magnifying glass to inspect a brochure's fine print. Some picture beautiful hotels, but in teeny-size letters say that substitutions may be made. Others state that rooms are "run-of-house." "Run-of-house means that the hotel gets to put you in whatever room they choose," Greenberg explains. "It might be the presidential suite, but most likely it'll be a room the size of a closet at the back of the hotel." Greenberg says the biggest mistake people make when booking tours abroad is buying into claims of "four-star hotels" without understanding what that really means. "We know what a four-star hotel is in the United States," he says, "but many countries use a star system that isn't necessarily a ratings system. Those stars aren't based on decor, amenities, ambience, architecture, or any of the other criteria we use in the United States. Often stars are just a designation by the government to indicate how much a hotel charges for a room, without making any kind of evaluation of its services." Thus, a four-star hotel abroad could just mean expensive, not luxurious.

When comparing different tours, if you simply book the cheapest one you're almost bound to be disappointed. Remember, your goal is value, the combination of cost and quality. There's probably a very good reason why one tour to Italy is $1,000 cheaper than any other. More expensive trips usually travel with smaller groups and offer nicer hotels, better tour guides, and include meals. Find out precisely what's included in the package price of any tour you're considering. Will you have to pay for meals? Admission to attractions? The airfare from your hometown? Also scrutinize the trip itinerary. Tours cramming too many things into too little time is a consumer complaint we've heard often. If a tour promises to visit a location you really have your heart set on, be aware that "visit" might mean five hours or five minutes. Make sure you'll have enough time to explore the places that interest you most. When shopping around for the perfect tour, keep these additional questions in mind.

- What's the average group size?
- What are the tour guide's qualifications?
- Will the same guide work the entire trip, or will there be several local guides?
- Are special skills or a certain physical ability level required?
- Are there optional excursions?
- If meals are included, must they always be eaten with the group, or can participants dine on their own?
- Are references available from two or three clients who've taken the tour before?

PROTECT YOURSELF: WATCHING OUT FOR YOUR WALLET

Buying a tour package can be a risky financial proposition since you're always required to pay in full, weeks, even months in advance. While most trips go off without a hitch, we've heard many horror stories of fly-by-night tour operators who take the money and run. And the government won't step in and help you recoup your losses. Although regulations vary from state to state, there are few laws on the books to protect the traveling public against unscrupulous tour operators. (See "Travel Fraud.") That's why you've got to protect yourself.

One of the most important things you can do is make sure your tour operator protects your deposit. Look for tour companies that put their clients' funds in an escrow account. (Some states require this by law.) That way, if the company goes belly-up, you have a better chance of getting your money back. Many reputable tour operators hold membership in one of the industry trade organizations, which require their members to follow a code of ethics. The United States Tour Operators Association also requires operators to post a $1 million bond or hold that sum in another form of security. Realize that any company can claim it keeps money in escrow or has a trade association membership. Don't take the company's word for it. Call the association it claims to belong to and get the name of the bank where it holds customer deposits in escrow. (See "Where to Turn for Help.")

As always, it's best to pay by credit card, but make sure you don't pay for your trip too far in advance. Most credit card companies allow only sixty days to dispute a charge after you get your bill, so if you pay too far ahead, you could lose the built-in protection that plastic provides. Also, before you put down a cent, make sure you fully understand a tour operator's cancellation and refund policies and get them in writing. Most travel packages have very strict penalties if you pull out. If you're forced to cancel after your final payment, there's a good chance you'll have to forfeit most of your money. This is a good reason to consider travel insurance.

There are several options when it comes to trip insurance. Some cover you only if you have to cancel due to serious illness, death, or other disaster at home or your destination. Other plans cover any expenses you incur if your flight is delayed or your baggage is lost, stolen, or damaged. More comprehensive policies include emergency medical insurance, which covers you if you get sick or are injured during a trip and need medical help or an emergency evacuation. You can buy trip insurance through your travel agent, tour operator, or an independent insurance company. All offer different types of plans at different prices, so you should shop around. Generally, you can expect to pay about $5 dollars for every $100 of basic coverage. Buying a policy through your tour operator is the most convenient, but it's often the least flexible and comprehensive. If you do purchase insurance through your tour operator, make sure the policy is underwritten by a separate entity so you're fully protected if the tour company goes bankrupt before your trip. Before you buy insurance, check your medical and homeowner policies to see what kind of coverage they offer when you travel. Then you can just buy trip insurance to fill in the gaps.

TRAVEL FRAUD

Most travelers have had at least one disappointing vacation. Travel fraud, however, goes far beyond disappointment. It's what turns your dream vacation into a screaming nightmare. Travel fraud comes in many different forms, and while most consumers think it will never happen to them, don't be so sure it can't happen to you.

SCHEMES, SCAMS, AND SWINDLES

The Federal Trade Commission (FTC) estimates that travel fraud costs consumers more than $12 billion a year. If you look at the number of complaints the FTC, state attorneys general, and Better Business Bureaus receive each year, travel-related fraud always ranks near the top of the list. From brokers of stolen plane tickets to bogus "travel clubs" that are really deceptive timeshare offers, travel-industry swindlers make a lot of promises but always fail to deliver. Take a look at a few scams the FTC has acted upon.

• A Massachusetts company offered immigrants "affordable" airfares to visit their homes in India and Africa. Victims prepaid their tickets, but the company never delivered and refused to provide refunds.

• A California firm sold tutorial kits that claimed to teach consumers how to become travel agents. It came with a travel agent I.D. card that the company said could be used to secure discounts, free upgrades, and insider perks for personal travel. In fact, the credentials rarely resulted in the promised discounts, and the kits were inadequate to allow the buyer to operate a travel business.

• For a $200 to $4,000 advance, a South Carolina company guaranteed it could resell consumers' time shares. The fees were collected but the properties were never sold.

• A Florida firm calling itself a "full-service travel agency" offered prepaid travel packages at discount rates in an effort to "promote tourism." The packages purportedly were sponsored by well-known hotel chains and airlines. However, the firm wasn't authorized to issue airline tickets, and the advertised hotels had never heard of the company. Consumers were promised refunds but never received them.

One of the biggest travel scams operating involves travel certificates. You open up your mailbox, and surprise! A colorful certificate tells you to "pack your bags" because you've been selected to "receive a Caribbean paradise cruise." On a cold and blustery day in New York City, we received just such a certificate. It sounded too good to be true, so we asked our bosses at NBC's *Today* show to send us on the trip so we could investigate.

JANICE AND JASON'S BIG ADVENTURE:
OUR TRAVEL DIARY

The certificate from Design Travel said we had been "certified to receive" a "fantasy holiday extravaganza," a "spectacular five day/four night cruise package." We would set sail from Florida on a luxury cruise to the Grand Bahamas, experiencing "Las Vegas-style shows, nonstop casino action, and endless meals onboard ship!" But to receive our trip to paradise, we had to call the special toll-free hotline within seventy-two hours.

Well, we didn't rush to the phone. We actually called a couple weeks after receiving the certificate and were told the offer was still good. Although the certificate certainly made it sound as if we had won something, we quickly learned this wasn't the case. Our "travel consultant" from Design Travel offered us "a vacation package valued at $1,200" that we could have for only $398 per couple. He said it was a special "promotional rate" being offered to create "word of mouth" for the cruise line. He also told us the ship was "exactly like the *Love Boat* without the bad actors." When we warned him that we didn't want to stay in shabby accommodations at our destination in Freeport, we were assured that the hotel was "newly renovated" and "near all the attractions" and that the rooms normally retailed for $120 a night. What the heck. NBC was paying, so we gave him our credit card number.

A week later we received a registration packet from a company called Cruises International. Upon reading over the material, we realized that our simple deal was getting complicated. We were required to give sixty days' notice before we wanted to take our trip and also had to provide an alternate date. Over the following weeks we would be asked to send additional money for things like reservation fees, taxes, port charges, and service fees. Before long, our total cost had risen to over $700, and that didn't include the airfare to get us from New York to the port in Fort Lauderdale.

Two months after our initial call, it was time to pack our bags (and our hidden cameras). As we set sail, it was evident this wasn't a *Love Boat* cruise as much as a five-hour shuttle. We later discovered that our unluxury ocean liner was actually a twenty-eight-year-old converted ferry boat. And, boy, did it look it. The "Las Vegas-style shows" turned out to be a steel-drum band. The "endless meals on-board ship" was a breakfast buffet we were rushed through. There was some gambling, but since we had set sail at dawn, the most popular activity onboard was sleeping. If you wanted a cabin, it cost an additional $40. Most folks got some shut-eye on the windswept deck after forking over $2 to rent a blanket.

When we arrived in Freeport and our "first-class hotel," we found a group of our fellow travelers trying to check in. None of the rooms was ready, so we were all herded to the "lounge" where we had to sit through a long sales pitch to buy various sightseeing tours. Still waiting for our room, we walked around the grounds of the hotel and videotaped the view. The entire property was surrounded by a twelve-foot-high fence topped with razor wire. We weren't sure if the hotel was trying to keep us in or keep others out. Either way, we felt more like inmates than guests.

When we were finally able to check in, many of our fellow travelers were very upset with their accommodations. "This was supposed to have been remodeled six months ago," said Mike, who came all the way from Maryland with his wife, Mary. The dresser and refrigerator in their room were both broken, the bathroom was filthy, and there were stains on the rug and bedspread. "I didn't expect to stay in the Plaza," said Mary, "but I did expect to stay in a clean hotel room." Remember, while NBC was paying for our trip, our fellow passengers had spent their hard-earned money and used their well-earned vacation days for this experience. Folks like Gene, who had bought the trip as a Christmas gift for his wife, Lena. After seeing the Cruises International promotional video at home in Iowa, this lovely middle-age couple assumed they'd be staying near the beach. But the hotel was over three miles from any shoreline, and the view from their window was of the infamous razor-topped fence. "We travel a lot," said Lena, "and this is the worst hotel I've ever stayed at." The hotel actually scared her so much that each night Lena barricaded the door of her room using chairs and a table.

Just about everyone we spoke to felt they'd been ripped off. "I'm a little embarrassed at myself for falling for it," said Helen, a young, single woman from Pittsburgh who took the trip on her own and sounded very depressed as she told us her story. Helen said that when she first saw the certificate, her instincts told her that the offer was too good to be true. However, when she called to inquire about the details, she signed up because "I couldn't believe that the salesman could be outright lying." Helen said she truly thought that she was one of the select few who were given the opportunity to take advantage of a special offer. But now, instead of feeling like a winner, she felt like a loser. In the end, she had wasted a week of precious vacation time and almost $1,800.

When we got back to the mainland, we tried to contact Cruises International, the company responsible for our "fantasy" vacation. When no one responded to our repeated phone calls, we decided to stop by the company's office in Altamonte Springs, Florida, with a camera crew in tow. We told the owner, Earl Brewer, we had just come back from taking one of his vacations and that many of our fellow travelers were complaining that the cruise was disappointing and the hotel substandard. Mr. Brewer was not pleased. "Darling, you're talking about a place I own," he told Janice. "I own [the hotel], and I'm very proud of it. It's a third world country. What do you want for the price you pay?" (By the way, the Bahamas Tourist Office was quite peeved to hear their country described as "third world.")

Brewer's son, Steve, went on to explain that Cruises International should not be held responsible for what the agent at Design Travel told us. He said that if consumers are unhappy with their trip, they should write so the problems could be investigated. He also claimed they respond to all complaints. But the Better Business Bureau told us they had revoked Cruises International's membership because of the number of complaints against the company. We then tried to talk with Design Travel but were refused an interview.

After our story aired, we received dozens of calls from victims of Design Travel, Cruises International, and other travel-certificate companies. We also heard from folks in a panic because they had just bought packages and wanted to know what to do. We even heard from employees of travel certificate companies who confirmed many of the tricks that are played on unsuspecting consumers. The government also got involved. A Florida judge ordered Cruises International to pay $12,500 in fines—the largest amount ever imposed by the state on a travel seller. Design Travel, of Santa Rosa, California, got hit hard too. The Florida consumer affairs department slapped it with a $10,000 fine for operating without a license and eventually ordered it to stop operating in the state because of all the complaints against it. And Design Travel's problems didn't end there. The attorney generals of California and Wisconsin filed suit against the company, as did the Federal Trade Commission as part of its "Operation Trip Up" fraud enforcement sweep. Both Design Travel and Cruises International have gone out of business, and at press time the court cases against Design Travel were still pending. (Keep in mind that other companies might bear the same names but are most likely not associated with the companies under investigation.)

Recently travel certificates have taken on new forms. Companies are now using new technology to perpetrate the scam. The Better Business Bureau issued an alert after one travel company sent unsolicited faxes offering travel packages similar to ours to offices nationwide. The "special promotional" offers were faxed in the form of a memo addressed to "All Staff," so many employees mistakenly believed the trips were sponsored by their company. The scam also has hit the Internet. Almost every month we receive personal emails offering the same old "paradise cruise" for a special promotional rate.

Don't be a victim. There are tons of scams out there, so be extremely skeptical of any unsolicited travel offers you receive, especially if they tell you that you've been "specially selected." Unless someone comes to your doorstep with a big check in his hands, trust us, you haven't won anything. We want your vacation to be fraud and frustration free, so before we bid you bon voyage, repeat after us: "If it sounds too good to be true, it probably is."

WHERE TO TURN FOR HELP

Air Travel
To lodge a complaint about airline service:
•Aviation Consumer Protection Division
U.S. Department of Transportation C-75
Room 4107
Washington, DC 20590
(202) 366-2220
www.dot.gov
To order a copy of the DOT's "Fly-Rights: A Consumer Guide To Air Travel," either download it free from the Web site (above) or send $1.75 to Consumer Information Center, Pueblo, CO 81009

Founded by Ralph Nader, this group works to promote passenger rights in the airline industry:
•The Aviation Consumer Action Project
Box 19029
Washington, DC 20036
(202) 638-4000

Travel Agents and Tour Operators
To check the number of unresolved complaints against a travel agency or tour operator, or to mediate a dispute with a member company, contact:

•American Society of Travel Agents
Consumer Affairs Department
1101 King Street
Suite 200
Alexandria, VA 22314
(703) 739-2782
www.astanet.com

To find an ASTA travel agent or tour operator in your area, call
(800) 965-ASTA or log on to their Web site (above). ASTA also
can direct you to agents and operators who specialize in certain
types of travel.

To find a "certified travel counselor" with at least five years experience and training in travel management, or to find an agent
who specializes in certain types of travel, contact:
•Institute of Certified Travel Agents
148 Linden Street
Box 812059
Wellesley, MA 02181-0012
(800) 542-4282
(617) 237-0280
www.icta.com

To check if your tour operator is a member or to order free
brochures, contact:
•United States Tour Operators Association
342 Madison Avenue
Suite 1522
New York, NY 10173
(212) 599-6599
(212) 599-6744 (fax)
(800) goustoa
www.ustoa.com

Fraud

To lodge a complaint about travel fraud, order brochures, or download them free from their Web site, contact:

•Federal Trade Commission
Consumer Response Center
Washington, DC 20580
(202) 326-3128
(202) 326-2012 (fax)
www.ftc.gov

▶ Top Ten Tips

1. *Shop early and often.* Start your search for plane tickets, hotel rooms, and travel packages as soon as possible to grab good bargains. However, even after you're booked, keep scanning ads and calling travel providers to see if prices have dropped. If they have, try to exchange for the better deal.

2. *Use all your resources.* When looking for the best prices, it always pays to shop around. Check out all your options, including travel providers' toll-free numbers, travel agents, consolidators, and the Internet. Always scan newspaper travel sections for special rates and promotions.

3. *Do your homework.* Check out the reputation of a travel agent or tour operator with the Better Business Bureau, state consumer protection office, American Society of Travel Agents, or United States Tour Operators Association. Be sure to ask how long the company has been in business. Many fraudulent companies change their names frequently as complaints mount against them.

4. *Be flexible.* The best bargains go to the most flexible travelers. Traveling during the off-season, flying on a weekday, staying over a Saturday night, and grabbing last-minute deals on the Internet are all ways to save big bucks.

5. *Never pay full price.* There's almost always a discount or promotion available. From membership discounts, to spe-

cial weekend getaway promotions, to half-price hotel directories, there's always a way to get a deal. But remember, you have to ask because travel providers don't always volunteer the lowest rates.

6. *Never take a travel brochure at face value.* Phrases like "first-class hotel," "steps from the beach," and "near all attractions" can be purposely misleading. Make sure to ask specific questions, such as exactly how many steps to the beach and how many miles to the attractions. Also, read all fine print very carefully.

7. *Review cancellation and refund policies carefully.* Before you put any money down, find out exactly what it will cost if you have to change or cancel your travel plans. For example, many plane tickets are nonrefundable and travel packages impose high penalties for cancellations. For peace of mind, consider trip cancellation insurance.

8. *Pay with plastic.* As with almost anything you buy, protect yourself by using a credit card when purchasing travel services. However, beware of paying too far in advance. Most credit cards give you only sixty days to dispute a charge after it first appears on your bill.

9. *Check your coverage.* Before you go anywhere, call your insurance agent and credit-card issuer to check if you're covered for things like loss of luggage, a rental-car accident, theft from your hotel room, and a medical emergency abroad. If you're not covered, consider buying additional travel insurance.

10. *Confirm your reservations.* No matter how you booked your trip, call the airline, hotel, or car rental company directly before you leave to make sure your reservation is in order. Also, travel with all your confirmation numbers in case something goes wrong.

Glossary

Alternate city: A city near your destination city that you fly to in order to save money on plane tickets. For example, flying into Providence instead of Boston.

Back-to-back ticketing: Using two round-trip tickets originating in opposite locations to avoid restrictions, such as Saturday-night stays, and still get a good fare.

CDW (collision damage waiver):   Insurance coverage offered by rental car companies that covers the consumer for damage or theft to a rental vehicle.

Commission override: A bonus an airline gives a travel agent on top of his or her regular commission for selling tickets on that airline.

Consolidator: A company that contracts with an airline or hotel for blocks of seats or rooms that might go unsold and then sells them to the public at a discounted rate.

CRS (computer reservation system):   A system used to ticket flights. There are four main systems in the United States, owned by different airlines: Sabre, Apollo/Galileo, System One Amadeus, and Worldspan.

Downgrade: Exchanging your plane ticket for one with a cheaper fare.

Excursion fare: A discounted nonrefundable airline ticket that usually requires at least twenty-one days' advance purchase, a Saturday-night stay, and other restrictions.

Hidden city: A city that is merely a stop on a plane's route, not your ticketed destination, but where you disembark to save money.

Nested ticketing: See "back-to-back ticketing."

Rack rate: The published list price for a hotel room, but a price you rarely should have to pay.

Suggested Reading

Best Fares Discount Travel Magazine. A monthly publication. $59.95 for a one-year subscription. Call (800) 880-1234.

Consumer Reports Travel Letter. A monthly newsletter. $39 for a one-year subscription, $5 per back issue. Call (800) 234-1970.

Gary Schmidt, *Fly for Less.* Oakdale, MN: Travel Publishing. Call (800) 241-9299.

Tom Parsons, *Insider Travel Secrets You're Not Supposed to Know.* Arlington, TX: Best Fares, USA. Call (800) 880-1234 or access the Web site, www.bestfares.com.

Wendy Perrin, *Wendy Perrin's Secrets Every Smart Traveler Should Know.* New York: Fodor's Travel Publications.

APPENDIX

HOW TO COMPLAIN

The transaction that takes place when goods are exchanged for money implies certain obligations. A purchase implies that the buyer is obligated to pay the merchant the requested price. The merchant is then obligated to surrender the item to the buyer. This simple concept has become very complicated in the service-oriented world of modern commerce, however. Expectations and obligations often collide, and as we all know, getting what you feel you deserve can be the most complicated part of any transaction!

Good customer service is difficult to define. Consumers and business owners often find themselves at odds over differing expectations. Are waitresses obligated to treat you nicely? What about police officers? While we contribute to the salary of both workers, most of us expect more consideration from the waitress. Does being a *regular* customer entitle you to extras? If so, is an establishment in the right if it makes you wait while staff fawns over its best clients? Is a merchant obligated to give you a full refund every time you come down with a case of buyer's remorse? Indeed, there are some very blurry lines in the customer service picture.

But there are times when you have no doubt you've been short-changed, cheated, or duped. Everyone has a story or two (dozen) about bad service, faulty products, or shoddy workmanship. Contrary to charm school wisdom, you can and should complain when you don't get what you pay for. A few assertive individuals get a kick out of complaining, but most of us have more enjoyable things to do with our time. As we've tried to illustrate throughout this book, there are complaint techniques you can use and each chapter provides information about the avenues specific to the industry it deals with. What follows is some expert advice for those who are starting the process because they, like Mick Jagger, just can't get no satisfaction.

GOOD TIMES CAN MEAN BAD SERVICE!
"Ironically, good economic times make it harder for companies to deliver customer service," says Claes Fornell, director of the University of Michigan Business School's National Quality Research Center (NQRC). The NQRC gives each sector of commerce a rating called the ACSI, American Customer Satisfaction Index. And while the American economy is currently enjoying boom conditions, customer satisfaction was down in two key industries at the end of 1997: discount and department store retail chains, and commercial banks. The reason, Fornell says, is that with unemployment well below 5 percent nationally and under 3 percent in some markets, retailers find it difficult to hire enough staff to wait on customers!

So while many consumers find themselves with more and more expendable income, they also may find themselves wrestling in the aisles over the salesperson's attention!

PREVENTIVE CUSTOMER SERVICE
As a purchaser of goods and services, you can do a lot to ensure that you get treated well and fairly. It's a simple but paramount piece of advice: Do whatever you can to get things off on the right foot. Attitude is crucial and communication is key.

Communication
Consider the importance of precise communication. Very few people are clairvoyant, especially when it comes to the purchase of services. The butcher, the baker, and the candlestick maker all need information about what you want and need from them. Let's not forget the hairdresser and the house builder! You will certainly benefit if you spend time preparing the service worker with details, pictures, descriptions, and/or facsimiles of what you have in mind. Get it out of your mind and down on paper if necessary!

372 APPENDIX

Attitude (Yours)

And your attitude can make or break the transaction. Sometimes you must sell people on the idea of giving you what you want. T. Scott Gross, in his book *How to Get What You Want from Almost Anybody,* says that if you want more than mediocre service, you must market yourself and your needs. You are vying for extra attention and energy. Be friendly. Be likable. Be enthused about what you want. It works.

Consider this true tale. A doorman in a high-rise apartment complex saw many apartments change hands with Realtors regularly shuffling in and out with prospective tenants. The Realtor commission on the sale or rental of these properties was a minimum of $2,000. Some units were vacant and others required an appointment to be shown. Often, however, the doorman had some discretion over when keys could be given to Realtors. A Realtor showed up with a client in tow, then requested the key to an available penthouse in an authoritative tone. The doorman did not know her personally so he inquired about whether she had made arrangements with the owner. She shoved her business card toward the doorman and snapped, "Sir, my name is Suzanne So and So and I'll have you know I hold a state-issued real estate license!" The doorman paused and responded, "Well, my name is Victor and I hold a driver's license. Have a nice day."

Suffice it to say, honey attracts more flies than vinegar.

Making the Best of a Bad Situation

It's a bummer to be the wronged consumer. If you feel you've genuinely been denied your due, you should take immediate action to make the best of a bad situation.

Complaining Dos and Don'ts

Many customer service experts, including M. Scott Gross and Steven Pollan, attorney and former CNBC *Steals & Deals* customer service answer man, contributed to the following list of complainer dos and don'ts.

1. *Do count to ten.* Consumers have been known to vent at helpless clerks and salespeople. Is your complaint legitimate? . . . or are you actually angry over an unrelated or past slight? A moment spent soul-searching can help you get the results you truly are looking for.

2. *Don't forget the facts.* Be an expert on your situation. Have every name, date, place, and time available. If you lack even one fact, your argument may be dismissed as frivolous or inaccurate.

3. *Do do it in person.* Letters sometimes can be ignored (more on letter writing later), and the phone can be too anonymous. In certain situations it's best to face the opposition! Plaster a huge smile on your face and plant your backside in a chair opposite the decision maker. It's difficult to disregard a warm body.

   Scott Gross cites one case where the face-to-face method worked beautifully was when Deirdre Martin had had an insurance claim denied. Her insurer claimed that a doctor visit was related to a preexisting condition. After much investigation she realized that her insurer had made a mistake about the date of a previous examination. All she needed was a note from the doctor's office outlining the accurate dates of her office visits. Over the phone the medical receptionist told her they were too busy and to have the insurance company call them instead. Deirdre recalls, "They were incredibly nasty. And I knew that the people at the insurer would never call so I decided to drive over to the doctor's office and ask them in person. It was like I was seven foot one instead of five foot one. My being there so disarmed them that they actually typed up the letter while I waited!"

4. *Don't disregard the rules.* It's frustrating being referred from one person to another, repeating the same story over and over. But if you follow the prescribed complaint process, you will gain clout and credibility. Complex complaint procedures are designed to frustrate the casual complainers of the world. The farther along you go in the

prescribed process, the more weight will be given to your arguments.

5. *Do push the up button.* If your request is denied, it may be because you are not dealing with the person who has the power to grant your wishes. Find your fairy godmother! If you don't get satisfaction, thank the person for her time, say you know she has done all that she could (even if she hasn't), and politely ask for the name of her superior. It's a nice touch to say that you will tell the higher-up how helpful she's been. Then take your problem upstairs.

TWO RINGS MAKE A WRITE

As we just stated, a face-to-face confrontation can be extremely effective. But some situations make such meetings impossible. The big cheese is the most protected person in any organization. George Steinbrenner probably doesn't take meetings with Yankee fans annoyed over being served a flat beer!

So sometimes you have to register your complaint via phone or letter. The phone is a handy tool for getting information about the policies, procedures, and players who can assist you while pursuing satisfaction, but it rarely suffices as a sole means of resolution, especially when money is involved. The spoken word disappears into thin air, but a letter creates a paper trail. Often you will improve your results by ringing up the decision maker and then following up with a letter or vice versa.

Writing to Make Things Right

For many, letter writing represents a roadblock to resolution. Lack of time and literary finesse can keep even the most righteous from pursuing redress. But fear not. What follows is a simple and straightforward form letter created by the Consumer Information Center that should provide a guideline when words fail you. Just fill in the blanks.

Sample Letter

(Your address)
(Your city, state, zip code)
(Date)

(Name of contact person):
(Title)
(Company name)
(Street address)
(City, state, zip code)

• Describe your purchase

• Name of product, serial numbers

• Include date and location of purchase

Dear (contact person):

On (date), I purchased (or had repaired) a (name of the product with serial or model number or service performed). I made this purchase at (location, date and other important details of the transaction).

Unfortunately, your product (or service) has not performed well (or the service was inadequate) because (state the problem).

• State the problem

Therefore, to resolve the problem, I would appreciate your (state the specific action you want). Enclosed are copies (copies, NOT originals) of my records (receipts, guarantees, warranties, canceled checks, contracts, model and serial numbers, and any other documents).

• Give the history

• Ask for specific action

• Enclose copies of documents

I look forward to your reply and a resolution to my problem, and will wait (set a time limit) before seeking third-party assistance. Please contact me at the above address or by phone at (home or office numbers with area codes).

• Set time for action or response

• Include how you can be reached

Sincerely,

(Your name)
(Your account number)

*Text in parentheses ( ) will change when you personalize your letter.
Source: Consumer Information Center

A WORD ABOUT CERTAIN INDUSTRIES

Some merchants concern themselves with keeping clients happy while others behave as if the customer is always wrong and usually a nuisance. Mark Green, author of *The Consumer Bible,* advises people to be extra careful when dealing with businesses that are complained about most often to the Better Business Bureaus. They include the following:

- •Retail sales
- •Home improvement companies
- •Service firms
- •Auto repair
- •Ordered products (catalog, telephone, mail order)

Retail and Ordered Products

Green suggests that consumers always check a seller's return policy before making a purchase. These policies are posted on store premises, on order forms, and on sales receipts. When a seller won't give you satisfaction, it sometimes helps to take your problem directly to the manufacturer, who may be more concerned with protecting the reputation of a brand name than a local retailer is.

Service Firms and Contractors

When purchasing services such as home improvement or auto repair, it is wise to discuss how disputes are handled prior to signing a contract or work order. Is a satisfaction guarantee or a parts warranty offered? Get it in writing. Many a firm is highly attentive when soliciting your business but turns up missing in action when you have a problem. Checking references is helpful . . . but of course you'll be given hand-picked references. Specifically request to speak to a former client who had a problem. You'll get a very clear picture of how the firm resolves complaint issues by speaking to someone who has been there.

Travel

From boarding imbroglios to baggage bungles, travel troubles can cause more than one kind of motion sickness. Travel disasters have been attributed to airlines, car-rental agencies, hotels, cruise lines, restaurants, customs departments, and travel agencies. Wendy Perrin, consumer news editor at Condé Nast *Traveler* magazine and author of *Wendy Perrin's Secrets Every Smart Traveler Should Know,* helps thousands of consumers a year get satisfaction and refunds from the travel industry. Perrin advises that an important element of getting justice is to determine your losses. Compare the amount you paid with the cost of what was delivered. What features of your trip did you not receive? Which weren't as advertised? How much extra did you have to pay to extricate yourself from a bad situation? Determine how much damage was done and assign to it a cash value.

If you can prove that you were wrongly overcharged, you probably will get a refund. If you can't document an out-of-pocket loss, then you probably won't. Perrin says to remember that many travel suppliers sell fantasy. If your complaint is based on unrealized expectations rather than a failure to deliver something specifically promised, don't expect much more than an apology letter.

OUR TOP COMPLAINT TIP: ASK AND YOU SHALL RECEIVE

And once you have determined your losses, be they tangible or intangible, you can get satisfaction only if you know exactly what will make things right, in your opinion. All the letters, meetings, and phone calls will be pointless unless you have a goal. Don't take the I'll-see-what-I-can-get approach. Is it a refund, exchange, or repair you want? Is it an apology or a policy change? Do you want an insolent employee reprimanded? Avoid being greedy or unreasonable. These behaviors will only stand in the way. Clearly state what you want in all letters, phone calls, and meetings. Decision makers want to deal with complainers who can cut to the chase. They do not have time to deal with complainers who are vague.

THE BIG GUNS
We've provided specific suggestions within each chapter, but certain consumer predicaments require that you bring in the big guns.

Better Business Bureaus
Each BBB is a nonprofit organization funded primarily by membership dues from local businesses. Consumers can use the BBB to get reports on businesses, information about charities, help with resolving disputes with companies, and consumer publications, brochures, and buying guides.

There are more than one hundred BBB offices in the United states. Each local office maintains files on companies with headquarters in its service area. But BBBs also carry some reports on companies that conduct business nationally. You can contact your local BBB first to see if it has the company report you are looking for and, if it can't help you, it will refer you to the office that can.

You can get the report right over the phone, although a few BBBs charge a small fee for the service to help pay for operating costs. The BBB will not recommend any business, but will give it either a satisfactory or an unsatisfactory rating. From the report you can also learn how long the company has been in business, how many complaints have been filed against it, and how many of those complaints are unanswered or unsettled. The report will also note if the company has been the subject of any enforcement actions taken by a government agency, such as the Federal Trade Commission or state attorney general's office. A few BBBs have databases available to do your own search right over the Internet.

If you have had a problem with a company and could not resolve it by dealing with the business directly, you can register a complaint with the BBB. You should submit your complaint in writing or on the BBBs Internet site (www.bbb.org). If the complaint cannot be satisfactorily resolved through communication with the business, the BBB may offer an alternative dispute settlement process, such as mediation or arbitration. However, keep in mind that BBBs are not consumer advocates; they are committed to acting as a neutral third party.

Consumer Protection Agencies

State and local consumer protection agencies conduct investigations, help resolve complaints, license and regulate certain types of businesses, promote consumer protection legislation, and provide information to consumers. If you have a question or a complaint about a local business, your city or county consumer office is probably your best bet. Usually you can find these local government agencies listed in the blue pages of your phone book. If not, contact your local city hall, chamber of commerce, or the consumer protection office located in your state capital. Usually each state's attorney general has a consumer affairs division.

We recommend calling any agency before sending in a complaint. That way you can be sure you're contacting the appropriate office and are following the correct procedures. In the if-all-else-fails department, some situations require government intervention or legal action. While we recommend you start with local consumer agencies, below is a list of various national agencies and organizations that may be able to assist you.

NATIONAL AGENCIES
AND ORGANIZATIONS

GOVERNMENT

Federal Trade Commission (FTC)
Consumer Response Center
6th Street & Pennsylvania Avenue, N.W.
Washington DC 20580
Phone: (202) 326-3128
www.ftc.com
The FTC doesn't resolve individual consumer disputes, but by filing a complaint, you can help it spot a pattern of law violations requiring law enforcement action as well as alert it to new scams that the public should know about. The FTC also has a wide variety of consumer brochures and buying guides available.

Consumer Information Center (CIC)
Pueblo, CO 81009
(888) 8-PUEBLO
www.pueblo.gsa.gov
A clearinghouse for federal consumer publications, the CIC has a consumer information catalog that lists more than 200 free and low-cost publications from over 40 government agencies. The most popular publication is the *Consumer's Resource Handbook,* a free guide that lists thousands of names, addresses, telephone numbers, and e-mail addresses of corporations, trade groups, state and local consumer protection offices, and federal agencies. It's an indispensable resource in any attempt to resolve a problem or complaint. Request the handbook by phone or mail, or download it from their Internet site.

ORGANIZATIONS

American Association of Retired Persons (AARP)
Consumer Affairs Section
601 E Street, N.W.
Washington DC 20049
Phone: (202) 434-6030
Fax: (202) 434-6466
www.aarp.org
AARP's Consumer Affairs Section advocates on behalf of midlife and older consumers. It has brochures and educational material on housing, insurance, funeral practices, eligibility for public benefits, financial security, transportation, and consumer protection issues.

Consumer Federation of America (CFA)
1424 16th Street, N.W., Suite 604
Washington DC 20036
Phone: (202) 387-6121
Fax: (202) 265-7989
CFA is a consumer advocacy and education organization. Issues on which it currently represents consumer interests before Congress and federal regulatory agencies include telephone service, insurance and financial services, product safety, health care, product liability, and utility rates. It also offers several consumer guides in book and pamphlet form.

Consumers Union (CU)
101 Truman Avenue
Yonkers NY 10703-1057
Phone: (914) 378-2000
Fax: (914) 378-2900
A nonprofit, independent organization, CU researches and tests consumer goods and services and disseminates the results in its monthly magazine, *Consumer Reports* (www.consumerreports.org), as well as other publications.

National Consumers League (NCL)
1701 K Street, N.W., Suite 1201
Washington DC 20006
Phone: (202) 835-3323
Fax: (202) 835-0747
www.natlconsumersleague.org
Founded in 1899, the NCL is America's pioneer consumer advocacy organization. The league is a nonprofit, membership organization working for health, safety, and fairness in the marketplace and workplace. Current principal issue areas include consumer fraud, food and drug safety, health care, the environment, financial services, and telecommunications. The league develops and distributes consumer education materials and newsletters.

National Fraud Information Center (NFIC)
P.O. Box 65868
Washington, DC 20035
Phone: (800) 876-7060 (toll free 9:00–5:00; TDD available)
Fax: (202) 835-0767
Email: nfic@internetmci.com
Web site: www.fraud.org
NFIC assists consumers in recognizing and filing complaints about telemarketing and Internet fraud. A project of the National Consumers League, the center's toll-free hot line provides consumers with information to help them avoid becoming victims of fraud, referrals to appropriate law enforcement agencies and professional associations, and assistance in filing complaints.

U.S. Public Interest Research Group (U.S. PIRG)
218 D Street, S.E.
Washington DC 20003-1900
Phone: (202) 546-9707
Fax: (202) 546-2461
Email: pirg@pirg.org
www.pirg.org/pirg

PIRG is a consumer advocacy group with offices in thirty-three states. The group lobbies and publishes reports on issues including credit bureau errors, bank fees and services, product safety, and the environment. U.S. PIRG doesn't handle individual consumer complaints directly but measures complaint levels to gauge the need for remedial legislation.

ADDITIONAL CONSUMER RESOURCES ON THE INTERNET

Federal Consumer Gateway (www.consumer.gov): A "one-stop" link to a broad range of federal consumer information resources available online.

Consumer World (www.consumerworld.org): A public service site that's gathered over 1,700 of the most useful consumer resources on the Internet.

The National Consumer Complaint Center (www.alexander-law.com/nccc): Sponsored by The Alexander Law Firm, the center provides a way of filing complaints with agencies that are interested in investigating and taking action for consumers.

ScamBusters (www.scambusters.com): A free electronic newsletter to help alert consumers about Internet scams.

Whether you're a consumer or an industry insider, we welcome your comments. You can contact us through our publisher or e-mail us directly at Tricks_of_Trade@hotmail.com.

We also hope you'll visit our Web page at http://members.tripod.com/~Tricks_of_the_Trade/index.html. It can lead you to hundreds of consumer resources on the Internet.

INDEX